THE ADEN EFFECT

Dr. Johan van Rooyen

notionpress.com
INDIA • SINGAPORE • MALAYSIA

ISBN

Hardcase 979-8-90510-349-0
Paperback 979-8-90479-298-5

Contents

PART ONE
THE FIRE
THE OLD MAPS ARE BURNING.
A NEW MAP IS BEING DRAWN.
ECONOMICS
POLITICAL SCIENCE
BUSINESS
FINANCE
INTERNATIONAL RELATIONS
OLD PARADIGMS
AI & TECHNOLOGY
ENERGY
WAR & SECURITY
INTEGRATED UNDERSTANDING
THE ADEN EFFECT
EDUCATION & KNOWLEDGE
CURRENCY & FINANCE
HUMAN COGNITION
TRADE & PRODUCTION
INSTITUTIONS & GOVERNANCE
FROM SEPARATE HEAPS
TO A SHARED FUTURE

Part One: The Fire

Introduction

The Afternoon in Chiang Mai

My son Aden is eleven years old. He sits across the room from me on an afternoon in April 2026, and in the space of perhaps thirty minutes he performs a sequence of actions that would, taken together, have been incomprehensible to anyone in any previous century and would still be difficult to explain to most of my colleagues.

The air outside is bad. The dry season in northern Thailand has merged this year with the smoke from fires across the border in Myanmar, where the war has gone on long enough that it has become part of the regional environment rather than an event within it. Agricultural burning adds to the load, and the natural fires that come with the dry heat add more. Chiang Mai sits in a valley between mountains, and the air, once it arrives, finds nowhere to go. It settles. The windows are closed. The purifier runs. This is the baseline now during April, and the children of this city have grown up understanding that the sky can become a problem, which is another thing my generation did not understand at their age.

Aden begins with his phone. He is studying science, working through material for his online American school, which operates from a location he has never visited and employs teachers he has never met in person. The curriculum is pitched above his age because he is academically ahead, which is something the placement process determined without my input, and which turned out to be correct. He absorbs the material quickly. Then, with no transition I can detect, he opens a different application on the same device and orders Lays crisps and candy to be delivered to our house, selecting items and confirming the purchase without any engagement with the money required. He completed a full semester of personal finance last year and received an A+ for his work. The distance between what he knows on the test and what he practices in the ordering is not visible to him. There is no friction between the two, because the device does not produce friction. The friction existed in my childhood. It does not exist in his.

Having ordered, he switches again, opens a music application, selects something I do not recognize, or like, and begins filming a short video of himself playing with our dog. The video will go somewhere. He does not explain where and I do not ask, because asking would mark me as someone who does not understand how the platforms work, and I am trying to preserve the small remaining authority I have. The dog, at least, is from my world. Dogs have been dogs for ten thousand years. Nothing else in the scene is from my world.

I am watching him while doing two things of my own. On one screen, I am following the latest developments in the Gulf conflict, the specific phase of which began with the closure of the Strait of Hormuz and has continued through a series of escalations that have reshaped energy markets, shipping routes, and the calculations of every government with exposure to Middle Eastern oil. On another, I am answering a message from Mansur, one of my students, who is from Uzbekistan and is preparing a TED talk on confidence. He has asked for my input on the structure of his argument. His cohort in my International Trade and Finance course includes students from Uzbekistan, Azerbaijan, South Korea, and Thailand. They are my window into how the emerging world is being experienced by the generation that will inherit it.

I take in the scene. My son ordering snacks without thinking about money, on a device he uses to study, on which he also creates content for audiences I cannot see. The war, which is not the kind of war the books in my library described, unfolding on a screen that updates faster than any news organization could once manage. The student, in another country, preparing to speak about confidence to an audience he will reach without any of the institutions that used to mediate such reach. The smoke outside, which is two wars and one changing climate compressed into a single visible phenomenon. And I, in the middle, trying to hold all of it in a single frame of attention, and largely failing.

This book is the record of that failure and the attempt to do better.

What This Book Is

What I am calling ***The Aden Effect*** is an attempt to describe, as clearly as I can, a transition that is happening faster than the institutions responsible for explaining it can keep up. The transition has been named in many ways by many observers. The fourth industrial revolution. The AI era. The age of disruption. The end of history's vacation. None of these names is wrong, exactly, and none of them is sufficient. What they miss is the specific feature of the current moment that makes it different from any previous transition, which is that the domains we have traditionally studied as separate, economics, politics, technology, military affairs, human cognition, environmental systems, are now interacting at speeds and intensities that make their separation a conceptual fiction. The transition is not happening in any one of these domains. It is happening in the feedback loops between them, and the feedback loops are what the old analytical tools were designed to ignore.

The book is written for a specific audience. It is written for educators who are trying to prepare students for a world the curriculum does not describe. It is written for decision makers who are aware that the advice they receive from consultants and institutions no longer maps onto the problems they face. It is written for economists who sense that their models have lost contact with the phenomena they claim to explain. It is written for scholars of international relations who know that the frameworks inherited from the Cold War cannot describe the multipolar, multi-stack, asymmetric environment that has replaced the world those frameworks were built for. It is not written for a popular audience, though anyone willing to follow the argument is welcome to read. It assumes the reader is familiar with the basic vocabulary of the domains it draws on, and it does not spend its pages on introductory material.

What the book will do is offer a framework for integrated analysis, a specific set of conceptual tools for thinking about phenomena that cross the old disciplinary boundaries. It will demonstrate the inadequacy of existing frameworks through cases that cannot be analyzed within any single discipline. It will name the feedback loops that are now doing the integration work the institutions have failed to do. And it will offer, in its closing sections, a provisional description of what is being settled in the aftermath of the fire, what institutional, cognitive, and civilizational arrangements are emerging to replace the ones that are failing.

What the book will not do is predict specific futures. The environment changes too quickly for predictions made even months ago to survive contact with the events that follow. What it will do instead is equip the reader with the conceptual apparatus to make their own informed judgments as new situations arise. This is a more modest ambition in one sense and a more demanding one in another. It is more modest because it does not claim prophetic authority. It is more demanding because it requires the reader to do ongoing analytical work rather than receiving conclusions, and the work is not easy.

The title refers to my son, whose name in its etymological origins means both *fire* and *settlement*. The choice of the name is deliberate. What is happening in the world is a fire, and the fire will produce a settlement, and the settlement is what the next generation will inhabit. The son in the scene above will live inside whatever the settlement turns out to be. The responsibility to get the analysis right is, in the end, a responsibility to him and to his generation, and the book does not pretend otherwise.

I hold a doctorate in business administration and teach online for an American university, working with students spread across Asia and the Middle East. My wife holds a doctorate and is active in research. She does not trust AI, and her skepticism has served as an essential corrective to my own thinking throughout the writing of this book. My son is eleven and does not yet know what kind of world he will inherit. None of us knows. What I can do is attempt to describe what is visible from where I sit, and to be honest about what I cannot see.

The chapters that follow are the attempt.

CHAPTER ONE

The Roosters and Their Heaps

Disciplines built their own heaps.
The world no longer fits inside any of them.

CHAPTER ONE

The Roosters and Their Heaps

Walk into any serious research university in the world today and you will find that economics and business are housed in different buildings, staffed by different faculty, governed by different committees, and subject to different tenure criteria. A professor of economics is not a professor of business. A professor of business analytics is not a professor of international relations. A professor of political science is housed somewhere else again, usually in a different college entirely, and the professors of engineering and computer science occupy yet another campus precinct with its own culture, its own funding streams, and its own assumptions about what counts as serious work. The students move between these buildings because they must, taking courses across the disciplinary map to complete their degrees. The faculty, in the main, do not. They stay inside the institutional structures that hired them, publish in journals their colleagues read, attend conferences with people who speak their vocabulary, and build careers on the assumption that their discipline is a coherent territory with its own internal logic. This is the structure that produced most of what we know as modern social science, and it is the structure that cannot survive the environment it now claims to describe.

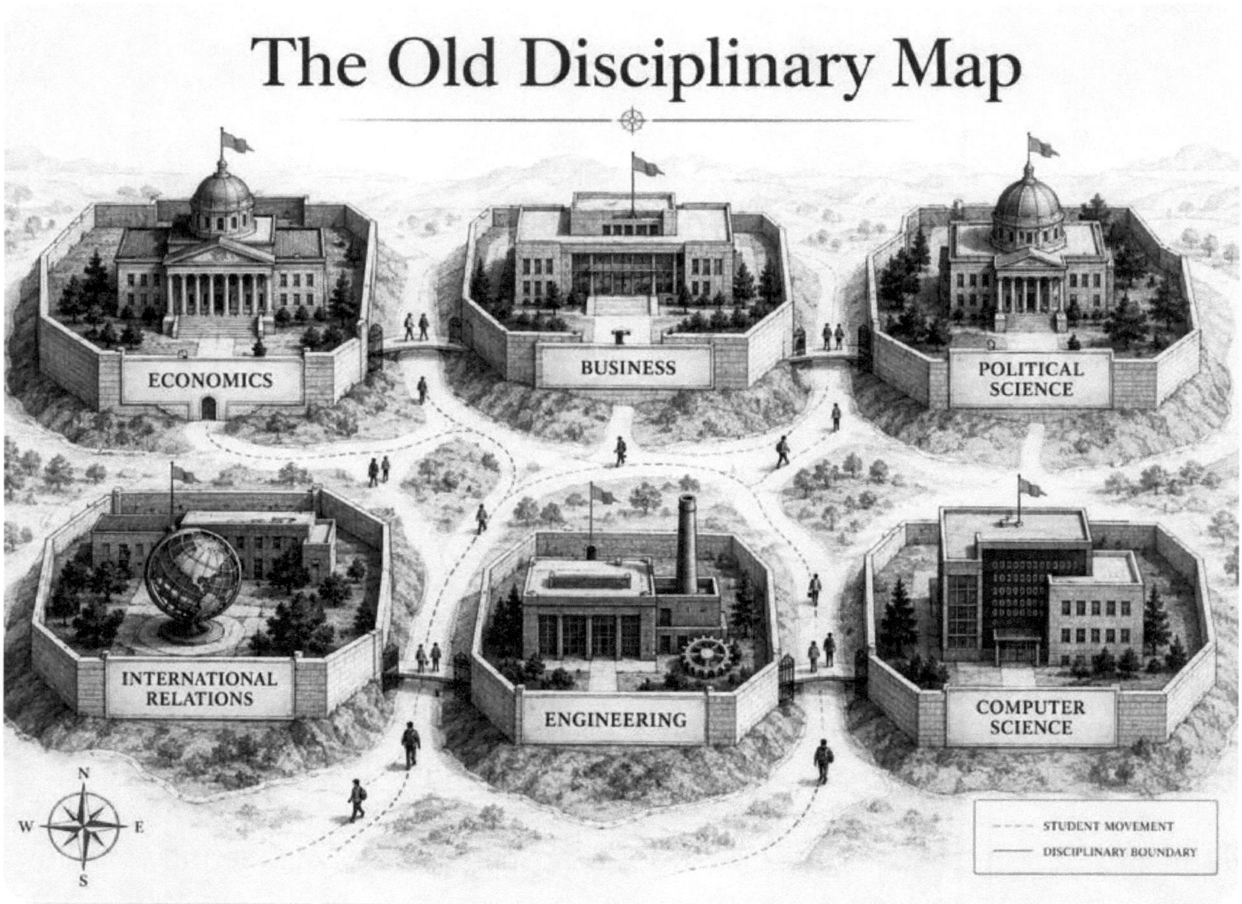

I have spent thirty years inside these structures. I was trained as an economist and then as a business scholar. I hold a doctorate in business administration from a British university and a graduate business degree from an American one. I am currently a professor of business analytics and international trade, and I teach students across Asia and the Middle East through an American institution that organizes its faculty into the same traditional departmental structure that every other research university uses. I know this system from the inside, and I am not writing from outside it. What I am doing is describing, with as much precision as I can, the specific ways in which the system has come to fail the students it serves, the problems it claims to address, and the world it tries to explain. The failure is not a failure of individual faculty. Most of my colleagues are capable and thoughtful people. The failure is structural, and it runs deeper than anyone wants to admit, because admitting it would require rebuilding careers and departments on foundations that do not yet exist.

Consider what happens when a student in my business analytics program tries to do honest work. Suppose the assignment is a marketing project, a standard case study of the kind that business schools have been running for seventy years. The student is asked to develop a marketing strategy for a product entering a new market. In the world the case method was designed for, the relevant variables were internal to the marketing discipline. Consumer segments. Price points. Channel strategy. Brand positioning. Competitive response. A good student could handle the case by reading the marketing literature, applying the marketing frameworks, and producing an analysis that would have been recognizable to a marketing professor in 1985 or 2005. The analysis would be judged on its fidelity to marketing theory and its plausibility as marketing practice, and the student would move on to the next case.

That world is gone. A student trying to do the same case today cannot honestly complete it within the marketing discipline. The product is digital, or has a digital component, which means the technology of how it is delivered shapes everything about how it can be marketed. The market is international, which means geopolitics determines whether the product can even be sold, and under what conditions, and in which currency, and with which data protections. The consumer base is formed by social media and algorithmic recommendation in ways that undermine every assumption the marketing literature was built on. The competitive environment includes AI-generated content that can replicate brand identity at zero marginal cost. The regulatory environment is set by overlapping national, regional, and platform-level authorities whose decisions cannot be predicted from any single framework. A student who produces a marketing analysis that ignores these dimensions produces a document that is technically competent within the marketing discipline and analytically useless in the actual environment. A student who includes these dimensions is accused of writing a paper that is not really about marketing anymore and is penalized for failing to stay within the boundaries of the assignment. The student is in an impossible position. The discipline is the impossible position.

I tell my students to incorporate the other disciplines regardless of whether the assignment technically calls for them, and I mark them on the integration rather than on the narrow disciplinary purity. This is my small act of resistance against the structure I work inside, and it produces better analysis than the alternative. But it is also a problem for the students, because other professors presumably, do not do this, and a student who learns to integrate in my course will presumable, be told by the next professor that their work is off-topic, undisciplined, or insufficiently focused. The institutional reward system is calibrated to the old disciplinary boundaries, and a student who learns to see across boundaries will be penalized as often as rewarded, which teaches them that the integration is personally risky even when it is analytically correct. This is one of the small cruelties of the current educational moment. We are training students to see the world as it is and then punishing them for having done so.

The disciplinary separations were not always this artificial. There was a period, roughly from the end of the Second World War through the end of the Cold War, when the separations worked reasonably well because the world they described was organized in the way the disciplines assumed. Economics could bracket political considerations because the major political questions about economic arrangements had been settled, provisionally, by the American-led liberal order. Political science could bracket economic considerations because the economic architecture was stable and the political questions were about elections, parties, and institutions within that stable architecture. International relations could focus on state-to-state interactions because the state was the dominant unit and non-state actors were secondary. Technology could be treated as an exogenous shock arriving from outside the economic system because the pace of technological change, while rapid, was slow enough that economic models could absorb it across decades. Human cognition could be treated as a stable background variable because the cognitive environment was reasonably constant across generations, shaped by television and print but not yet by anything that fundamentally altered attention or preference.

This is the world that produced the frameworks most of my colleagues presumably, still teach. Heckscher-Ohlin on factor endowments. Adam Smith on the invisible hand and equilibrium. Ricardo on comparative advantage. Keynes on aggregate demand. Friedman on monetary policy. Modern portfolio theory. The Cold War IR frameworks of Waltz, Mearsheimer, and Keohane. The organizational theory of Chandler and Williamson. The marketing frameworks of Kotler and Porter. Each of these bodies of work is serious, each of them captured something real about the world it was built to describe, and each of them now fails in specific ways that the discipline housing it is institutionally incapable of addressing. The failures are not failures of the original thinkers. Adam Smith was not wrong about equilibrium as he understood it. He was working with the world in front of him, and his model was adequate for that world. The failure is what happens when a model designed for one world is applied unchanged to another world that has different structural properties, and when the institutions housing the model refuse to acknowledge that the transfer has broken down.

Take Heckscher-Ohlin. The model is elegant and it does specific work. It explains why countries trade the way they do based on their factor endowments. Countries with abundant capital export capital-intensive goods. Countries with abundant labor export labor-intensive goods. Countries with abundant land export land-intensive goods. The logic is tight and the predictions are testable and for much of the twentieth century the model explained actual trade patterns well enough to be a foundational element of international economics. Every undergraduate in the field is taught it. Every graduate economist can derive it. Every trade policy analyst uses its intuitions even when not invoking the model by name.

Now ask what happens when AI enters the picture. AI is not labor in the traditional sense. It does not eat, sleep, form families, demand wages, organize unions, or participate in democratic politics. It is not capital in the traditional sense either, because it does not sit passively in factories the way machinery does. It is something else, a factor of production that combines features of labor and capital without fitting cleanly into either category, and it is being deployed across industries at a pace that neither the labor force nor the capital stock has ever approximated. A country with abundant compute infrastructure and trained models has an endowment that Heckscher-Ohlin cannot name. A country that lacks these things cannot substitute its traditional labor endowment for them, because the productivity gap is too large to close through price adjustment. The entire development ladder that Heckscher-Ohlin implicitly supported, the logic by which poor countries could climb through labor-intensive exports into more capital-intensive production over time, depends on labor being valuable because rich countries need it. If AI makes cognitive and increasingly physical labor replicable at scale without human workers, the ladder breaks, and countries that were supposed to climb it have nowhere to go.

There is a further complication that goes even deeper. Heckscher-Ohlin treats land as one of three factors, and the model assumes that productive activity requires land in meaningful proportions. Agricultural production is land intensive. Manufacturing historically required substantial industrial land for factories. Resource extraction obviously requires land. The productive geography of nations was mapped onto their land endowments. But a data center that does the work of a thousand office workers requires almost no land. A cluster of servers producing economic value that once required a whole city requires acres, not square kilometers. If the emerging productive factor requires minimal land, then the land endowment that Heckscher-Ohlin treated as a primary variable becomes secondary, and countries that were previously constrained by their land poverty may no longer be. Singapore becomes richer, not because it grew, but because the productive factors stopped requiring what it lacked. Countries with vast land but poor digital infrastructure become relatively poorer, not because they shrank, but because what they have stopped mattering as much. The model did not anticipate this because it was built for a world in which physical production required physical space, and the physical space has become largely decoupled from the output.

The pattern is not that one old model has failed. The pattern is that the major frameworks inherited from the twentieth century fail in similar ways: each assumes a stable boundary that the current world has already crossed.

Old Framework	*What It Assumed*	*What Has Changed*	*Why It Fails Now*
Heckscher-Ohlin	Countries trade according to factor endowments: land, labor, and capital.	AI, compute infrastructure, data, models, and digital systems have become productive factors that do not fit cleanly into the old categories.	The model cannot properly name or measure the new endowments shaping trade and development.
Equilibrium Theory	Supply and demand adjust toward balance through price signals over time.	Different parts of the system now move at radically different speeds: software adjusts quickly, energy infrastructure slowly, geopolitics instantly.	The system no longer reliably converges toward equilibrium; it oscillates around shocks, delays, and political constraints.
Comparative Advantage	Countries should specialize where they are relatively most efficient.	Nearshoring, friendshoring, security-shoring, and strategic redundancy now matter as much as efficiency.	Efficiency is no longer the dominant logic of production; resilience and security have become economic values.
Petrodollar Logic	Currency choice is mainly an economic decision based on liquidity, depth, and efficiency.	Currency choice is increasingly shaped by security guarantees, sanctions risk, geopolitical alignment, and parallel settlement rails.	Money is no longer just a medium of exchange; it is becoming geopolitical infrastructure.
GDP-Centric Measurement	National success can be measured primarily through output, growth, and monetary transactions.	Countries increasingly optimize for stability, legitimacy, resilience, happiness, sustainability, and strategic autonomy.	GDP captures part of the outcome but misses the deeper objectives driving state behavior.
Disciplinary Specialization	Complex problems can be divided into separate fields and analyzed independently.	AI, energy, war, finance, trade, cognition, and politics now interact as one system.	The most important dynamics occur between disciplines, exactly where the old academic structure is weakest.

The issue is therefore not whether each model still contains insight. Many of them do. The issue is whether they still describe the operating environment with enough accuracy to guide students, policymakers, executives, or governments. Increasingly, they do not.

I can hear the defenders of the model already. They will say that Heckscher-Ohlin is a long-run theoretical framework, that it was never meant to apply in detail to every moment, that AI can be incorporated as a form of capital with some modifications to the model. All of this is technically defensible. It is also beside the point. The question is not whether the model can be patched. The question is whether the patched model still captures what is driving trade patterns, and whether students trained on the original model will be able to extend it correctly to the new environment, and whether policy-makers will be able to use it to make sensible decisions. My observation, from inside the teaching of this material, is that the patches accumulate faster than the model can absorb them, and students who learn the patched version are less effective at applied analysis than students who abandon the model altogether and reason from first principles about the actual environment. The model has become a pedagogical ritual rather than an analytical tool and preserving it in the curriculum is partly a matter of professional inertia and partly a matter of faculty identities that have been built around teaching it.

Adam Smith and equilibrium present a related but distinct problem. Smith was building his framework at a time when economic adjustment was slow enough that the equilibrium concept made practical sense. Supply and demand would find their balance because the process of finding it was slow relative to the underlying structure of production. Factories took years to build. Shipping routes were established over decades. Consumer preferences changed across generations. In such a world, the equilibrium framework produced useful predictions because the system was genuinely trying to reach equilibrium and had time to do so. Old uncle Adam Smith, as I sometimes call him with affection in my lectures, was working with the tempo of the world he lived in, and his intuitions served that tempo well.

The tempo has changed. Supply now adjusts at software speeds in some domains and not at all in others, and the unevenness is itself the problem. A factory in Shenzhen can retool in weeks for a new product category. An oil refinery cannot. A data center capacity can be spun up in months. A rare earth mine cannot be opened in under a decade. Demand shifts at the speed of TikTok in consumer goods, and at the speed of geopolitical crisis in commodities, and at the speed of regulatory whiplash in financial services. The equilibrium concept assumes that supply and demand are both responsive to price signals at roughly comparable speeds, and that the adjustment process will converge. Neither of these assumptions now holds. Supply in some sectors responds faster than price signals can be generated. In other sectors, supply cannot respond at all on any relevant timescale. Demand fluctuates faster than supply can track, then shifts again before the tracking is complete. The system does not converge to equilibrium. It oscillates around absences.

What I observe in my finance classes is that students trained on equilibrium models arrive at policy recommendations that would have worked in 1985 and cannot work now. The recommendations have the logical form of equilibrium analysis. If supply is restricted, price rises, which draws new supply, which brings the system back toward balance. In a world where the supply of energy can be restricted by a missile fired from a proxy force on a coastline, and the supply of semiconductors can be restricted by an export control announced by a presidential tweet, and the supply of fertilizer can be restricted by a war between two specific countries that happen to produce a third of the world's output, the equilibrium logic does not apply. The supply is not responsive to price. It is responsive to politics, to military events, to regulatory decision, and to the speed at which these factors can interact. The equilibrium framework cannot absorb this because its underlying ontology assumes that supply and demand are economic variables responding to economic forces. In the current environment, both are political variables being deployed as political instruments.

Which brings us to the third major failure, which is the concept of comparative advantage. Ricardo's framework is the intellectual cornerstone of free trade economics, and it has been the default operating assumption of international trade policy for two centuries. Countries should produce what they produce relatively most efficiently, trade for the rest, and the whole system benefits. The argument is mathematically elegant, and it has been used to justify trade liberalization across every major economic negotiation since the General Agreement on Tariffs and Trade was signed. The assumption underlying it is that economic efficiency is the dominant consideration in production decisions, and that factors outside the economic calculus can be treated as boundary conditions that do not fundamentally alter the analysis.

That assumption has collapsed, and the language that has emerged to describe the collapse tells you what has replaced it. Nearshoring. Friendshoring. Security-shoring. Each of these terms names a logic that is not comparative advantage. Nearshoring produces the good where it is geographically proximate to the market, even when this is more expensive, because distance itself has become a risk. Friendshoring produces the good where it is politically aligned with the buyer, even when the friend is less efficient, because alignment is a form of insurance. Security-shoring produces the good where it cannot be leveraged against you, even when the secure location is far from optimal, because the risk of being held hostage by a supplier exceeds the cost premium of redundant capacity. Each of these logics trades economic efficiency for a different kind of value, and the value being purchased is resilience, autonomy, or strategic insurance. Ricardo cannot price any of these things, because Ricardo assumed they did not need to be priced. They were free. They were provided by the liberal order, the American security umbrella, and the stable institutions of the postwar period. Now they are scarce, and every serious actor is paying for them, and the name of what is being paid for is not comparative advantage.

The consulting industry has spent the last four decades advising multinational corporations based on comparative advantage logic. Optimize the supply chain. Source the cheapest input globally. Manufacture where labor is cheapest. Assemble where tariffs are lowest. Ship where transport is most efficient. The frameworks produced elegant presentations with efficient-frontier diagrams and cost breakdowns by geography. They also produced the fragility that the world has been discovering since the pandemic. Every company whose CEO congratulated himself on a lean just-in-time supply chain in 2019 was congratulating himself on a structural vulnerability that would be exploited within two years. The advice was not wrong within its own framework. It was wrong because the framework assumed a world that was no longer the one the company was operating in, and the consultants did not know this because their own training was calibrated to the same vanished world.

The petrodollar case is perhaps the clearest example of how thoroughly the old economic frameworks fail to describe what is happening, and it is worth examining in some detail because it illuminates the broader pattern. The petrodollar system was established in the early 1970s through an agreement between the United States and Saudi Arabia. In exchange for American security guarantees, Saudi Arabia would price its oil exclusively in dollars and reinvest its oil revenues in US Treasury bonds. This arrangement, replicated across the Gulf, produced the invisible architecture that made the dollar indispensable to global trade. Oil was denominated in dollars, therefore every country that needed oil needed dollars, therefore the dollar was the required medium of international settlement, therefore the United States could run persistent deficits without the capital flight that would have crushed any other currency. The architecture was not just about oil. It was about the dollar's systemic role in everything, because oil was the base layer and every other trade rode on the same rails.

What the economic models told us about this arrangement was that it was stable because it was efficient. The dollar was the most liquid currency, the US Treasury market was the deepest, the American financial system was the most developed, and therefore rational actors would continue to use the dollar because alternatives were inferior. The models could not see, and did not attempt to see, that the arrangement was stable because it was backed by security guarantees, and that the security guarantees were the real collateral. When the security guarantees weakened, the economic rationale for the arrangement weakened with them, and the system would begin to fracture not because the dollar became less liquid but because the underlying guarantee had eroded.

This is what we are now watching. In June 2024, Saudi Arabia chose not to formally renew its exclusive commitment to dollar-priced oil. Since then, the Kingdom has built technical infrastructure for yuan settlement, including a seven-billion-dollar currency swap with China and participation in the mBridge digital payment platform, which processed over fifty-five billion dollars in transactions by November 2025. The dollar's share of global foreign exchange reserves has fallen from seventy-one percent in 1999 to approximately fifty-seven percent in 2025, the lowest level since 1994. During the 2026 Strait of Hormuz crisis, Iran began charging yuan-denominated transit tolls for vessels passing through the strait, creating the first operational petroyuan corridor in history. Chinese vessels moved freely. Western-linked tankers faced delays or redirection. This is not the dollar being replaced by the yuan. The yuan still accounts for under two percent of global reserves. It is something different. It is fragmentation. The monolithic dollar-based settlement system is bifurcating into parallel rails, and different transactions are moving on different rails depending on the political relationships of the parties involved.

No standard economic model can describe what is happening here, because the models assumed that currency choice was an economic decision. The Saudi move to the yuan is not an economic decision in the sense the models imagine. It is a security decision with economic expression. The Saudis are not choosing the yuan because it is more efficient than the dollar. It is not. They are choosing to maintain the option of yuan settlement because the security arrangement that made exclusive dollar pricing rational has weakened, and they need insurance against the possibility that it weakens further. The economic variable is being driven by the political variable, and the old models treated the political variable as exogenous. In this environment, it is the main event.

The broader point that emerges from the petrodollar case is that economics has historically assumed it could treat geopolitics as a boundary condition. Wars happen, governments change, alliances shift, and these things affect economic variables, but the underlying logic of economic activity can be analyzed within its own terms. This assumption worked during periods of political stability because the political variables were genuinely stable enough to bracket. It does not work now, because the political variables are the dominant forces driving economic outcomes, and any analysis that treats them as boundary conditions is analyzing the wrong thing. The question is no longer how economic actors optimize within a political environment. *The question is how political decisions shape the space of possibility for economic action, and this is a question the economic discipline was not built to answer.*

Consider the Hungarian case, which is unfolding as I write this chapter. In January 2026, a Russian drone strike damaged the southern branch of the Druzhba pipeline that carries oil through Ukraine to Hungary and Slovakia. Flow to Hungary was interrupted. Viktor Orbán, then Prime Minister of Hungary, responded by blocking a ninety-billion-euro European Union loan to Ukraine, linking the two issues. Croatia offered its Adria pipeline as an alternative and was accused by Hungary and Slovakia of charging three times the European average for transit. Slovak Prime Minister Robert Fico escalated by threatening to cut emergency electricity assistance to Ukraine if the pipeline was not restored. The dispute paralyzed a twentieth European Union sanctions package against Russia. In early April 2026, Orbán lost a decisive election to Péter Magyar, a conservative former government insider who ran on what he called system change but who also opposes EU military aid to Ukraine. On April 21, 2026, Ukrainian President Volodymyr Zelensky announced that the pipeline had been repaired and could resume operations, paving the way for Hungary to lift its veto on the European loan.

What is this? An economist looking at it through the traditional lens would see a trade disruption, an infrastructure repair issue, a political dispute, an election outcome. The disciplinary vocabulary has words for each of these separately. What it does **not** have is a framework for describing what the episode actually is, which is economic infrastructure being used as a political instrument by multiple actors simultaneously, in an environment where the infrastructure itself has been weaponized by a third party as part of an ongoing war, with the economic consequences flowing back into electoral politics in the affected country, which in turn shapes the geopolitical landscape for the next round of the same dispute. The oil was not blocked because of scarcity. The pipeline was not repaired because of technical readiness. The election was not decided only by the pipeline issue, but the pipeline issue was decisive enough to shape which party could credibly govern. Economics describes part of this. International relations describes part of this. Political science describes part of this. None of them describe the integration, and the integration is where the actual action is.

This is what I mean when I say the roosters are standing on their heaps pretending that the landscape has not changed around them. The economist analyzing the pipeline dispute in economic terms is not wrong within the terms of the discipline. The international relations scholar analyzing it in IR terms is not wrong either. Each of them can produce a coherent paper within their field, publish it in a journal their colleagues read, and receive tenure for having done so. But neither of them captures what is actually happening, and a policymaker who draws on analysis in isolation will make decisions that reflect the partial understanding of the partial discipline. What the policymaker needs is the integrated analysis, and the integrated analysis is not being produced by anyone whose career depends on disciplinary affiliation, because the academic reward system does not value it. The reward system values disciplinary purity. The world demands integration. The gap between what is valued and what is needed is the gap the disciplines cannot close from within their current structure.

There is one more failure I want to name before closing this chapter, because it completes the picture of what has broken. The standard economic framework assumes that the purpose of economic activity is to maximize output, measured primarily through gross domestic product, which itself is measured primarily through monetary transactions. Economic growth is defined as GDP growth. National success is defined as higher GDP per capita. Development is defined as the path by which poor countries grow their GDP. This framework has been so deeply embedded in economic thinking that alternatives have been treated as exotic curiosities rather than as serious challenges to the measurement apparatus.

Bhutan has been measuring Gross National Happiness since 2008, when the concept was formally instituted in the Bhutanese constitution. The framework has four pillars, which Bhutan describes as sustainable and equitable socio-economic development, environmental conservation, preservation and promotion of culture, and good governance. It has nine domains of happiness and uses a specific methodology for weighing them. It has a policy screening tool that evaluates government proposals against the framework before implementation. Most relevantly for our purposes, Bhutan has demonstrated that a country can be governed with reference to a measurement system that is not GDP and that the results are defensible. The country has seventy-two percent forest cover protected by constitutional mandate. It is the first carbon-negative country in the world. It has free universal healthcare and school curricula focused on mindfulness and sustainability alongside academic achievement. In 2011, the United Nations General Assembly passed resolution 65/309, drawing on Bhutan's approach, urging member nations to measure happiness and well-being. The International Day of Happiness was declared the following year. Several developed countries, including New Zealand, Scotland, and Finland, have adopted well-being frameworks alongside GDP measurement.

The Gulf states operate with a different but related logic, one that does not formally reject GDP but in practice subordinates it to stability, ruler legitimacy, and long-term transition planning. The question that preoccupies Gulf leaders is not whether GDP will grow next quarter. It is how to manage the transition from an oil-dependent economy to whatever comes after oil, while maintaining social stability and ruler authority, within a regional security environment that is actively deteriorating. GDP growth is one consideration among several. Sovereign wealth funds, Vision 2030-style development plans, citizenship policies for expatriate populations, religious legitimacy, and diplomatic positioning are others. An analysis that treated these governments as GDP maximizers would miss what they are doing, which is managing a multi-variable optimization in which GDP is a constraint and an input rather than the objective function.

Hungary has been cut off from its traditional oil supply not because of scarcity but because the political geometry of the conflict puts the pipeline in a war zone and the war zone interacts with EU decision-making in ways that neither the pipeline operators nor the oil buyers nor the governments involved fully control. A GDP-based analysis of Hungary's situation would capture none of this. The relevant variables are political legitimacy, EU membership tensions, relations with Russia and Ukraine, historical grievances, domestic electoral dynamics, and the specific negotiating position of a country whose governing party has just lost an election. The economic impact on GDP is real, but it is downstream of all these other factors, and an analysis that started from GDP and worked outward would miss everything that mattered.

What all of this points to is that economics as a discipline has been operating with a measurement framework that was always culturally specific and is now being openly rejected by countries with significant populations and significant influence. Bhutan is small, but its example has been endorsed by the United Nations. The Gulf states are not small. Hungary is not small. China's measurement of national success has been heterodox by Western standards for decades, and the fact that its economy has grown at rates that Western models could not predict without being able to explain why should have triggered more disciplinary reflection than it did. The GDP-centric framework is not a universal framework. It is the framework of a particular moment in a particular set of countries, and the moment is ending faster than the discipline is prepared to acknowledge.

The sum of all this, across Heckscher-Ohlin and equilibrium and comparative advantage and the petrodollar and GDP itself, is that the core analytical tools of economics were built for a world that had specific structural features which no longer obtain. The tools were never intended as universal. They were intended as descriptions of the world in front of the people who built them. The people who built them understood this. Adam Smith would not have been surprised to learn that his equilibrium framework did not describe every possible economic arrangement. He was writing about the eighteenth-century commercial economy of Britain, and he knew it. The problem is that his successors elevated his framework to universality and taught it to generations of economists as if it described any world rather than the specific world it was built for. Heckscher and Ohlin were describing twentieth-century trade patterns. Ricardo was describing early nineteenth-century trade. None of them were trying to capture a world in which AI replaces labor, land becomes optional for production, supply cannot respond to price, currency choice is a security decision, infrastructure is a political weapon, and measurement itself is contested.

The roosters, by which I mean the specialists who dominate each disciplinary heap, are not bad people. They are people doing what their training has prepared them to do. The trouble is that the training itself is now an impediment to seeing what is happening. The economist who has spent a career elaborating equilibrium model has committed to a framework that cannot describe current economic dynamics. The international relations scholar who has spent a career refining Cold War theories has committed to a framework that cannot describe a multipolar, multi-stack, asymmetric world. The business strategist who has spent a career optimizing within the Porter framework has committed to a framework that cannot describe an environment where the rules of competition are being rewritten by political actors using economic instruments. The specialists cannot simply update. Their careers, their reputations, their curricula, their textbooks, their graduate students, their recommendation letters, all of it is built on the frameworks they are being asked to abandon. Update is easy to say and impossible to execute within the current institutional structure.

Which is why the integration, when it comes, will not come from within the existing disciplines. It will come from the margins, from practitioners, from scholars who have left the reward systems or who have secured enough distance from them to think freely, and from a new generation of students who were never fully trained into the old boundaries because they encountered the integrated environment before the disciplinary walls could harden around them. My students in Tashkent and Azerbaijan and Karachi and Islamabad are in a better position to see what is happening than my colleagues in Boston and London, because my students have not yet been taught to separate what is connected. My job, as I understand it, is to help them preserve that native integration through their training rather than losing it. The job of this book is to help the readers who are still inside the old disciplinary heaps find a way to see past their walls.

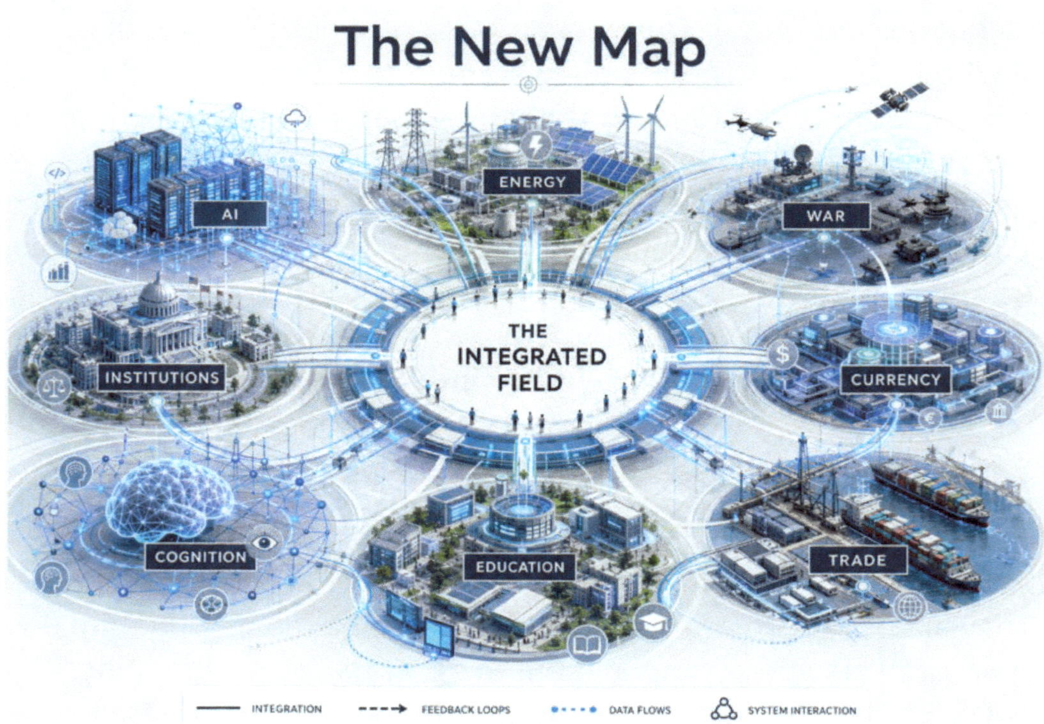

The rest of Part One is about what is burning in the fire that the old structures cannot see. Chapter Two examines the specific cases that cannot be analyzed within any single discipline and must be analyzed across all of them. Chapter Three names what is being consumed, which is not civilization or capitalism or democracy as such but a specific configuration of institutional and intellectual habits that was built for a window that has closed. The chapters that follow are about what is emerging from the combustion. The rest of the book is the attempt to describe it honestly.

One last observation before we move on. My wife, who does not trust AI and who reads everything I write with a particular kind of attention I value precisely because it is not mine, pointed out that the argument of this chapter can be read as hostile to the disciplines themselves. It is not. The disciplines produced real knowledge about real phenomena, and that knowledge remains valuable. What is being challenged is not the work the disciplines have done but the claim that the work still captures the phenomena it was built to describe. A map that was accurate in 1985 is not a false map. It is a map of 1985, and the person who uses it to navigate 2026 is making a mistake that the map itself cannot be blamed for. The mistake is the use of the map, not the map. What we need now is new maps, drawn for the territory as it is, and the drawing of those maps is what the rest of this book attempts. The roosters will not like the new maps. The roosters are not the intended audience. The intended audience is the people who need to navigate the territory and who know, at some level, that the old maps are no longer working. This book is for them.

— CHAPTER TWO —
THE CASES THAT DO NOT FIT
Five cases. One argument.
The world is changing in ways the old frameworks cannot see or explain.
1. HORMUZ
When the Unknown Reshapes the Known
Geography as leverage
Currency of power
From petrodollar to petroyuan
2. RARE EARTHS
The Elements That Reshape Power
Nd Pr Dy
Tb Eu Y
Not just commodities
Configured value
Tech, geopolitics, policy, military
3. REGIONAL WAR
When Conflict Ripples Everywhere
Beyond the battlefield
Supply chains fracture
Finance and politics move first
4. AI & PLATFORMS
When Intelligence Becomes Infrastructure
Platforms shape reality
Information is power
Control is influence
5. DIGITAL MONEY
When Money Becomes Code
Parallel financial systems
Different rules
Same technology, different sovereignty
ECONOMICS
INTERNATIONAL RELATIONS
BUSINESS STRATEGY
SECURITY STUDIES
GEOPOLITICS
FINANCE
TECHNOLOGY
LAW & POLICY
ENVIRONMENT
OLD FRAMEWORKS, INCOMPLETE MAPS, FALSE ASSUMPTIONS.
OUTDATED
Interconnected. Nonlinear. Unpredictable. Real time.
THIS IS THE NEW REALITY.
THE WORLD CANNOT BE UNDERSTOOD WITH TOOLS BUILT FOR A WORLD THAT NO LONGER EXISTS.
DIFFERENT DISCIPLINES. → DIFFERENT MODELS. → DIFFERENT ASSUMPTIONS. → NONE OF THEM ENOUGH. → INTEGRATION OR IRRELEVANCE.

CHAPTER TWO

The Cases That Do Not Fit

If the previous chapter argued that the disciplinary frameworks have lost contact with what they describe, this chapter shows the loss in action. Five cases follow. Each one resists analysis within any single field. Each one carries part of the argument the next chapters will need.

Hormuz: When the Unknown Reshapes the Known

Most readers of this book can name the leader of the United States, the capital of the United States, and the currency of the United States. The same readers, in most cases, cannot name the supreme leader of Iran, the capital of Iran, or the currency of Iran. This asymmetry of recognition is not incidental. It reflects the cognitive geography of the world the readers were trained in, in which the major powers occupied the foreground and everywhere else was background. The background was assumed to react to the foreground. Foreground actors made decisions and the background adjusted. This was the implicit operating assumption of every framework of international economics, international relations, and global business strategy that came out of the Cold War period. The actors who mattered were the ones whose names were in the news. The ones whose names were not in the news did not matter, except as variables that the major actors managed.

The Strait of Hormuz crisis demolished this assumption. A country whose leader is unfamiliar to most Western readers, whose capital is geographically vague in their imagination, and whose currency they could not name, exerted decisive influence on the global economy of the country whose leader, capital, and currency are known to every literate person on earth. The mechanism was geographic and political rather than economic in any traditional sense. Iran sits on the northern coast of the Strait of Hormuz, through which approximately one-fifth of the world's seaborne oil passes. When the conflict between Iran and Israel escalated into direct strikes between the two countries, and when the United States entered the conflict in support of Israel, Iran responded by making the strait functionally impassable for vessels not paying the costs Iran demanded. The economic geography that everyone knew was turned into a tollbooth. The country with the smaller economy, the smaller military, and the smaller global recognition reset the operating conditions of the world's largest economy and its closest allies in a matter of days.

The economic textbooks have a vocabulary for some of what happened. Oil prices spiked. Shipping insurance costs surged. Container rates jumped as carriers rerouted around the Cape of Good Hope. Refining margins were disrupted in countries dependent on Gulf crude. Inflation expectations adjusted upward in every economy that imports energy. All of this is recognizable as a supply shock, and the standard analytical frameworks could process it as such. What the frameworks could not process was the second-order consequence, which was that the shock revealed and accelerated a structural shift in how the global financial system itself operates.

The shift involves what is now being called the petroyuan corridor. As Iran throttled the strait, it began conditioning passage of certain vessels on payment of transit tolls denominated in Chinese yuan rather than in US dollars. Chinese-flagged vessels and vessels carrying oil to Chinese buyers moved through with relative ease. Western-linked tankers faced delays, redirection, and additional friction. This was not a market response. It was a deliberate policy intervention that bifurcated the global oil trade into two parallel settlement systems within the geographic space of a single shipping lane. The dollar-priced barrels and the yuan-priced barrels were physically identical, extracted from the same fields, transported on similar vessels. They differed only in the currency of payment and the identity of the buyer. The political geography of the conflict had inserted itself into the financial architecture of the trade.

Behind this development lies a longer story that the standard frameworks have also failed to absorb. The petrodollar system was established in the early 1970s through agreements between the United States and Saudi Arabia, in which the Kingdom committed to pricing oil exclusively in dollars and recycling its oil revenues into US Treasury bonds, in exchange for American security guarantees. This arrangement, replicated across the Gulf, produced the invisible architecture that made the dollar indispensable to global trade. Every country needing oil needed dollars. Every dollar earned from oil sales returned to the American financial system as Treasury purchases, allowing the United States to run persistent fiscal deficits that any other country would have been punished for by capital flight. The petrodollar was not an economic phenomenon. It was a security arrangement with economic expression. The economic models, treating it as economic, missed the foundation on which it rested.

That foundation has been visibly weakening. In June 2024, Saudi Arabia chose not to formally renew its exclusive commitment to dollar-priced oil. Since then, the Kingdom has built technical infrastructure for yuan settlement, including a seven-billion-dollar currency swap with China and participation in the mBridge digital payment platform, which processed over fifty-five billion dollars in transactions by November 2025. The dollar's share of global foreign exchange reserves has fallen from seventy-one percent in 1999 to approximately fifty-seven percent in 2025, the lowest level since 1994. The decline has been gradual but consistent, and it reflects not a sudden loss of confidence in the dollar but a systematic effort by central banks worldwide to diversify their holdings and reduce dependence on a single settlement system. The Hormuz crisis accelerated what was already happening, by exposing the contradiction at the heart of the petrodollar arrangement: the security guarantees that backed it have weakened, and Gulf states have begun behaving as if they recognize this.

The economist analyzing all of this within the framework of currency markets sees a story about reserve diversification and gradual de-dollarization. The political scientist analyzing it within the framework of international relations sees a story about American hegemonic decline and the rise of a multipolar order. The military analyst sees a story about asymmetric warfare and the failure of conventional power projection against determined regional actors. The energy specialist sees a story about supply chain vulnerability and the need for diversified routing. Each of these analyses captures part of what happened. None of them captures the integration, which is that a single event simultaneously shifted the financial architecture, the geopolitical landscape, the military doctrine, and the energy economics in ways that interact with each other and that none of the disciplines can analyze in their interaction. The petrodollar fragmentation and the Hormuz interdiction and the cost-exchange ratio failure of expensive Western naval assets against cheap Iranian drones and the political reshaping of Gulf state positioning are not four separate phenomena. They are four faces of one phenomenon, and the phenomenon has no name in any existing curriculum.

What the case demonstrates, beyond any specific analytical point, is that recognition no longer maps to power in the way the old frameworks assumed. A country whose name is not in the daily news of the major Western capitals can reshape the operating assumptions of the global economy from a position of geographic and political leverage that no economic model would have predicted to be decisive. The actor whose currency is unknown is the actor introducing currency innovation that the actors with known currencies cannot prevent. The asymmetry has inverted. The frameworks built on the older asymmetry have not caught up, and the policy advice flowing from them is now consistently wrong, because it assumes a world in which the recognition gradient still runs in the direction it ran in 1995.

Druzhba: Infrastructure as Political Weapon

If Hormuz shows what happens when geography becomes a deliberate chokepoint, the Druzhba pipeline case shows what happens when economic infrastructure becomes a deliberate political weapon, and how the weaponization cascades through electoral politics in ways that no infrastructure analysis can capture. The case is unfolding as I write this chapter, and the specific events span the period from late January through April of 2026.

The Druzhba pipeline is one of the longest oil pipelines in the world, completed during the Soviet period, designed to carry Russian crude westward to Eastern European countries that were then part of the Warsaw Pact. After the collapse of the Soviet Union, the pipeline continued operating through Ukraine into Hungary, Slovakia, and the Czech Republic. After the Russian invasion of Ukraine in 2022, the European Union imposed sanctions on Russian oil but provided exemptions for landlocked countries that had no immediate alternative supply, allowing Hungary and Slovakia to continue importing Russian crude through the southern branch of Druzhba on the basis that no realistic substitute was available.

On January 27, 2026, a Russian drone strike damaged the southern branch of the Druzhba pipeline inside Ukrainian territory. Flow to Hungary and Slovakia was interrupted. The repair was technically complex, requiring weeks of work in a war zone, with continued Russian targeting risk. The interruption fell across the European winter, when energy demand was at its peak.

What followed was not a technical story about pipeline repair. It was a political story in which multiple actors used the disruption as leverage for unrelated objectives. Hungarian Prime Minister Viktor Orbán, who had maintained close ties to Russian President Vladimir Putin throughout the war and whose political coalition depended on cheap Russian energy as part of its economic platform, responded by blocking a ninety-billion-euro European Union loan to Ukraine that had been approved in principle the previous December. Orbán linked the two issues explicitly, stating that Hungary would not approve the loan until Russian oil resumed flowing through the pipeline that had been damaged by Russian strikes. The other European Union member states viewed this as a breach of the principle of sincere cooperation, since the disruption was caused by Russia and the loan was intended to support the country defending itself against Russia, but Hungary had veto power over the loan and used it.

Slovak Prime Minister Robert Fico escalated the situation further. On February 21, 2026, Fico issued a direct ultimatum to Ukrainian President Volodymyr Zelensky via social media, declaring that if oil transit through the Druzhba pipeline was not restored by Monday, February 23, he would instruct the Slovak state grid operator to terminate all emergency electricity assistance to Ukraine. The Ukrainian Ministry of Foreign Affairs condemned the threat as energy blackmail, noting that ultimatums should be directed at the Kremlin rather than at Kyiv, but the threat itself was credible enough to require diplomatic management. Croatia offered its Adria pipeline as an alternative supply route to both Hungary and Slovakia. Both countries declined the offer, accusing Croatia of charging transit fees three times the European average, though the underlying objection was political rather than commercial. Zelensky pointed out that the refusal proved the dispute was not about energy security but about a preference for maintaining a financial relationship with Russia, since the Croatian alternative was technically viable and Hungary and Slovakia had chosen not to use it.

Through February and March, the dispute paralyzed a twentieth European Union sanctions package against Russia, since both Hungary and Slovakia simultaneously vetoed it. The Hungarian electoral campaign approached against this background, with Orbán framing the energy disruption as evidence of Ukrainian aggression against Hungary and as justification for his policy of resistance to deeper European Union integration on Ukraine. He lost the election in early April 2026 to Péter Magyar, a conservative former government insider who had founded a new party and run on what he called system change, but who also opposed European Union military aid to Ukraine and indicated he would maintain Hungary's veto until oil flows resumed.

On April 21, 2026, Zelensky announced that the Druzhba pipeline had been repaired and could resume operations. Magyar, the prime minister-elect, indicated he would lift the veto on the European loan once flows restarted. The dispute that had paralyzed European Union policy for three months ended with a technical repair announcement that returned the situation to its pre-January state, except that the political damage had reshaped the Hungarian government, the European Union's sanctions trajectory, the credibility of European cooperation, and the relationship between Ukraine and the two member states that had treated its wartime infrastructure as bargaining material.

The same pipeline system was being used by another actor for a different political objective at the same time, and this is the part of the story that completes the pattern. The northern branch of Druzhba, which carries oil through Russian territory to German refineries, has historically been used by Kazakhstan to ship its own crude to European customers under transit arrangements with Russia. In April 2026, Russia announced that it would stop transit of Kazakh oil to Germany via Druzhba beginning May 1, 2026. The announcement was not framed as a commercial decision and not justified through technical considerations. It was a political decision by Russia to deny supply to Germany at a moment when Germany had emerged as one of the leading European providers of military aid to Ukraine, when European energy security remained fragile, and when fracturing European coalition discipline was an explicit Russian strategic objective. The same pipeline system was simultaneously being weaponized by multiple actors for different purposes. Russia targeted the southern branch through Ukraine to disrupt Hungarian and Slovakian politics in ways favorable to Russian interests. Russia announced halting Kazakh transit through the northern branch to punish Germany for its support of Ukraine. Hungary and Slovakia used the southern branch disruption to extract concessions from the EU on unrelated policy. Ukraine used the timing of repairs to influence the loan and sanctions packages. Kazakhstan, which is not a party to the war and which depends on the pipeline for export revenue, finds its commercial access cut off as collateral damage of decisions made for political reasons by an actor that controls the transit territory but does not own the oil being transited.

This is what infrastructure looks like when it has become political arsenal across the board. No single actor controls the system. Every actor with leverage over any segment of it is using that leverage to advance objectives that have nothing to do with oil. The pipeline was built to move crude from production zones to refineries. It now moves crude when the political alignment of every actor along its length permits the movement, and it stops moving when any of those actors finds it advantageous to interrupt. The commercial function of the pipeline has not disappeared, but it has been demoted from primary purpose to secondary effect. The primary purpose, in practice, is whatever political objective the actor with current leverage is pursuing, and the actor with current leverage changes with each episode.

What is this case? An energy economist analyzing it within the framework of oil markets sees a transient supply disruption in a regional pipeline with manageable economic consequences. A political scientist analyzing it within European Union politics sees a member state veto being used to extract concessions on unrelated policy. An international relations scholar sees Russian information warfare exploiting infrastructure vulnerability to fragment Western coalition support for Ukraine. A military analyst sees a successful demonstration of how strikes on civilian-coded infrastructure can produce strategic effects far exceeding their tactical cost. Each of these analyses captures part of the case. None of them captures what happened, which is that a single drone strike triggered a cascade through energy infrastructure, electoral politics, alliance management, sanctions policy, and the legitimacy of European decision-making, and that the cascade was deliberate at every step, with multiple actors using different parts of the same infrastructure for different political objectives that had nothing to do with oil.

The deeper observation is that infrastructure that was built as economic plumbing is now being used as political arsenal, and the actors using it understand exactly what they are doing. The Russians targeted the pipeline knowing that the disruption would affect Hungarian and Slovakian politics in ways favorable to Russian interests. Orbán used the disruption knowing that Hungarian voters would blame Brussels and Kyiv rather than Moscow if the message could be controlled. Fico used the situation knowing that threatening Ukrainian electricity would force European Union attention to his demands. Zelensky timed the repair announcement knowing it would unlock the loan and the sanctions package. Every party understood that the pipeline was not really about oil. It was about the political effects that could be extracted from controlling, disrupting, and restoring the flow of oil. The economic analysis treats the pipeline as a piece of infrastructure with a function. The political analysis treats it as an asset to be deployed. Neither describes what was actually happening, which was that the pipeline became, simultaneously, both of these things and several others, and the actors involved were optimizing across all the dimensions at once.

The Lights Switched Off: COVID, Masks, and the Forgetting

The third case shifts register from international politics to domestic experience, and it is also the case that has been most thoroughly forgotten despite being the most universally lived. Between early 2020 and the end of 2022, the global economy was deliberately switched off and back on by political decisions of unprecedented scope. Borders closed. Schools closed. Workplaces closed. Travel was conditioned on vaccination status that determined whether individuals could earn a living, attend a relative's funeral, or move freely within their own countries. Companies that had operated profitably for decades went bankrupt within months because their revenue collapsed and their costs did not. Supply chains that had been optimized over a generation were disrupted in ways that have not fully recovered. Governments printed currency at scales that produced the inflation cycle the world is still working through. Children lost approximately two years of normal schooling, with consequences in cognitive development and social formation that are now beginning to appear in measurable form. Several million people died from the virus or from the consequences of the response to the virus, depending on how one counts and which deaths one attributes to which cause.

And then, within roughly thirty months of the most acute disruptions, the entire phenomenon was switched off in public discussion as completely as it had been switched on. The institutions that imposed the restrictions stopped reviewing them. The intellectual class that argued various positions during the period stopped revisiting their arguments. The policy frameworks that were rewritten under emergency conditions remained in place without being examined. The people who lived through it largely stopped discussing it. A historical event of this magnitude does not normally disappear from active discussion within three years of its conclusion. Wars are discussed for generations. Financial crises are studied for decades. The 1918 influenza pandemic remained a medical and policy reference point for the rest of the twentieth century. COVID was the largest disruption to global movement, commerce, and individual liberty since the Second World War, and the conversation about it has effectively ended. The silence is itself a phenomenon worth analyzing, because it indicates something about the analytical capacity of the institutions that should be performing the analysis. They cannot, or will not, engage with what just happened, and the disengagement is now part of the data.

The masks are useful as a case because they were the visible symbol of the larger phenomenon, and because their cycle illustrates in compressed form what the broader disruption did at scale. Between early 2020 and the end of 2022, the global production and consumption of medical face masks underwent a complete supply-demand cycle, including the construction of new manufacturing capacity, the establishment of mandatory consumption protocols, the cultural transformation of the product into a political marker, the substantial decline of the protocols, and the obsolescence of much of the new capacity. No equilibrium model can absorb a cycle of this compression. Every reader of this book has personal experience of the cycle, which is part of what makes it a useful entry point. Each reader will remember the specific mask requirements they navigated, the specific moments when those requirements changed, the specific arguments that surrounded the changes, and the specific point at which the requirements quietly stopped being enforced.

In early 2020, when the SARS-CoV-2 virus began its global spread, mask supply collapsed almost immediately. Existing manufacturing capacity, which had been built around predictable healthcare and industrial demand, could not accommodate the sudden requirement that essentially every person in the developed world wear a mask in essentially every indoor public setting. Hospitals competed with governments for whatever supply existed. Governments competed, in some cases redirecting shipments destined for other countries. Manufacturers in China, which produced the majority of the world's masks at the time, scaled production rapidly but could not match demand. Prices spiked. Counterfeits proliferated. New manufacturing lines were established at speed in countries that had previously imported all their masks, often with public funding designed to ensure domestic supply security.

This phase, which lasted roughly through the middle of 2021, looked like a textbook case of supply responding to demand under duress. The economic frameworks were comforting in their familiarity. Price signals were drawing capital into manufacturing capacity, the new capacity was scaling, and over time the supply would catch up with the demand and equilibrium would be approached. The frameworks did not warn that by the time the new capacity reached full operational scale, the demand would have shifted to something the supply was not designed for, and that the meaning of the product itself would have changed in ways that the supply chain could not respond to.

By mid-2022, the cultural and political environment around masks had transformed. In some communities, masking remained a serious public health practice, observed conscientiously and continuously. In others, it had become a political marker, with refusal to wear a mask serving as a signal of opposition to government overreach and willingness to wear one serving as a signal of compliance with authority. In still others, masks had become fashion accessories, with patterned and branded versions sold as expressions of personal style. In yet others, they had become objects of fear, worn by individuals whose sense of risk had not adjusted to the changing epidemiological situation. The same physical object, manufactured to the same specifications, signified completely different things in different contexts within the same week. A factory producing surgical masks in 2022 was producing a single product that simultaneously fulfilled multiple demand functions that did not share any common analytical structure.

Then the demand collapsed. Not gradually but suddenly, across most jurisdictions in late 2022 and through 2023. Mask mandates were lifted. Compliance enforcement ended. The masks themselves did not disappear, but the requirement to wear them did, and consumption fell to a fraction of its peak. The factories that had been built or expanded during the panic phase faced overcapacity that could not be rationalized through gradual demand decline, because the decline was not gradual. The investment had been justified based on demand that no longer existed, and the assets had no productive alternative use, since their specialization was the source of their value. Government stockpiles, accumulated at scale during the height of demand, began expiring in warehouses while policy debates about whether masks had ever been effective reignited in the academic literature, in court filings, and in political campaigns.

My own observation of this cycle includes a detail I want to record because it captures the absurdity in compressed form. In one phase, I flew from Chiang Mai to Tashkent. Uzbekistan is a doubly landlocked country in Central Asia, which is to say it is one of only two countries in the world that is landlocked and bordered entirely by other landlocked countries. Its connection to the global pandemic was indirect, mediated through the same airline networks and information flows that connected everywhere to everywhere. On the airplane, the cabin crew reminded passengers continuously to wear their masks correctly, to keep them over the nose, to replace them if they became wet, to dispose of them properly. The protocol was rigorous and the enforcement was visible. Outside the airplane, in Tashkent itself, the mask compliance was light to nonexistent in many settings, because the population was navigating its own relationship with the protocols based on local conditions, which were not the conditions assumed by the airline's global procedures. The contrast was not anomalous. It was the global pattern in compressed form. The protocol was universal. The local realities were varied. The connection between the protocol and any actual epidemiological logic was tenuous in many specific contexts, and everyone involved at some level knew this and continued the rituals because the rituals had become the point.

The spectacle of senior medical authorities wearing two masks simultaneously in 2021, without any clinical evidence that double masking provided proportional protection benefit and with substantial evidence that proper fit of a single mask was the actual variable, captured the same dynamic at the elite level. The ritual had detached from the function. The performance of compliance had become the substance of the practice.

This was visible to anyone watching closely. It was rarely discussed openly in the institutions whose authority depended on the performance, because discussing it would have undermined the authority itself. The performance continued because the alternative was to admit that the institutional response had outrun its evidentiary basis, and no institution wanted to make that admission while it was still acquiring authority by maintaining the performance.

What does the standard economic framework do with this case? It can analyze the supply response and the price signals through the panic phase. It can analyze the overcapacity and the asset write-downs through the collapse phase. It cannot analyze the cultural transformation of the product, the political weaponization of compliance, the institutional incentive to maintain rituals beyond their evidentiary basis, or the way that all of these factors fed back into the demand curve in ways that no price signal could capture. The economic analysis treats demand as a function of price and income. Mask demand during this period was a function of regulation, identity, ideology, fear, fashion, and institutional ritual, and these factors moved demand in ways that prices and incomes could not predict and that the supply chain could not respond to.

The deeper observation is about the tempo, and about what the silence after the tempo indicates. The classical equilibrium framework assumed that supply and demand would adjust at roughly comparable speeds, and that the adjustment process would converge. The mask cycle compressed an entire supply-demand-collapse sequence into approximately thirty months, with the cultural and political dynamics moving even faster within the cycle. No supply chain can respond at this tempo. No capital allocation framework can be informed by signals that change quarterly. No business strategy built on traditional demand forecasting can survive a market in which the demand function is being rewritten by political and cultural forces that do not consult the demand forecasters. The equilibrium framework is not wrong about the principles of supply and demand. It is wrong about the speed at which they operate in the current environment, and the speed mismatch is the kind of structural problem that no patching of the model can fix. But there is a further point. The disciplines failed to predict what happened during COVID, which is a forgivable failure given the unprecedented nature of the event. They are also failing to retrospectively analyze what happened, which is a more fundamental failure because retrospective analysis is supposed to be the easiest thing the disciplines do. The masks, the bankruptcies, the school closures, the vaccine-conditioned mobility restrictions, the supply chain destruction, the printed currency and its inflationary aftermath, the cognitive losses in children, the deaths from causes we do not agree on how to count, all of this happened, and it is being collectively forgotten because no analytical framework exists that can hold it together as a coherent object of study. Each discipline has its piece. None of them has the whole. The whole is what was lived through, and the whole has been allowed to slip out of public discussion because nobody knows how to discuss it without exposing the inadequacy of their own analytical apparatus.

Rare Earths: When Geology Becomes Geopolitics

The fourth case is the most structural, and it is where the integration of economics, geopolitics, technology, and military strategy becomes most undeniable. It concerns the global scramble for rare earth elements and other strategic minerals, which have become the chokepoints of the technological economy in the same way that oil chokepoints defined the twentieth century. The case is current, unfolding in real time, and the most instructive examples are Myanmar and Ukraine, with Niger, the Democratic Republic of Congo, Greenland, and Taiwan as supporting context.

Rare earth elements are a group of seventeen metallic elements with specific properties that make them essential for many technologies of the current era. They are used in permanent magnets for electric motors, in wind turbine generators, in advanced electronics, in precision-guided weapons, in electric vehicle batteries, and in the high-temperature applications required for advanced manufacturing. Despite their name, they are not particularly rare in the earth's crust. They are difficult to extract economically because they are typically found in low concentrations and require complex chemical processing to separate. The processing is energy-intensive, environmentally destructive, and concentrated in a small number of facilities globally. China holds approximately ninety percent of the world's rare earth processing capacity, even though it does not hold ninety percent of the underlying deposits. The processing dominance, not the extraction dominance, is the source of Chinese leverage in this domain.

Myanmar is now the largest external supplier of rare earth raw materials to Chinese processing facilities. Approximately fifty-seven percent of China's rare earth imports came from Myanmar in 2024, with the share rising. The mining occurs in the northern frontier regions of Myanmar, particularly Kachin State and Shan State. These regions are not under the control of the Myanmar military government, the formal recognized state authority of the country. They are administered by ethnic armed organizations that have fought the central government for decades and that maintain various degrees of relationship with Beijing. The Kachin Independence Organization controls some of the deposits in Kachin State. The United Wa State Army, an armed group with longstanding ties to Beijing, controls deposits in Shan State. The mining operations are conducted by Chinese companies in partnership with these armed groups, with environmental and labor practices that would not be permitted in any jurisdiction with functional regulatory oversight. Workers, many of them recruited from Myanmar's collapsed formal economy after the 2021 military coup, work in conditions that produce documented health crises and environmental contamination, with toxic runoff poisoning rivers that flow downstream into Thailand and Laos and ultimately into the Mekong, affecting tens of millions of people who depend on these waterways for food and water.

This is the supply chain on which the global green energy transition partly depends, and on which advanced military systems including precision-guided weapons partly depend. The mineral that goes into a wind turbine generator in Germany, an electric vehicle in California, or a guided missile in Texas may have been mined in territory controlled by a Burmese ethnic armed group, processed at a Chinese refinery using inputs from a war zone, and sold into a global market that does not see and does not want to see the chain of custody. The standard economic analysis of any of these end products treats the mineral inputs as commodities purchased on world markets at prevailing prices. It does not treat them as outputs of a specific political and military arrangement that combines Chinese strategic interest, ethnic armed group governance, Myanmar military instability, environmental devastation, and the willingness of end users not to inquire too closely about the origin of their inputs. All these factors are part of the actual supply chain, and none of them have a place in the standard analytical frameworks of trade or production economics.

Ukraine presents a different but related case. The country sits on substantial deposits of lithium, titanium, uranium, and several other minerals critical to the energy transition and to defense applications. Most of these deposits are either under Russian occupation, in territory contested by active fighting, or within range of Russian artillery and missile strikes. Mining, which requires substantial fixed infrastructure and long-term capital commitments, is impossible under these conditions for any commercial operator. The deposits are valuable in principle and inaccessible in practice, which makes them assets that exist primarily as bargaining chips rather than as productive resources.

On April 30, 2025, the United States and Ukraine signed an agreement that the Trump administration called a rare earth deal. The agreement established a joint reconstruction investment fund, capitalized in part by future revenues from Ukrainian natural resource extraction. The fund covered minerals including rare earth elements but also titanium, lithium, uranium, oil, and natural gas. Ukraine retained ownership of the underlying resources and the right to determine what would be extracted and where. The United States acquired preferential rights to mineral extraction and a fifty percent share of royalties, rents, and license fees from new projects. The framing of the deal, in the public statements of both governments, was that this was an exchange of mineral access for continued American support of Ukraine in its war with Russia. The Ukrainians accepted the deal because they needed the support. The Americans pursued the deal because they wanted access to the minerals on terms favorable to American interests. Both parties understood that the minerals being negotiated were largely inaccessible under current conditions and would remain so until the war ended on terms that would allow commercial development.

In August 2025, reports emerged that the Trump administration was considering a parallel proposal to Russia that would offer Russian access to rare earth deposits in Ukrainian territories under Russian occupation, as part of a broader package of incentives intended to bring an end to the war. The same minerals, in this proposal, would be accessible by Russia under Russian-controlled administration of the relevant territories. The proposal was structured as a peace incentive, but its analytical structure was identical to the Ukraine deal. Mineral access was being offered as compensation for political behavior. The minerals themselves had no fixed sovereignty in the analytical frame the negotiators were using. They were assets to be allocated in negotiations whose primary subject was peace and security, not commercial extraction.

This is not how comparative advantage works. There is no version of Ricardo's framework that can describe minerals being offered to multiple parties simultaneously as bargaining chips in negotiations whose primary subject is the cessation of armed conflict. The minerals do not change locations. The geological deposits are where they are. What changes is the political configuration that determines who can access them, and the access is being negotiated as part of broader settlements in which the minerals are inputs to political calculations rather than outputs of economic optimization. The same physical mineral has different value depending on who controls the territory it is in, who is willing to provide security for the extraction, and what political concessions the buyer is willing to make to gain access. This is a different ontology of value than the standard economic framework was built to handle.

Niger provides another version of the same pattern. France's nuclear power generation, which produces approximately seventy percent of the country's electricity, depended significantly on uranium imported from Niger for decades. The arrangement was a legacy of French colonial relationships in West Africa, maintained through a combination of commercial contracts, security cooperation, and the institutional infrastructure that France had built across its former colonies. In July 2023, a military coup in Niger overthrew the elected government, and the new junta moved to expel French military forces and to renegotiate the terms of resource extraction. The junta aligned with Mali and Burkina Faso, both of which had experienced their own coups, in a regional bloc with stronger ties to Russia than to France. The uranium that France had relied on became suddenly contingent on the political alignment of a country that France could no longer take for granted, and the implications cascaded through French energy policy, French industrial competitiveness, and French foreign policy in Africa more broadly.

The Democratic Republic of the Congo holds most the world's known cobalt reserves. Cobalt is essential for the lithium-ion batteries that power electric vehicles and grid storage. Chinese companies have made substantial investments in Congolese cobalt extraction over the past two decades, and Chinese influence in the country's resource sector is now structural rather than incidental. Western automakers attempting to secure cobalt supply for their electric vehicle programs find themselves negotiating with intermediaries who are themselves negotiating with Chinese-aligned operators in a country whose security situation is unstable. The cobalt itself is fungible in the sense that any cobalt molecule is identical to any other. The supply chain through which it moves is not fungible. Different routes carry different geopolitical implications, and the choice of route affects everything from final product pricing to the strategic vulnerability of the buyer's industrial base.

Greenland has emerged as an unexpected addition to this picture, partly because of climate change. The melting ice cover is exposing mineral deposits that were previously inaccessible. The strategic value of these deposits, including rare earths and uranium, has drawn the attention of multiple major powers, with American interest expressed in unusually direct terms by recent administrations. Denmark's sovereignty over Greenland, which had been treated as settled for decades, has become a subject of active diplomatic discussion in ways that would have seemed bizarre even a few years ago. The geological reality is that climate change is reshaping the value of land in specific places, and the geopolitical consequences are flowing from the geological reality rather than from any change in the strategic doctrine of the involved parties. Land that was worth little when frozen is worth a great deal when its mineral content becomes accessible, and the value reshapes the politics in ways that the politics did not anticipate.

Taiwan represents the most consequential case in this category, even though Taiwan does not have rare earth deposits in any meaningful quantity. What Taiwan has is the world's most advanced semiconductor fabrication infrastructure, concentrated primarily in the Taiwan Semiconductor Manufacturing Company. The advanced chips that enable the AI economy, the chips that train large language models and that power data center operations and that make modern electric vehicles possible, are produced in Taiwan. The strategic value of Taiwan is no longer primarily about its position in the first island chain or its symbolic significance to the Chinese Communist Party's national project. It is about the fact that the global digital economy depends on a small number of fabrication facilities in a single geographic location that is contested by the second-largest economy in the world. The economics of this dependency cannot be modeled within the conventional trade frameworks. The frameworks assume that production will respond to price signals and that supply chains will diversify in response to risk. In semiconductor fabrication, the capital requirements and the technological complexity are such that diversification on relevant timescales is impossible. The dependency is structural and the structural dependency is itself a strategic asset, both for Taiwan and for the actors negotiating around it.

What ties the rare earth and strategic mineral cases together is a general observation that the chapter has been building toward. The value of physical resources is now determined by their position in chains of technological and political dependency that did not exist when the resources were first identified, and that change continuously as the technology stack evolves and as the political landscape shifts. A cobalt deposit in 2005 was a moderate commercial asset. The same deposit in 2025 is a strategic asset that nation-states are willing to negotiate around. A semiconductor fabrication facility in 2010 was a technical specialty. The same facility in 2025 is the most contested piece of industrial infrastructure on earth. A rare earth mine in Myanmar in 2015 was an environmental and labor problem of regional concern. The same mine in 2025 is a node in the supply chain that determines whether the German wind energy industry can meet its production targets. The underlying physical assets have not changed. The configuration that gives them value has changed, and the value has moved with the configuration.

This is what I mean when I say that value has become configuration-dependent rather than substance-dependent. The standard economic framework treats value as emerging from the intersection of supply and demand for a relatively stable category of good or service. The frameworks have always had some recognition that demand can shift, but the recognition was for demand shifts within stable categories. What the rare earth cases demonstrate is that the categories themselves are not stable. What counts as a strategic mineral is determined by what technology requires it, and the technology requirements are evolving faster than the mineral extraction can adapt. What counts as a fungible commodity is determined by the supply chain through which it moves, and the supply chains are increasingly differentiated by political affiliation. What counts as a tradable good is determined by whether the political environment permits the trade, and the political environment is being actively reshaped by the trade itself. The economic categories that the textbooks treat as foundations are themselves outputs of processes that the textbooks do not analyze.

The War in the Numbers

The fifth case is different in character from the first four because it is not a single event with multiple dimensions but a single event whose consequences appear in unexpected places, in industries with no apparent connection to the conflict, in the routine quarterly financial reports of corporations whose primary business has nothing to do with energy, with the Middle East, or with military affairs. The Iran war that began in late February 2026 has, within weeks, written itself into the income statements and balance sheets of luxury houses in Paris, semiconductor manufacturers in Hsinchu, advertising holding companies headquartered in Paris, and asset management firms in New York, in ways that no analyst would have predicted from the war's stated objectives or geographic scope. The case is not about the war itself. It is about the speed and reach of the second-order transmission, and what the transmission tells us about the actual structure of the global economy beneath the disciplinary surface that economists, strategists, and corporate analysts have been looking at.

Consider European luxury, an industry whose primary business is selling handbags, watches, jewelry, and apparel to high-net-worth consumers globally. The Middle East accounts for a relatively small percentage of total sales for the major luxury houses, typically in the mid-single digits. The standard analytical frameworks of the luxury sector treat the region as one geographic market among several, with its growth driven by tourist spending in Dubai, the wealth of Gulf nationals, and the broader regional economy. None of these frameworks anticipated what happened in the first quarter of 2026. When the United States and Israel attacked Iran in late February 2026 and the Strait of Hormuz crisis followed, store closures in Dubai, Bahrain, and Kuwait followed within days, driven by airport closures and security concerns. Tourist flows into the region collapsed. The high-net-worth consumers who had been spending in the Middle East largely stopped traveling there. The Russian, Chinese, Indian, and Saudi tourists who account for approximately sixty percent of luxury spending in the United Arab Emirates, according to Morgan Stanley estimates, redirected their consumption elsewhere or postponed it indefinitely.

The financial consequences arrived in the quarterly reports filed in mid-April 2026. LVMH, the world's largest luxury conglomerate, reported first-quarter revenue of nineteen point one billion euros, down six percent on a reported basis, with the Iran war costing the group a full percentage point of organic growth. The CFO of LVMH explained on the earnings call that when the conflict began in March, demand in the affected region deteriorated by between thirty and seventy percent depending on the specific shopping center or business. Kering, which owns Gucci and several other brands, reported that Gucci's revenue declined fourteen-point-three percent to one point three five billion euros, with the Iran war contributing to the decline alongside ongoing brand-specific challenges. The Kering CEO told analysts that beyond the local impact, the key consideration was the potential effect on global tourism flows and the broader macroeconomic environment, which the company was monitoring closely. Hermes, the luxury sector's perennial outperformer and historically the most resilient player in the industry, reported that activity was significantly affected by the Middle East situation, with Middle East sales down thirteen-point -four percent year-on-year. Hermes shares fell eight-point-two percent on the day of its results, a figure that reflects how much the stock had been priced for continued immunity to the sector's broader problems. Across the luxury sector, the combined market capitalization loss since the start of the Iran war exceeded one hundred billion dollars, with LVMH and Hermes each losing more than forty billion in value within weeks.

Moncler, the Italian luxury house known for its down-filled jackets, illustrates a more diffuse version of the same pattern. Moncler reported that its Middle East sales fell by fifty percent in March, but the head of strategic planning told analysts that this did not have a meaningful direct impact on the business because the Middle East accounts for less than two percent of total Moncler sales. The interesting figure was elsewhere. Moncler's overall EMEA revenue was down one percent for the first quarter, and the executives attributed this dip not to weak Middle East sales but to reduced tourist flows into Europe. Wealthy customers from overseas who would normally travel to European cities to shop at Moncler stores were not making those trips, because the decline in flights connected to the Middle East crisis had reduced tourist traffic into Europe more broadly. The transmission mechanism is worth pausing on. A military conflict in the Middle East reduced global aviation activity, which reduced tourist flows into European retail districts, which reduced revenue for a luxury house whose direct Middle East exposure was already minimal. The chain runs from regional war, through global aviation networks, through tourist behavior, into European store traffic, into a Q1 revenue figure reported in Milan. No standard analytical framework for luxury retail handles this transmission cleanly, because the framework assumes that revenue impacts are localized to where the disruption occurred, and what Moncler's numbers demonstrate is that the impact propagates through global networks in ways that disconnect cause from location.

None of this would have appeared in any economic forecast made before late February 2026. The frameworks that luxury analysts use to model the sector treat geopolitical events as exogenous shocks that affect specific regions for limited periods. The frameworks do not handle situations in which a regional conflict simultaneously closes airports across the affected zone, redirects tourist flows globally, disrupts supply chains for materials and components, and reprices the strategic value of the entire region for high-net-worth consumers worldwide. The luxury houses themselves did not predict the magnitude of the impact. Their CFOs are now describing the effects in real time on earnings calls, using language that suggests they are still trying to understand what just happened to their numbers.

The semiconductor industry presents a different version of the same pattern, with consequences that are potentially more severe because they ripple into every product that contains an advanced chip. The mechanism is helium. Helium is a colorless, odorless gas with no effective substitute for several critical applications in semiconductor manufacturing. It is used to cool the superconducting magnets in lithography equipment, to flush toxic residue after wafer washing, to maintain the precise temperature conditions required for the most advanced chip production. The fabrication of advanced semiconductors cannot continue without helium, and the helium supply has no easy alternative path.

Approximately one-third of the world's helium supply comes from Qatar, specifically from the Ras Laffan Industrial City facility, which is the largest liquefied natural gas plant on earth and produces helium as a byproduct of LNG production. In early March 2026, Iranian missile and drone strikes hit Ras Laffan as part of the broader regional conflict. Helium production at the facility halted. Approximately five point two million cubic meters of helium per month went offline. Liquid helium evaporates within roughly forty-five days, which means that stranded inventory in cryogenic containers cannot simply be held until shipping resumes. The supply gap will outlast the conflict itself by months even in the most optimistic scenarios.

The consequences are arriving across the global semiconductor industry. TSMC, the Taiwan Semiconductor Manufacturing Company, produces the world's most advanced chips and depends entirely on imported helium, with Qatar as a primary source. Samsung and SK Hynix in South Korea are similarly exposed, with South Korea sourcing over seventy percent of its helium from Qatar. Helium spot prices roughly doubled within weeks of the Ras Laffan strikes. China, which sources fifty-four percent of its helium from Qatar, saw helium prices jump from seventy-six yuan per cubic meter in early March to one hundred seventy yuan within weeks, a one hundred twenty percent increase. The Taiwan Semiconductor Industry Association called on the Taiwanese government to begin stockpiling helium. Japanese helium firms began limiting sales. The largest semiconductor manufacturers globally have indicated they have buffer inventories that can manage the short-term disruption, but the buffers have time limits, and a sustained outage at Ras Laffan would force production cuts that would propagate into every industry dependent on advanced chips, which is most of the modern industrial economy.

The standard economic analysis of the semiconductor industry treats inputs as commodities purchased on world markets at prevailing prices, with supply chain risk considered as an abstract category requiring some redundancy and stockpiling. The standard analysis does not handle the situation in which a single missile strike in a single facility in a single country, in a war ostensibly about a different country and different objectives, takes one-third of a critical input offline for months, and where the input has no substitute and where the affected industry produces components that go into nearly every product in the modern economy. The transmission mechanism from a strike on Ras Laffan to the production schedule of an advanced chip fabrication line in Hsinchu is invisible to any framework that analyzes the chip industry within its own boundaries. The transmission becomes visible only when the analyst is willing to integrate across the boundaries of energy production, military conflict, materials science, and supply chain economics. No undergraduate semiconductor course teaches this. Few graduate courses do. The professionals managing the affected supply chains are learning it as the disruption unfolds, in real time, with no framework to guide their response.

Advertising and corporate transformation services provide the third domain of unexpected impact. Publicis Groupe, headquartered in Paris and operating globally as one of the largest advertising and marketing services holding companies, reported its first quarter 2026 results in mid-April. The headline numbers were strong, with organic growth of four-point-five percent and reported revenue growth of nine point four percent. Buried within the results were two specific impacts of the Iran war that no advertising-industry analyst would have included in their forecasts a quarter earlier. First, organic revenue in the Middle East and Africa region declined five-point-one percent, reflecting the regional disruption. Second, and more consequentially, the war reduced client visibility globally and weighed on capital expenditure heavy transformation projects. Publicis Sapient, the consultancy arm of the group that handles digital and technology transformation work for major corporations, slowed materially in Q1 because clients across the global client base became more cautious about committing to large multi-year transformation projects in the face of geopolitical uncertainty. Arthur Sadoun, the chairman and chief executive of Publicis Groupe, addressed the situation on the earnings call, noting that the war had affected the technology practice and that client visibility had reduced even in markets geographically distant from the conflict.

This is the second-order transmission at its most diffuse. A war in the Middle East affects the digital transformation budget of an industrial corporation in Germany or a financial services firm in the United States, not because the corporation has any direct exposure to the Middle East but because the geopolitical uncertainty propagates through risk-adjusted decision-making at the level of corporate capital allocation. The CFO of the German industrial firm reads the news, talks to her board, considers the macroeconomic environment, and decides to defer the transformation project that was planned for Q2. Multiplied across thousands of corporate decision-makers globally, the deferral becomes a measurable slowdown in the consultancy revenue of Publicis Sapient, which appears in the Publicis Groupe quarterly report, which is read by analysts who attempt to model the relationship between geopolitical events and advertising sector performance. The relationship is real, but it does not fit any standard analytical framework, because the standard frameworks treat advertising sector performance as a function of consumer spending and brand strategy rather than as a function of corporate risk perception in distant industries facing distant geopolitical concerns.

Asset management provides the fourth domain. Larry Fink, the chairman and chief executive of BlackRock, the world's largest asset manager with assets under management measured in the trillions, gave an interview to the BBC in late March 2026 in which he addressed the Iran war directly. The substance of his analysis is worth quoting because it captures the limit of what even the most sophisticated financial actor can offer in this environment. Fink described two extreme outcomes for the war and refused to predict anything in the middle. In the first scenario, global powers reach an accommodation with Iran, Iranian oil and Venezuelan oil return to the world market, and oil prices fall to approximately forty dollars per barrel, producing what Fink called a scenario of abundance and growth. In the second scenario, the conflict continues without resolution, Iran remains a threat to trade and to the Strait of Hormuz, and oil prices stay above one hundred dollars and approach one hundred fifty dollars per barrel for years, producing what Fink called a stark and steep recession. Fink stated explicitly that he saw no plausible middle scenario between these two extremes.

The significance of this is not the specific scenarios. The significance is what it tells us about the analytical situation of the most powerful financial actor in the world. The chairman of BlackRock, with access to the deepest market data and the most sophisticated quantitative analysis available anywhere, looked at the Iran war and reported that he could not produce a probabilistic forecast with anything resembling normal confidence intervals. He could only describe two extreme outcomes and acknowledge that no one knew which would obtain. This is not how asset management is supposed to work. The discipline assumes that managers can construct probability-weighted scenarios, can hedge against the major risks, can position portfolios to capture opportunity while protecting against downside. What Fink described was a situation in which the standard methodology had broken down, where the binary nature of the possible outcomes made conventional hedging strategies inadequate, and where even an actor with BlackRock's resources could only wait to see which extreme would arrive. He did not say BlackRock was unaffected. He said the analytical framework his industry uses cannot price what is actually happening, which is a more honest and more troubling admission than any specific prediction would have been.

Across these four corporate cases, what emerges is a pattern that the standard frameworks cannot describe. A regional military conflict simultaneously affects luxury sales in geographies it does not touch, semiconductor production in countries not party to the war, advertising and consultancy revenue from clients with no direct exposure to the region, and the analytical capacity of asset managers whose business is precisely to handle this kind of uncertainty. Each impact is real, measurable, and visible in financial reports filed with regulators. Each impact would have been invisible to the standard analytical frameworks of the affected industries before the events unfolded. The frameworks did not predict, and do not now explain, what is appearing in the numbers. The numbers are appearing anyway, because the underlying integration is real, even when the analytical frameworks treat it as not their problem to handle.

This is the structural observation the chapter has been building toward, expressed in the most current possible form. The economy is not divided into the sectors that the disciplines and the trade press assume it is divided into. It is a single integrated system in which a strike on a Qatari LNG facility produces effects that flow within weeks into the cosmetics counter at Sephora, the chip in your laptop, the consultancy budget at a German manufacturer, and the portfolio allocation at a New York pension fund. The transmission paths are real, and they are operating now, in real time, generating the financial results that corporate executives are reporting and that investors are responding to. The frameworks that should be analyzing these transmissions remain organized around assumptions about sectoral independence that have been false for a generation and are now visibly false in every quarter's earnings reports. The Iran war is not just a Middle East story. It is a luxury story, a semiconductor story, an advertising story, an asset management story, and many other stories simultaneously, and the simultaneity is the substance of what is happening, not a complication that can be bracketed for the convenience of disciplinary analysis.

Case	*What It Looks Like at First*	*What It Actually Shows*	*Disciplines Forced Together*
Hormuz	An oil supply shock in the Middle East	Geography, military pressure, currency settlement, and global finance becoming one event	Energy, geopolitics, military strategy, currency systems, trade
Druzhba	A pipeline disruption	Infrastructure becoming political arsenal and electoral leverage	Energy, EU politics, war, infrastructure, elections
COVID Masks	A public health product cycle	Demand shaped by regulation, fear, identity, ritual, supply chains, and institutional authority	Public health, economics, sociology, politics, logistics
Rare Earths	Strategic minerals and supply chains	Value becoming configuration-dependent rather than substance-dependent	Geology, technology, military strategy, environment, trade
War in the Numbers	Corporate earnings affected by war	Regional conflict appearing inside luxury sales, helium supply, advertising budgets, and asset management models	Finance, war, energy, consumer behavior, supply chains

What the Cases Show Together

The five cases presented in this chapter share a structural feature that I want to name explicitly before closing. In each case, the standard analytical frameworks of one discipline can describe part of what happened, and in each case the integration across disciplines is what is doing the analytical work. The Hormuz case combines geography, military strategy, currency settlement, and political asymmetry. The Druzhba case combines infrastructure, electoral politics, alliance management, and information warfare. The mask case combines public health, supply chain economics, political identity, and institutional ritual. The rare earth cases combine geology, industrial policy, military competition, and the configuration-dependent nature of contemporary value. The corporate financial cases combine military events, energy markets, supply chain dynamics, consumer behavior, and risk perception across industries that no analytical framework treats as a coherent set. Each case looks different at the surface. Each case has the same underlying structure, which is that no single discipline can describe it, and the disciplines together can describe it only if they are willing to coordinate in ways that the academic reward systems do not currently support.

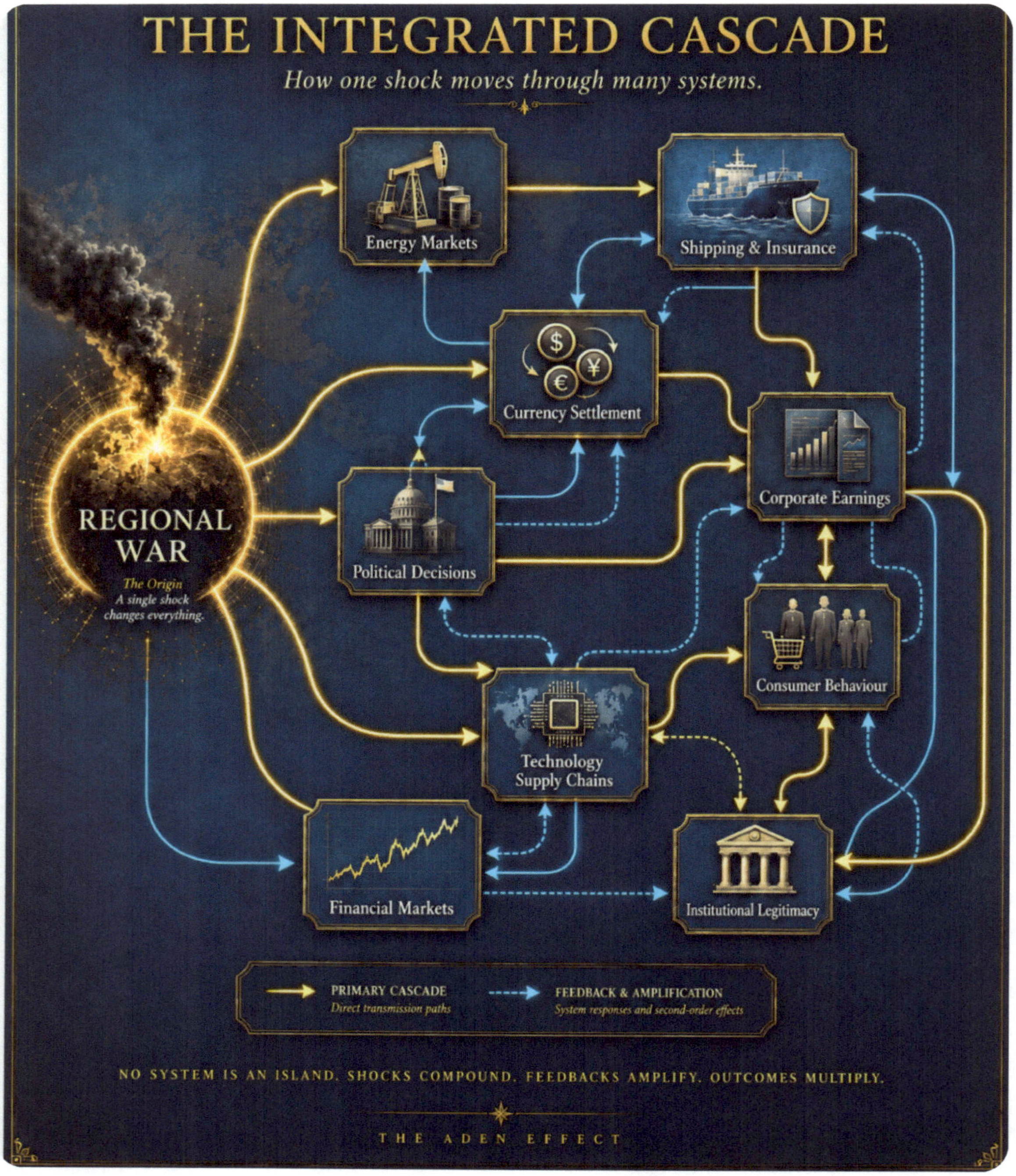

This is not a complaint about academic specialization. Specialization has produced real knowledge, and the knowledge remains valuable. The complaint is about the gap between the specialized knowledge and the integrated phenomena that the specialized knowledge cannot describe. The gap was small enough during the postwar period that the disciplines could function as if their separate analyses added up to a coherent picture. The gap is now large enough that the separate analyses are actively misleading when applied to the integrated phenomena, because the analyses treat the phenomena as decomposable in ways that lose what is happening.

The reader who has followed the cases will have noticed that the integration is not a matter of adding more variables to the existing models. It is a matter of changing the underlying ontology of what is being analyzed. Hormuz is not an oil supply event with political complications. It is a single event that is simultaneously economic, military, currency-financial, and political, and the simultaneity is the substance of the event. Druzhba is not a pipeline disruption with political consequences. It is a single sequence in which infrastructure, electoral politics, alliance management, and military strategy were being operated as a coordinated weapon system by multiple actors with different objectives, and any analysis that separates the components misses the coordination. The masks were not a public health intervention with cultural side effects. They were a single product whose meaning, function, and economic role were being continuously rewritten by political and cultural processes that were operating faster than the supply chain could respond. The rare earths are not commodities with strategic implications. They are physical materials whose value is being constituted moment by moment by configurations that span technology, geopolitics, environmental policy, and military doctrine, and that change as any of these factors change.

The next chapter takes this observation and asks what is being consumed in the fire that the old structures cannot see. The disciplines are failing, but they are failing because the world they were built to describe is itself changing in specific ways that the chapter will name. The fire is not the failure of the disciplines. The fire is the transformation of the underlying conditions, of which the disciplinary failure is one consequence among many. To understand what is happening, we must look past the failures of the analytical tools and at the changes in the substance that the tools were trying to grip. That is the work of Chapter Three.

CHAPTER THREE

WHAT IS ACTUALLY BURNING

Old structures built for a world that no longer exists.

We are not facing isolated problems. We are living through an integrated cascade. Understanding it requires new tools, broader lenses, and honest thinking.

CHAPTER THREE

What is Actually Burning

Four scenes before the argument, because the argument of this chapter is easier to see when it has already been lived in.

Aden is sitting at the kitchen table with his phone and a graph he has generated. He is eleven years old. He has asked me to check his work, which I always do because the checking is one of the few remaining ways I can still be useful to him academically. The graph plots student age against the grade level the student occupies in school, using data he has gathered from his online school's published distributions. He is testing a hypothesis, which is that the relationship between age and grade level is not quite linear in the way one might expect, because there are compression effects at the upper end where students accelerate and at the lower end where students are held back. He has generated the chart, calculated the correlation coefficient, identified the outliers, and is now considering whether his initial hypothesis should be modified. I look at him, and I do the arithmetic in my head. I first encountered the word hypothesis at university. I was nineteen. He has just used the word without explanation, in a context where the word is doing exactly the work it is supposed to do. The gap between his intellectual operations at eleven and my own intellectual operations at his age is approximately eight years of formal education. The gap has closed because the tools have arrived to close it, and the tools have arrived in the last three years of his life. I am not sure what to do with this observation. I record it.

Tulkin is one of my students in International Trade and Finance. He is preparing a presentation on the United States-Mexico-Canada Agreement and its current status, which requires him to account for the most recent developments in the ongoing tariff disputes, supply chain reconfigurations, and political maneuvering around the agreement's review. He writes to me to apologize for the delay in submitting his draft. He explains that he had to use AI to find out what had happened in the last two days, because the situation was moving faster than the standard news sources could summarize, and he needed to integrate multiple streams of reporting before he could understand what he was supposed to be presenting. I read his message and I think about what he has just described. A student of international trade could not independently track what was happening in international trade over a forty-eight-hour period. The information moves faster than unassisted human monitoring can process. He reached for the tool. He wrote a solid presentation. He did not think of this as failure. He thought of it as adaptation. He is correct.

Years ago, in a different role at a different institution, I was responsible for coordinating the curriculum of an MBA program. A situation arose in which one of the professors, teaching a course that touched on macroeconomic indicators, was informing students that GDP was an insignificant measure with no real meaning. I looked into what he was teaching and concluded that his position was not based on any sophisticated critique of the GDP framework but on a failure to understand what GDP was supposed to measure, how it was constructed, or what work it did in macroeconomic analysis. He was not arguing against GDP from a position of understanding. He was dismissing it from a position of not understanding. After the appropriate procedural steps, he was asked to resign and did so. This happened before the arrival of the current generation of AI tools. It was a straightforward case of a professor teaching something he did not understand, and the correction was to remove him from teaching. I have not thought about him in years.

I am thinking about him now because this chapter will make an argument about GDP that could superficially resemble his. I will argue that GDP has become a less adequate measure of what it was designed to measure, that the phenomenon of national economic activity has changed in ways that the GDP framework does not capture well, and that alternative frameworks like Bhutan's Gross National Happiness and the various well-being indices emerging from other countries are doing analytical work that GDP cannot do alone. This argument sounds like his argument. It is not his argument. He was wrong because he did not understand what he was critiquing. I am making a specific claim about a framework I understand, at a moment when the framework's adequacy is visibly declining. The distinction matters, and it matters for reasons beyond defending my own position. The distinction matters because the whole chapter is about what happens when frameworks that were once adequate become inadequate as the world changes around them, and it is possible to critique frameworks honestly only if you first understand what the frameworks were trying to do.

The smoke outside the window is still here. It is April 2026 in Chiang Mai, and the air quality index today is in the range that would be considered emergency conditions in any Western capital and that the children of this city treat as the ordinary spring weather because it has been their ordinary spring weather for most of their lives. The smoke is from multiple sources. Agricultural burning. Natural dry-season fires. But most of it, this year, is from the continuing civil war in Myanmar, where ethnic armed groups and the military junta have been fighting for territorial control since the 2021 coup. Some of the territory being fought over contains rare earth deposits. The deposits are being extracted, processed in Chinese facilities, and exported as components of the green energy infrastructure that European governments are building in response to climate concerns expressed by voters who are also breathing smoke, though from different fires in different locations. The whole system, from the Myanmar hillside to the German wind turbine, operates across domains that no single discipline can describe. The particulates in my son's lungs originate in a war whose economic logic connects to a climate policy whose moral logic connects to an industrial strategy whose political logic connects back to the war. And my son, doing hypothesis testing at eleven, will inherit all of it.

Categories Are Not Stable Anymore

The first thing being burned is the assumption that the categories we use to describe economic and social reality are stable natural kinds rather than historical constructions. The disciplines treated labor, capital, land, nation-states, currencies, firms, trade, and war as foundational entities that could be studied in their own right, with their internal dynamics analyzed through specific frameworks and their interactions studied across frameworks. This treatment made sense during a period when the categories were stable enough that the disciplines could take them as given. The categories are not stable now.

Consider labor. For two centuries, labor was the paradigmatic factor of production whose distinctive features were embodiment, temporality, and reproduction. Labor was performed by humans. It took time. It wore out. It required rest and nutrition. It reproduced itself through families and communities, through schools and hospitals. It accumulated skill across working lives and transmitted skill across generations. The entire political economy of the modern era grew up around labor as this specific kind of thing. Democracy developed partly because workers became citizens. Social insurance developed because workers aged. Education systems developed because labor required formation. The labor unions, the political parties, the welfare states, the citizenship frameworks, the immigration policies, all of this rested on labor being what it was, which was embodied human work that had to be performed by people who also had to live somewhere and be educated and eventually retire.

AI is dissolving labor as a stable category. Not by replacing all human labor. By producing a new kind of productive capacity that has some features of labor and some features of capital and some features that are genuinely new. A large language model trained on human text produces cognitive output that was previously available only from trained human workers.

The model does not eat, sleep, form families, age, or retire. It does not have a country. It does not vote. It does not require education because it already encodes the relevant knowledge. It does not need healthcare. Its productive capacity can be scaled by adding compute, without the social reproduction that scaling a human workforce requires. This is not capital in the traditional sense either, because capital sat passively in factories while workers operated it, and AI acts rather than waiting to be acted upon. It is something else, and the labor category and the capital category are both being stretched to accommodate it in ways that distort both categories without resolving the underlying confusion.

The confusion matters because entire institutions were built on the assumption that labor was labor and capital was capital. Labor law assumed human workers with human rights and human vulnerabilities. When the work is increasingly done by AI, labor law does not automatically cover the new entity, and the humans who trained the AI, operated the AI, or were displaced by the AI find themselves in legal categories that were not designed for their situation. Taxation assumed a stable relationship between earned income and taxable capacity. When the productive unit is software rather than a worker, the tax base shifts in ways that fiscal authorities have not yet figured out how to handle. Immigration policy assumed that countries needed workers from other countries when domestic workers were scarce or expensive. When productive capacity can be added through compute rather than through migration, the logic of immigration changes in ways that the immigration policies have not yet absorbed. The category of labor was doing analytical work across dozens of institutional domains, and the dissolution of the category is creating institutional gaps that nobody has the authority or the mandate to close.

Labor is also being dissolved through a different mechanism that predates the current AI wave and that my own working life illustrates. I hold a South African passport. I live in Thailand. I teach online for an American university. My students in any given semester are physically located in Uzbekistan, Pakistan, Bhutan, Sri Lanka, Azerbaijan, South Korea, and Thailand. My labor is performed in Chiang Mai, purchased in the United States, delivered across Central and South Asia, and invoiced in whatever currency the arrangement specifies. Thai labor law does not meaningfully cover me. American labor law does not meaningfully cover me. The labor laws of the student countries have no claim on me. I work in a space that exists between jurisdictions, enabled by connectivity infrastructure that the legal frameworks have not caught up with. I am not an unusual case. There is now a substantial global population of what I think of as netizens, workers whose primary economic community is networked rather than geographic, who include professionals at the top of their fields operating in this mode by choice because it is how their work is efficiently done. The category of netizen labor breaks several frameworks at once. It breaks Heckscher-Ohlin because my labor is not part of the Thai labor endowment even though I am physically in Thailand. It breaks the GDP framework because the value of my labor flows through jurisdictions that do not coherently account for it. It breaks immigration policy because I am not an immigrant in any traditional sense. It breaks the assumption that the nation-state is the container within which labor markets operate. The AI dissolution of labor produces non-human productive capacity. The netizen dissolution of labor delocalizes human productive capacity from geographic containment. Both are happening simultaneously. Both break the labor category. The frameworks that depend on labor being what it was cannot absorb either dissolution, let alone both together.

Consider the nation-state. For three centuries, the nation-state was the paradigmatic unit of political organization, characterized by territorial sovereignty, monopoly on legitimate violence within its borders, exclusive currency and legal systems, and the authority to enter into binding agreements with other nation-states. International relations as a discipline was built on the nation-state as the fundamental unit. Economics treated the nation-state as the container within which markets operated and the unit across which trade was measured. Political science studied politics as what happened inside nation-states. The entire architecture of analysis assumed that the nation-state was where the action was.

The nation-state is now one kind of actor among several, sharing the stage with platforms, networks, transnational firms, cities, and non-state armed groups, each of which exercises some of the functions that used to be reserved to states, and none of which fits the nation-state category. A global platform like Meta or Google or TikTok operates across every national jurisdiction, sets rules for its users that the users follow more consistently than they follow their national laws, controls information flows that used to be the responsibility of national media systems, and generates tax obligations in national frameworks that were built for firms with territorial presence. A transnational firm like TSMC or ASML or Saudi Aramco exercises influence over national economic outcomes in ways that no single nation-state can contain or direct. A city like Dubai or Singapore or Shenzhen functions as a semi-autonomous economic zone with its own regulatory environment, tax structure, and labor policies, not fully under the authority of the nation-state that nominally contains it. An armed group like the Houthis or Hamas or the Kachin Independence Organization exercises territorial control and military capability in zones that the nominal nation-state does not reach. The analysis that takes the nation-state as the fundamental unit cannot describe a world in which the nation-state is one actor among several, and the relationships among these actors are what determines what is actually happening.

A territory like Somaliland breaks the nation-state category in yet another way, by exercising every functional attribute of a nation-state while lacking the formal recognition that the international system requires for nation-state status. Somaliland has its own currency. It has its own passport. It has its own military. It has held multiple credible democratic elections with peaceful transitions of power since declaring independence in 1991. It has maintained internal security for more than three decades in a region where the nominal state next door, Somalia, has not managed to do so. By every functional criterion of what constitutes a nation-state, Somaliland is a nation-state. By the criterion that matters for the international system, which is diplomatic recognition by other nation-states and membership in international bodies, Somaliland is not a nation-state. Which definition the analyst uses determines what can be seen, and the two definitions have come apart in a way the discipline cannot coherently handle. The gap between functional reality and formal recognition is itself now one of the structural features of the international system, and the disciplines that work with the nation-state category have no framework for navigating it.

Somaliland matters for the current moment for a reason that extends beyond the category-breaking observation. The territory sits at the southern end of the Bab el-Mandeb strait, which along with the Strait of Hormuz controls global maritime trade between Europe and Asia. Berbera port, on the Somaliland coast, is the natural alternative infrastructure for regional maritime access when the main Red Sea routes are disrupted. The Houthi campaign against Red Sea shipping, conducted from Yemen since late 2023, has made this alternative infrastructure suddenly valuable in ways it was not five years ago. Container shipping companies have rerouted around the Cape of Good Hope to avoid Houthi missiles and drones, adding two weeks and substantial cost to Europe-Asia voyages, and every alternative that reduces this cost has acquired strategic weight. Somaliland, without nation-state status, controls a port that the international system needs, and the need is increasing as the primary routes become less reliable. The Ethiopia-Somaliland Memorandum of Understanding of January 2024, which gave Ethiopia sea access through Berbera in exchange for partial Ethiopian recognition of Somaliland, triggered a regional crisis precisely because an unrecognized state was able to negotiate a sovereign economic arrangement with a recognized state that rearranged the regional landscape. The same pattern of asymmetric leverage that defines the Houthis now defines Somaliland, in a different register. The Houthis use cheap weapons to endanger expensive shipping. Somaliland uses geographic position to offer an alternative when the shipping is endangered. Both are non-state actors, in the formal sense the international system uses, that are determining what global commerce actually does, while the recognized nation-states struggle to categorize what is happening to them.

Consider currency. For most of the twentieth century, currency was what nation-states issued and what circulated within and between nation-states as the medium of exchange and the store of value. The Bretton Woods system organized national currencies under the dollar. The post-Bretton Woods system of floating rates preserved the basic logic that currencies were national artifacts used for national and international transactions.

The petrodollar arrangement we discussed in Chapter Two reinforced this, with oil priced in dollars and the dollar serving as the settlement currency of global trade. Economics treated currency as a national variable, and the international monetary system as a system of interactions among national variables.

Currency is now fragmenting in ways that the national-currency framework cannot describe. We discussed the petroyuan corridor in Chapter Two. We can add to that the mBridge digital payment platform, the Saudi-China yuan swap arrangements, the UAE-India rupee-dirham settlement for specific trades, the various cryptocurrency systems that operate outside any national jurisdiction, the stablecoin architectures that peg digital tokens to national currencies while operating independently of the issuing governments, the central bank digital currencies being developed by multiple countries that will likely be incompatible with each other. The monolithic global currency system, in which all transactions ultimately cleared through dollar-denominated infrastructure, is bifurcating and multiplying. A transaction in 2026 might be denominated in dollars, settled in yuan, hedged in a stablecoin, and recorded on a ledger maintained by a consortium that does not include any central bank. What counts as currency in this environment is no longer a simple matter. It depends on the purpose, the counterparty, and the political relationship between the parties, and the same nominal dollar can function differently depending on which rail it moves through.

The disciplines have concepts for some of what is happening. Monetary economists can analyze reserve diversification. International political economists can analyze hegemonic decline. Fintech specialists can analyze specific digital currency designs. Nobody has a coherent framework for the integrated phenomenon, which is that the category of currency itself is being restructured into something that no longer has the unified meaning the discipline assumed. When the category dissolves, the analyses that depend on the category being stable dissolve with it, and the replacements have not yet been built.

The general pattern is the same across labor, nation-state, currency, firm, trade, and war. Each of these categories was a historical construction that served as a foundation for analytical work during a specific period when the categories were stable enough to be taken as natural kinds. The categories are not stable now. They are being reshaped by AI and by platform technology and by asymmetric warfare and by climate change and by demographic shifts and by the interactions among all of these. The reshaping is proceeding faster than the disciplines can absorb, and the disciplines are producing analyses that treat the categories as if they were still stable, which produces analyses that are increasingly wrong in specific ways that the disciplines cannot self-correct from within their current frameworks.

The Separations Are Gone

The second thing being burned is the idea that the domains we have been analyzing separately can be analyzed separately. Chapter One described the institutional separation of economics, politics, technology, military affairs, and human cognition into different disciplines, different departments, and different journals. Chapter Two showed through cases that the phenomena these disciplines claim to describe are actually integrated in ways that the disciplines cannot capture. What is now burning is the assumption that the separations were ever descriptive rather than merely convenient.

The assumption was that the separations reflected real distinctions in how the world was organized. Economic life was thought to have its own logic, political life its own, technological development its own, military affairs its own, and human cognition its own. The logics interacted, but each could be analyzed in its own terms first, and the interactions could be handled as secondary adjustments. This assumption worked adequately during a period when the coupling between the domains was relatively loose. Technology changed slowly enough that its effect on the economy could be absorbed as gradual productivity growth. Military affairs operated in a separate sphere from economic life for most of the population. Politics had its own cycles that did not directly shape daily economic activity for most actors. Human cognition was stable enough across generations that economic models could treat preferences as exogenous.

None of this is true now. Technology changes faster than the economy can absorb it, with AI capabilities being released in cycles measured in months and each release forcing economic adjustments that the previous release had not anticipated. Military affairs operate continuously in economic life through infrastructure weaponization, supply chain disruption, cyber operations, and information warfare, none of which respect the conceptual boundary between military and civilian activity. Politics directly shapes economic outcomes through sanctions, export controls, industrial policy, immigration policy, and regulatory decisions that move faster than economic actors can adapt. Human cognition itself is being reshaped by the information environment that humans now live inside, with implications for consumer behavior, labor market outcomes, and political preferences that no stability assumption can capture.

What this means for analysis is that the integration is not a problem to be handled through interdisciplinary coordination. It is the substance of what is happening. An analysis that separates economics from politics from technology from military affairs from cognition misses the specific shape of any actual phenomenon, because actual phenomena now take their specific shape from the interactions across these domains. The Strait of Hormuz crisis was not an oil price event with political complications. It was an event whose nature was constituted by the simultaneous operation of military, currency, political, and cognitive forces, and any analysis that separates these forces produces a different event than the one that actually occurred.

The implication for the disciplines is that they cannot be rescued by better interdisciplinary cooperation, because interdisciplinary cooperation still assumes the disciplines are the primary unit of analysis and the cooperation is an enhancement. What is required is different. What is required is to abandon the discipline as the primary unit and to take the integrated phenomenon as the primary unit, with disciplinary tools serving as instruments for understanding aspects of the phenomenon rather than as comprehensive frameworks for understanding it as a whole. This is a significant change. It is resisted by every institutional incentive in the current academic structure. It is also, in my judgment, unavoidable, because the disciplines that refuse to make the change will continue producing analyses that do not describe the phenomena they are supposed to describe, and the analyses will be progressively discredited by reality, and the discipline itself will lose its authority to speak on the subjects it claims to cover.

Meaning Is Configuration-Dependent Now

The third thing being burned is the assumption that the meaning of objects, practices, and measurements is stable enough to support analysis. The mask case in Chapter Two showed the same physical object carrying incompatible meanings simultaneously across different communities. The rare earth cases showed the same mineral having wildly different strategic values depending on who controlled the territory it sat under. The petrodollar case showed the same financial instrument operating as different things on different settlement rails. What is emerging from these cases and others is that meaning has become configuration-dependent in a way that challenges the foundations of how the disciplines have analyzed everything they analyze.

The disciplines operated on the assumption that objects and practices had stable meanings that could be taken as given in analysis. A dollar was a dollar. A mask was a mask. A worker was a worker. A firm was a firm. A country was a country. The meanings were given by the category the object or practice belonged to, and the categories were the ones we just discussed under the first thread. When those categories were stable, meanings were stable. When those categories dissolve, meanings dissolve with them, and the disciplines find themselves analyzing objects whose meaning is itself in question.

Consider GDP, since I have committed to discussing it. Gross Domestic Product is a measurement framework, not a thing in the world. It was designed in the 1930s and 1940s, during a specific period when the question of how to measure national economic activity had a reasonably clear answer. Economic activity meant the production and exchange of goods and services within national borders, measurable through transactions that had monetary prices. GDP captured this. It did not capture household production, volunteer work, environmental costs, or the value of free time, but it did capture a real thing, which was the monetary economic activity of a country over a period. For most of the twentieth century, that thing was what people cared about when they asked whether the economy was growing, and GDP was an adequate measure of it.

What has happened is that the thing itself has changed in ways that GDP does not capture well. First, a growing portion of economic activity happens through transactions that are either free at the point of use or priced in ways that do not reflect the value being transferred. Free services provided by digital platforms have enormous economic value to users but contribute to GDP only through the advertising revenue of the platforms, which is a fraction of the value being transferred. Open-source software infrastructure underlies much of the digital economy but is not captured in GDP except through the wages of developers, who mostly work on it as an adjunct to other paid work. Social media, search, navigation, translation, and many other services generate consumer value that GDP does not capture. A country whose citizens use Google Maps billions of times a year has received enormous value that GDP does not measure, because the user pays nothing at the point of use.

Second, cross-border digital flows do not map cleanly onto national borders, which GDP requires for its territorial definition. A Vietnamese developer working for an American firm, paid in dollars deposited in a Singapore bank, using tools hosted on cloud infrastructure in multiple jurisdictions, is contributing to economic activity that no single country's GDP captures coherently. The activity is real. The output is real. Where the GDP accrues is a matter of convention, and the conventions were designed for an era when economic activity was mostly territorially bounded.

Third, GDP measures activity but not the sustainability of the activity or the well-being it generates. A country that grows its GDP by depleting its aquifers, polluting its air, and exhausting its workers shows up as growing. A country that sustains its ecological base, maintains the health and happiness of its population, and builds long-term capacity shows up as flat. The GDP measurement does not care about the distinction. For decades, this limitation was acknowledged but treated as a minor technical issue. It is not a minor issue when the ecological and human costs of GDP-maximizing behavior are themselves becoming the dominant economic problems of the era.

Fourth, and this is perhaps the largest of the current inadequacies, GDP cannot distinguish between output produced by human labor and output produced by AI assistance or automation. A consultant who bills a client ten thousand dollars contributes the same ten thousand to GDP whether she wrote the report over three weeks of unassisted work or assembled it in thirty minutes from AI-generated drafts. The framework registers the transaction, not the production process. When the relationship between transaction price and labor input breaks, as it is breaking now across every professional services domain, GDP is measuring something other than what it was designed to measure. The problem extends beyond professional services. A customer service operation that employed five thousand representatives ten years ago may employ five hundred representatives today, with AI systems handling the bulk of inquiries, producing equal or better service at much lower employment, wages, and supporting economic activity. GDP shows the first configuration as more economically significant than the second, even though the second produces the same output with less resource consumption. A road built by five hundred workers over two years enters GDP through a different profile than the same road built by automated equipment with twenty supervisors in six months, even though the final infrastructure is identical. The AI contribution itself is largely invisible to the framework. When you use AI to do three hours of work in a few minutes at a cost of a few cents, GDP registers the few cents, not the value of the work. The producer captures the surplus indirectly through higher margins or more output, but the direct value creation by the AI does not appear as production. The framework was designed to measure monetary transactions for goods and services produced by human labor within national borders. Each element of that design is weakening. What GDP captures is becoming a smaller share of what the economy actually does, and the framework has no internal mechanism for self-correction because the inadequacies are built into its definition rather than arising from measurement errors.

Bhutan's Gross National Happiness framework, which I discussed in Chapter One, is one attempt to address the inadequacy. It measures nine domains of well-being, applies a specific methodology, and screens government policy proposals against the framework. Several other countries have developed parallel well-being measures alongside GDP. The United Nations has endorsed the broader principle. None of these alternatives has displaced GDP as the headline measure of economic success, but the erosion of GDP's authority is visible and proceeding, because the measurement framework is increasingly perceived as capturing something less important than what it claims to capture.

Here is where I have to be careful. When I say GDP has become a less adequate measure, I am not saying what the professor I had to let go was saying. He was saying GDP was insignificant without understanding what it measured. I am saying GDP measures something specific, that something was a reasonable proxy for economic success during a specific historical period, and that the thing it measures has changed in ways that make the measure less adequate as a proxy for what we care about. The distinction is between dismissing a framework and understanding the conditions under which a framework ceases to be adequate. The first is easy and wrong. The second is harder and necessary. I make the distinction because the chapter is about what is burning, and part of what is burning is the stability of meaning itself, and the stability of meaning of a measurement framework is a specific case of the larger phenomenon.

The broader implication is that every measurement, every category, every analytical framework the disciplines use is subject to the same dynamic. The framework was designed for a world in which the thing it measured was relatively stable. The thing has changed. The framework now measures a less adequate version of what it was designed to measure. The discipline must either acknowledge this and rebuild the framework or continue using the framework while the gap between what it measures and what matters grows. The professional incentives tend toward continuing to use the framework. The analytical consequences of continuing to use the framework are that the analysis becomes progressively less useful, and the discipline that produces the analysis becomes progressively less authoritative.

Discontinuity Is Normal Now

The fourth thing being burned is the assumption that the future is approximately the present with adjustments. All of modern planning, all of modern forecasting, all of modern insurance pricing, all of modern capital allocation, all of modern career development, all of modern education rests on some version of this assumption. We can plan for the future because the future will mostly resemble the present, with some changes we can estimate through extrapolation. The assumption worked well during periods of stable growth, moderate technological change, and limited geopolitical upheaval. It does not work now.

Consider the last six years. A global pandemic shut down the world economy for roughly eighteen months, producing consequences that include supply chain disruption, inflation, debt accumulation, political polarization, and educational losses that will affect a generation. A major war in Europe disrupted energy and food markets globally, forcing the restructuring of European defense spending, trade patterns, and diplomatic alignments. A war in the Middle East closed a strait through which one-fifth of the world's seaborne oil passes, disrupted global luxury markets, threatened semiconductor production, and accelerated the fragmentation of the dollar-based settlement system. AI capabilities evolved from curiosities to foundational technologies in roughly three years, reshaping education, labor markets, creative industries, and military affairs. Climate patterns shifted regionally in ways that forced population movements, agricultural adjustments, and insurance industry stress. A reconfiguration of American trade policy disrupted global supply chains with weeks of warning. None of these events would have been predicted with any precision from a baseline of 2018. Each of them had consequences that cascade through multiple other domains. The cumulative effect is that the last six years have included more discontinuities than the previous thirty, and the pattern shows no sign of slowing.

The discontinuities are not random shocks distributed around a stable trend. They are themselves the pattern. The world is producing discontinuities faster than the planning frameworks can absorb them, and the planning frameworks are still assuming that discontinuities are rare deviations from a stable baseline. When a planning framework assumes discontinuities are rare and discontinuities are normal, the framework produces plans that do not survive their own assumptions. The plans are not wrong because the planners were incompetent. The plans are wrong because they assume a kind of world that is no longer operating, and the plans continue to be produced because no alternative framework has replaced them.

This has specific consequences for every institution that depends on stable forecasting. Insurance companies cannot price risk accurately because the risk distributions are not stable. Pension funds cannot project returns over forty-year horizons because the economic environment that would generate those returns cannot be assumed to exist. Universities cannot design curricula for careers their students will pursue because the careers do not yet exist and existing careers are disappearing on timescales shorter than a degree program. Militaries cannot plan force structures for future conflicts because the nature of future conflicts is being rewritten by technological changes measured in months. Governments cannot plan tax revenues because the economic activity that generates revenue is moving across jurisdictions faster than tax authorities can adapt. Individuals cannot plan careers, marriages, retirements, or inheritances with the confidence that their grandparents had, because the assumptions that supported confident planning have weakened.

My own teaching illustrates the problem at a smaller scale. Planning an International Trade and Finance course for a full semester used to be straightforward. The case studies chosen in August would still be the right case studies in December, because the underlying trade environment changed slowly enough that the cases remained current. This is no longer possible. The cases I would use in week twelve do not exist in week one, and the cases I chose in week one has been overtaken by week twelve. I now teach a subject that is being rewritten while I teach it, and I have to adjust the syllabus continuously to match what is happening in the world the syllabus is supposed to describe. Some foundations do stay the same. Supply and demand still operate. Incentives still matter. Comparative advantage retains explanatory value within its limits. But the foundations that remain stable are surrounded by a growing envelope of activity that has been absorbed into political theater, where trade decisions are made for political reasons that serve political narratives, and the political reasons override the economic logic often enough that teaching the economic logic in isolation produces students who cannot explain what they are observing. The tariff announcements that arrive as social media posts and reverse as social media posts a week later. The sanctions packages that are negotiated for their domestic political effects and abandoned when the effects are achieved.

The trade agreements that are signed for photo opportunities and ignored in practice. All of this is now continuous, and it shapes the actual flow of global commerce in ways that the economic framework treats as exogenous. Teaching international trade in 2026 requires integrating the political theater as a constitutive element of the subject, not as a complicating factor that can be bracketed for analytical convenience. The frameworks that treated it as bracketed produce graduates who are systematically unprepared for the environment, they will work in.

The psychological and social effects of this are visible but rarely named explicitly. A generation that cannot plan its future with the confidence that previous generations had responds by either foreshortening its planning horizon or by abandoning planning entirely in favor of shorter-term optimization. This shows up in housing markets, in marriage rates, in birthrates, in investment patterns, in political behavior. It shows up in the psychological literature as increased anxiety and decreased sense of agency. It shows up in the consumer economy as a shift away from durable long-term goods and toward experiential consumption and subscription services. It shows up in the labor market as reduced loyalty to employers and increased willingness to move frequently. All of these shifts can be analyzed as individual preferences, but they are also rational adaptations to an environment in which long-term planning has become less feasible, and the adaptations aggregate into patterns that no individual framework can explain.

The analytical implication is that the planning and forecasting apparatus of modern institutions needs to be rebuilt on assumptions that take discontinuity as normal rather than exceptional. This is not a call for shorter planning horizons. Shorter horizons are themselves an adaptation that has costs. It is a call for different kinds of planning, planning that builds in flexibility, redundancy, and the capacity to absorb surprises, rather than planning that assumes surprises are rare enough to ignore. The engineering principle of designing for the failure modes rather than for the expected operating conditions is closer to what the current environment requires than the economic principle of designing for the equilibrium that will be approached over time. The equilibrium will not be approached. The system will continue to produce surprises, and the institutions that survive will be the ones that are designed to handle surprises rather than to plan them away.

What Is Burning	*Old Assumption*	*What Has Changed*	*Why It Matters*
Stable Categories	Labor, capital, land, currency, firms, and nation-states could be treated as stable analytical units.	AI, platforms, digital labor, non-state actors, and fragmented currency systems are dissolving these categories.	The models built on these categories become less accurate when the categories themselves change.
Separate Domains	Economics, politics, technology, military affairs, and cognition could be studied separately.	These domains now interact continuously and shape one another in real time.	Integrated phenomena cannot be understood through separated disciplines.
Stable Meaning	A dollar, a mask, a worker, a country, or GDP meant roughly the same thing across contexts.	Meaning now depends on configuration, platform, politics, identity, settlement rail, and institutional setting.	Analysis fails when it assumes fixed meanings for things whose meaning is changing.
Continuity	The future would mostly resemble the present, with adjustments.	Discontinuity has become normal: pandemics, wars, AI, climate shocks, sanctions, and trade disruptions arrive faster than institutions can adapt.	Planning must shift from prediction and optimization to resilience, flexibility, and failure-mode design.

What Is Left After the Fire

This chapter has named four things that are being consumed. The stability of categories. The separations between domains. The stability of meaning. The assumption of continuity. Each of these was a foundation of the analytical frameworks that Chapters One and Two described as failing. Each of them is being lost, and the loss is the reason the frameworks are failing. What is burning is not the disciplines themselves but the conditions under which the disciplines could operate with their current assumptions.

Three more things are also burning, and I name them here so they do not slip through the cracks even though I will develop them in later chapters. Scale as the generator of value is burning, and Chapter Eight will address this through the asymmetric warfare and asymmetric economics patterns that are emerging. Trust in credentialed institutional authority is burning, and Chapter Five will address this through the accountability collapse that AI decision-making is producing. The separation between observer and observed is burning, and Chapter Six will address this through the cognitive restructuring that AI collaboration is producing in the humans who use it. All of these are parts of the same fire, and the chapter would not honor its title if it pretended that the four threads it developed were the whole of what is being lost.

What remains, though, is not nothing. The fire is transforming, not destroying. Something will emerge from the combustion, and the emergence is what the rest of this book is about. Part Two develops the framework for integrated analysis that takes the collapsing separations as its starting point and builds analytical tools that work across them. Part Three examines what is being built to replace the institutional and cognitive arrangements that are failing. Part Four returns to the personal question of how to live inside this transition and what we owe to the generation that will inherit whatever the settlement turns out to be.

Before we turn to the constructive work, I want to say one thing directly that the diagnostic chapters have circled without stating plainly. The fire is not a tragedy. It is also not a liberation. It is a historical event of large scale whose character will be determined partly by how the actors living through it respond. The actors who refuse to see what is burning will be consumed by the burning. The actors who celebrate the burning will be complicit in destroying what should have been preserved. The actors who see clearly, who name what is being lost without sentimentality and what is emerging without triumphalism, who hold both the diagnosis and the response in view, are the actors whose work will matter most during the transition. This book is written for those actors, and the remaining chapters are an attempt to equip them with frameworks that can survive the environment in which they will be used.

My son is still at the kitchen table. He has moved on from his hypothesis testing to something else, some other project I have not yet examined. He is eleven years old. The fire is burning the world he will inherit, and whatever settlement emerges from the fire is the world he will live in for most of his life. I owe him a clear-eyed account of what is happening. I owe him the frameworks to understand it. I owe him the honesty to say that nobody yet knows how it ends. And I owe him the commitment to keep trying to see clearly, and to write what I see, for as long as I can. This book is partly that attempt. The remaining chapters are where the attempt moves from diagnosis to construction. Part One ends here. Part Two begins with the feedback loops that are doing the integrating work the disciplines cannot.

PART TWO
THE INTEGRATION
FROM DIAGNOSIS TO DIRECTION.
FROM SEPARATION TO SYNTHESIS.
DISCIPLINARY SILOS
ECONOMICS
POLITICS
OLD MODELS
FRAGMENTED ANALYSIS
OUTDATED ASSUMPTIONS
LINEAR THINKING
INTEGRATED UNDERSTANDING
SYSTEMS THINKING
FEEDBACK LOOPS
CROSS-DOMAIN INSIGHTS
ADAPTIVE FRAMEWORKS
ACCOUNTABILITY & ETHICS
RESILIENT INSTITUTIONS
A FRAMEWORK FOR THE COMPLEX WORLD.

Part Two: The Integration

Diagnosis without prescription is a kind of cowardice. The first three chapters of this book have argued that the disciplinary frameworks have failed, that the failures appear in specific events that no single discipline can explain, and that the failures rest on changes in the underlying world that the disciplines were not built to handle. If the book stopped there, it would be one more catalogue of what is broken, and the world has many of those already. The reader who has followed Part One has earned the right to ask what to do, and the author who wrote Part One has the obligation to attempt an answer. Part Two is that attempt.

The attempt has a specific character that I want to name before the work begins, because the character will determine how the chapters that follow should be read. What Part Two offers is not a new theory of integrated phenomena. It is too early for theory, because theory requires that the underlying patterns have stabilized enough to be captured in formal terms, and the patterns have not yet stabilized. What Part Two offers instead is a framework for analysis, which is something more modest and more useful at the current moment. A framework gives the analyst tools for thinking, vocabulary for naming, and structure for organizing what would otherwise be a mass of unrelated observations. It does not predict. It does not claim completeness. It does not pretend that the next iteration will not improve on it. What it does is give serious people a way to begin the analytical work that the disciplines have failed to begin, with the understanding that the work itself will refine the framework as it proceeds.

Three chapters carry the framework. Chapter Four names and describes the feedback loops that are doing the integration work the disciplines have refused to do. The loops connect domains that the disciplines treat as separate, and the connections are the substance of contemporary phenomena rather than the noise around them. Chapter Five examines the collapse of accountability that AI-human hybrid decision-making produces and argues that this collapse is the most important political problem of the next decade because accountability is the foundation of legitimate authority. Chapter Six addresses the new cognitive ground, including the changes in human cognition produced by the information environment we now inhabit, the observer-observed problem when the analytical tools are themselves participants in the phenomena being analyzed, and the implications for what serious thinking looks like in the current moment. The three chapters do different work but they share a structural feature, which is that none of them can be reduced to the categories of any single existing discipline, and the integrations they describe cannot be separated into disciplinary components without losing what is most important about them.

The work of Part Two will be more demanding than the work of Part One. Diagnosis is the easier movement, because the diagnostic work proceeds by demonstrating that something is wrong, and the wrongness is observable once it is pointed at. Construction is harder. Construction proceeds by proposing tools that may or may not work, and the working has to be tested against phenomena that are themselves moving. The reader who found Part One persuasive may find Part Two more contentious, because the framework I propose can be argued with in ways that diagnosis cannot. This is appropriate. The framework should be argued with. Better frameworks will emerge from the arguments, and the arguments themselves are part of the work that the current moment requires.

I want to name one more thing before Chapter Four begins. The framework is being built in real time, against an environment that is itself changing as the framework is being written. By the time you read this, some of what I describe will have been overtaken, and some of the cases I use to illustrate the framework will have been replaced by newer cases that demonstrate the same patterns in different forms. This is not a flaw in the work. It is the condition of any work that takes the current moment as its subject. The framework is meant to outlast the cases that illustrate it, by being useful for analyzing whatever cases the reader encounters, including the cases that will exist when the reader picks up the book and the cases that emerge after the book has gone to press. If the framework cannot do this, it has failed at what it was attempting. If it can, it has done the work the moment requires. The judgment of whether it succeeds belongs to the reader, and the test will not be whether the cases I use are still current but whether the framework helps the reader make sense of cases that are.

Part One ended with my son at the kitchen table, doing hypothesis testing at eleven, and with the obligation I owe him to provide a clear-eyed account of what is happening. Part Two is the next move in meeting that obligation. He will not read this book for years. By the time he does, the specific arguments may have aged in ways that are visible to him but were not visible to me. What I hope, and what the framework attempts, is that the underlying analytical apparatus will still be useful when he encounters it, even if the specific examples have been replaced by his own. This is the test I am writing toward. It is the only test that ultimately matters.

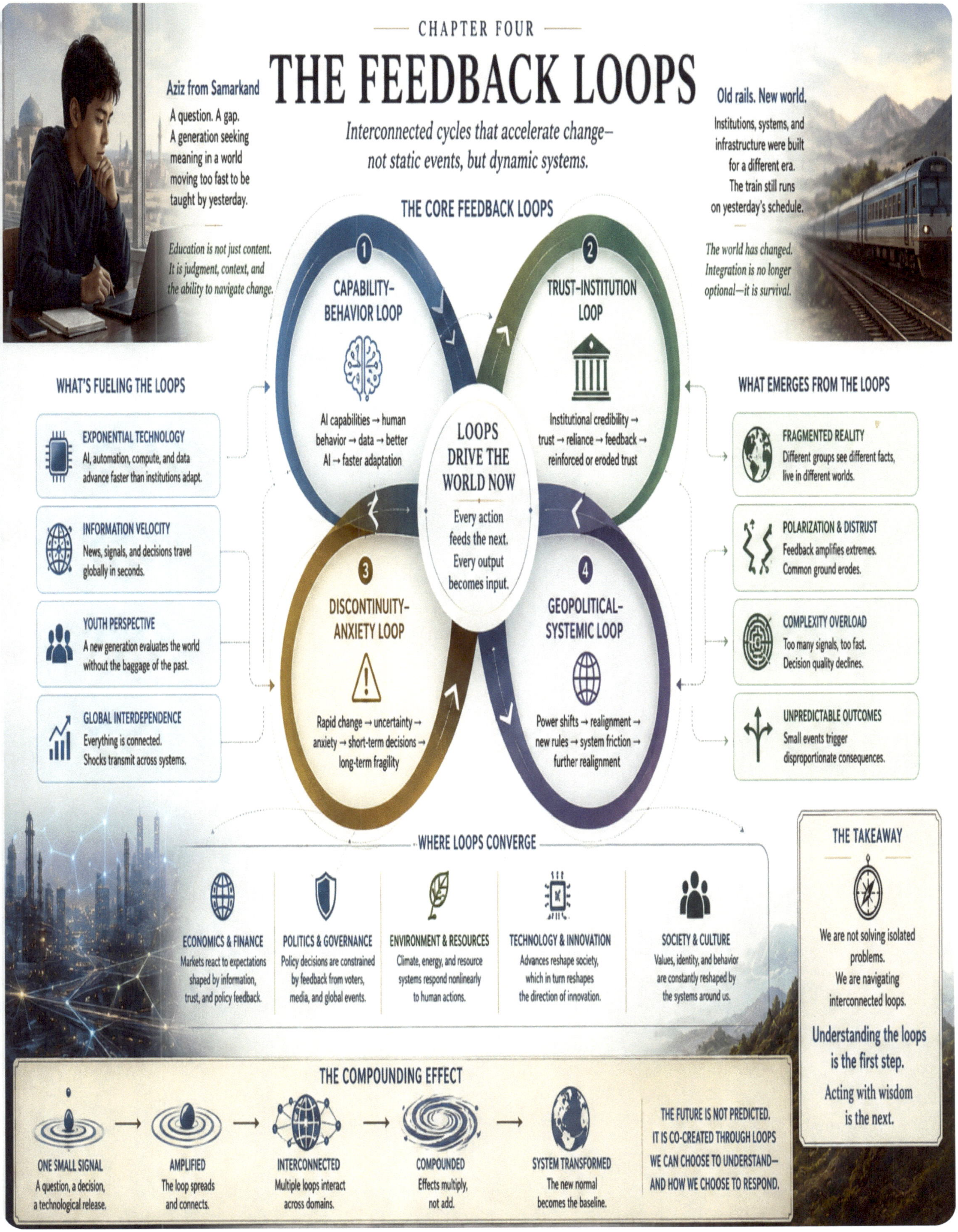
CHAPTER FOUR
THE FEEDBACK LOOPS
Interconnected cycles that accelerate change–
not static events, but dynamic systems.
Aziz from Samarkand
A question. A gap.
A generation seeking meaning in a world moving too fast to be taught by yesterday.
Education is not just content. It is judgment, context, and the ability to navigate change.
Old rails. New world.
Institutions, systems, and infrastructure were built for a different era.
The train still runs on yesterday's schedule.
The world has changed. Integration is no longer optional—it is survival.
THE CORE FEEDBACK LOOPS
1 CAPABILITY-BEHAVIOR LOOP
AI capabilities → human behavior → data → better AI → faster adaptation
2 TRUST-INSTITUTION LOOP
Institutional credibility → trust → reliance → feedback → reinforced or eroded trust
3 DISCONTINUITY-ANXIETY LOOP
Rapid change → uncertainty → anxiety → short-term decisions → long-term fragility
4 GEOPOLITICAL-SYSTEMIC LOOP
Power shifts → realignment → new rules → system friction → further realignment
LOOPS DRIVE THE WORLD NOW
Every action feeds the next. Every output becomes input.
WHAT'S FUELING THE LOOPS
EXPONENTIAL TECHNOLOGY
AI, automation, compute, and data advance faster than institutions adapt.
INFORMATION VELOCITY
News, signals, and decisions travel globally in seconds.
YOUTH PERSPECTIVE
A new generation evaluates the world without the baggage of the past.
GLOBAL INTERDEPENDENCE
Everything is connected. Shocks transmit across systems.
WHAT EMERGES FROM THE LOOPS
FRAGMENTED REALITY
Different groups see different facts, live in different worlds.
POLARIZATION & DISTRUST
Feedback amplifies extremes. Common ground erodes.
COMPLEXITY OVERLOAD
Too many signals, too fast. Decision quality declines.
UNPREDICTABLE OUTCOMES
Small events trigger disproportionate consequences.
WHERE LOOPS CONVERGE
ECONOMICS & FINANCE
Markets react to expectations shaped by information, trust, and policy feedback.
POLITICS & GOVERNANCE
Policy decisions are constrained by feedback from voters, media, and global events.
ENVIRONMENT & RESOURCES
Climate, energy, and resource systems respond nonlinearly to human actions.
TECHNOLOGY & INNOVATION
Advances reshape society, which in turn reshapes the direction of innovation.
SOCIETY & CULTURE
Values, identity, and behavior are constantly reshaped by the systems around us.
THE TAKEAWAY
We are not solving isolated problems.
We are navigating interconnected loops.
Understanding the loops is the first step.
Acting with wisdom is the next.
THE COMPOUNDING EFFECT
ONE SMALL SIGNAL
A question, a decision, a technological release.
AMPLIFIED
The loop spreads and connects.
INTERCONNECTED
Multiple loops interact across domains.
COMPOUNDED
Effects multiply, not add.
SYSTEM TRANSFORMED
The new normal becomes the baseline.
THE FUTURE IS NOT PREDICTED.
IT IS CO-CREATED THROUGH LOOPS
WE CAN CHOOSE TO UNDERSTAND—
AND HOW WE CHOOSE TO RESPOND.

CHAPTER FOUR

The Feedback Loops

Aziz is from Samarkand. He is twenty years old. He is one of my students in Business Analytics, and yesterday he asked me a question that turned into a longer conversation than either of us had planned. He wanted to know whether I thought he should continue with his university education. The question was not about money. His family could afford his studies. The question was about whether the studies themselves were worth the time. He had noticed that most of his subjects were teaching him history. The frameworks were old. The case studies were old. The textbooks had been written for a world that he could see, around him, was no longer the world he was living in. He could access the same material faster through Claude, with more detail and better tailored to his actual questions. So why was he sitting in lectures? Why was he completing assignments that asked him to apply frameworks his professors knew were inadequate to phenomena the frameworks did not describe?

I gave him my honest answer, which was that he was largely right and that the situation he described was not going to be fixed by his university because the university could not see itself clearly enough to fix it. The new courses being added were old maps with newer typography. The frameworks being taught were the same frameworks I had been describing in this book as failed. He was correct that he could access the historical material more efficiently through AI. What he could not access through AI, I told him, was the judgment to know what to do with the material. AI is excellent at producing answers. It is not yet capable of telling him which questions are worth asking, which answers matter, which discussions to enter and which to avoid, which decisions to make when the analysis runs out. The judgment calls are still his to make, and the judgment is forming in him whether he notices it or not, partly through formal education that is increasingly inadequate, and partly through conversations like the one we were having, and partly through his own observation of the world he is preparing to enter. The university is one input among several, and he should not abandon it but he should also not expect it to do the work he assumes universities are supposed to do.

He thought about this for a moment and then he thanked me. He said he wished we had more time, but he had to leave to catch his train. The train left at a specific minute. The minute had been determined by a timetable inherited from infrastructure built during the Soviet period, on rails laid down by an empire that collapsed before Aziz was born, in a country that has rebuilt itself politically twice since the rails were laid. Missing the train would cost him substantially more inconvenience than continuing the conversation would have cost. So he left. The conversation was unfinished. The conversation will probably remain unfinished, because the phenomena Aziz was asking about are not the kind that get finished in conversations. They are the kind that get worked through across years of living, with occasional clarifying exchanges along the way.

I want to start this chapter with that exchange because the exchange contains, in compressed form, most of what the chapter is about. Aziz was experiencing several things simultaneously. He was experiencing the gap between what his university was teaching and what the world was doing, which is the trust-institution-formation problem. He was experiencing the cognitive transformation produced by AI access to information, which is the capability-behavior problem. He was experiencing the fear that the discontinuities he was watching in the world would render his preparation useless, which is the discontinuity problem we discussed in Chapter Three. He was experiencing the contradictions of living simultaneously inside a new informational environment and an old physical infrastructure, the train running on its old schedule while the questions in his head were entirely new. And he was experiencing, although he did not name it this way, the necessity of forming his own judgment because no institution was going to form it for him on terms adequate to the situation he would inhabit.

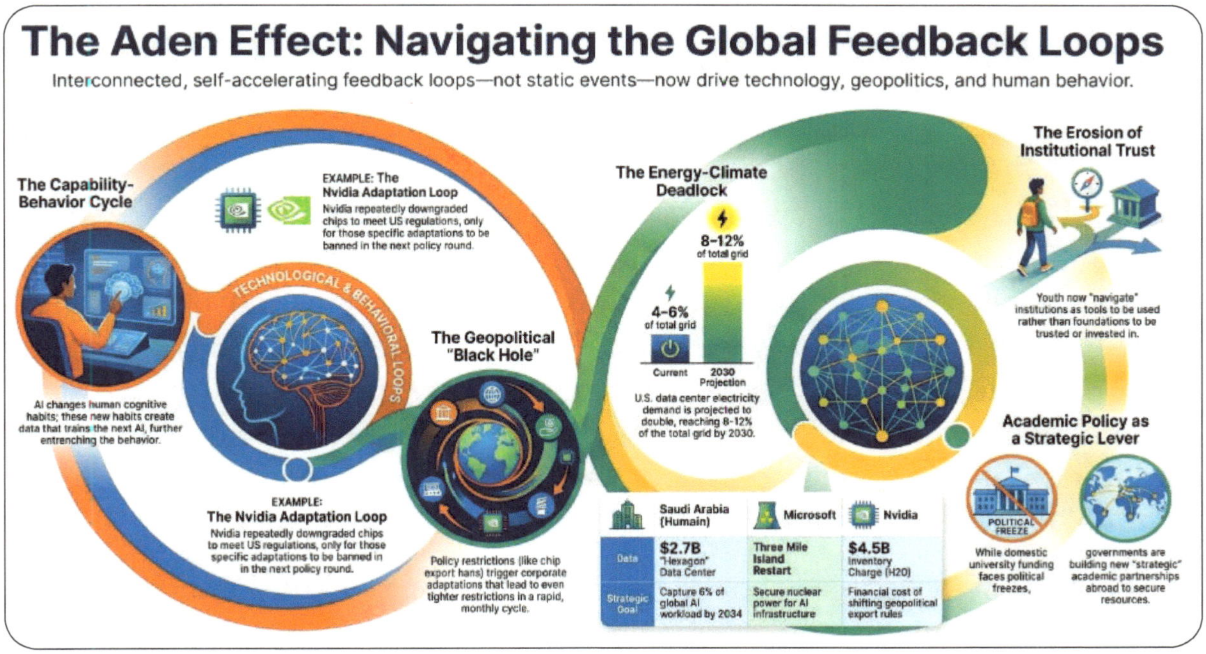

None of these experiences can be analyzed separately. The trust problem produces the cognitive transformation produces the discontinuity anxiety produces the judgment necessity, and each of them feeds back into the others. Aziz cannot resolve any of them in isolation, and any analytical framework that treats them as separate problems will miss what is happening to him. The chapter is about the loops that connect these phenomena, and the loops are what I am asking you to start seeing as the unit of analysis. Not the discrete phenomena that the disciplines have been trained to analyze. The loops in which the discrete phenomena are embedded, where the actual dynamics of contemporary life are operating.

The Capability-Behavior Loop

The first loop runs between AI capabilities and human cognitive behavior. New AI capabilities reach users. Users adapt their thinking, working, and communicating to take advantage of the capabilities. The adaptations produce data that becomes training material for the next generation of AI capabilities. The next generation is more aligned with the new patterns of human use, which accelerates the adaptation. The cycle compresses. Each iteration shortens the time between capability release and behavioral integration, and each iteration also shortens the time between behavioral integration, and the next capability release that builds on it. The loop is not stable. It does not converge. It accelerates.

Consider what happens to a single cognitive activity, the production of written analysis. Five years ago, a student writing an analytical paper would read sources, take notes, organize an outline, draft a first version, revise, and submit. The cognitive activity included reading comprehension, synthesis, structural reasoning, and prose generation, and each of these activities was practiced repeatedly across the work. Three years ago, AI tools became capable enough to assist with prose generation, and students who used them shifted some of the cognitive load away from sentence-level production toward higher-level structural and editorial decisions. Today, AI tools are capable enough to handle the synthesis and the structural reasoning if the student knows how to prompt them well, and the student's cognitive activity has shifted further, toward question formulation, source evaluation, and judgment about which AI outputs to accept and which to discard. The same word, paper, refers to a different cognitive activity than it did five years ago, even when the final document looks similar. The activity itself has been restructured, and the restructuring has happened largely without explicit acknowledgment by the institutions that grade the papers.

This is the first half of the loop. AI capabilities change what humans do when they think. The second half is what happens to AI capabilities as a result. The text that the next generation of models' trains on includes the text being produced now by humans using AI assistance. If the next generation is trained on text generated through human-AI collaboration, the next generation will be more fluent in the patterns of that collaboration. It will anticipate what the human prompter wants more reliably, will generate outputs that fit more cleanly into human-AI workflows, and will be more aligned with the cognitive style that the previous generation produced in its users. The training is not random. It is biased toward the styles of thought that AI users have been developing, because those are the styles that show up in the recent text. The next generation reinforces those styles by being better at supporting them, and the users who adopted the styles in the first place find themselves working with tools that are progressively more attuned to their adopted patterns.

The compounding is the part that the standard frameworks miss. A static analysis of AI use would describe how a particular tool affects a particular task. A loop analysis describes how the tool affects the user, who produces data that affects the next tool, which affects the user further. The static framework gives you a snapshot. The loop framework gives you a trajectory. The trajectory is what matters for understanding where this is going, because the question is not what AI does to thinking right now but what the iterating loop does to thinking across multiple cycles.

Aziz is in the loop. He is twenty years old. He has been using AI tools since he was sixteen or seventeen, which means his analytical maturation has occurred entirely inside the capability-behavior loop. His native cognitive patterns include AI as a participant in a way that mine do not, because I formed my analytical habits before the loop began compressing at its current rate. When he asks whether he should continue his studies, the question is being asked from inside the loop, and his available answers are also being shaped from inside the loop. He cannot step outside it to evaluate it from a stable external position, because the position from which he would evaluate it is itself being shaped by the loop. This is true for him, and it is true for everyone now, and it is also why the standard educational frameworks cannot evaluate themselves usefully. They are inside the loop they are trying to evaluate, and the evaluation tools they have are themselves products of the loop's earlier iterations.

This does not mean that nothing useful can be said. It means that the analysis must acknowledge its own position inside the phenomenon being analyzed, which is something the disciplines have generally been unwilling to do because acknowledging it requires giving up the pretense of external objective analysis that the disciplines have used to legitimize their authority. The honest analysis is one that says, openly, that the analyst is also a participant, that the analytical tools are also products of the loop, and that the conclusions reached are provisional precisely because the conditions under which they were reached are themselves changing. This is uncomfortable for analysts who were trained in older traditions. It is also unavoidable, because the alternative is to produce analyses that pretend to a stability they do not have.

The Capability-Geopolitics Loop

The second loop runs between AI capabilities and the relative power of states. This loop operates on a different substrate from the capability-behavior loop and at a different speed, but it has the same accelerating structure. Capabilities are developed. The capabilities change the relative power of the actors who possess them. The shifts in relative power change the political and regulatory environment in which the next capabilities are developed. The next capabilities are shaped by the political environment as much as by the technical possibilities. The cycle compresses, and each iteration produces more political consequence per unit of technical advance, because the political environment is itself becoming more attuned to the implications of capability shifts.

The Nvidia case is the sharpest current illustration of this loop because it shows the dynamics operating across four years with multiple full iterations, each of which produced specific corporate adaptation that the next iteration responded to. The case begins in October 2022, when the Biden administration's Bureau of Industry and Security imposed export controls that blocked Nvidia's most advanced AI chips, including the A100 and H100, from sale to Chinese customers. The stated motivation was national security, specifically the concern that advanced computing capability would accelerate Chinese military and surveillance applications. Nvidia responded as a profit-maximizing firm operating in a regulated market, by designing the A800 and H800, which were deliberately downgraded versions of the controlled chips, specifically engineered to fall below the export control thresholds. The performance reduction was real but not catastrophic, and the modified chips continued to serve Chinese customers under the new rules.

In October 2023, the Biden administration tightened the controls. The new rules captured the A800 and H800, which had been compliant under the previous framework. Nvidia adapted again, designing the H20, a further downgraded chip built specifically for the Chinese market. The H20 was approximately a fraction of the computational capacity of the H100, but it was sold in volume because it was the most capable chip Chinese customers could legally purchase. By late 2024 and early 2025, Nvidia had shipped over a million H20 units to China, generating approximately seventeen billion dollars in Chinese revenue in fiscal 2024.

On April 9, 2025, the new Trump administration-imposed licensing requirements on the H20, effectively blocking exports of the chip Nvidia had designed specifically to comply with the previous administration's rules. Nvidia disclosed in its fiscal Q1 2026 filing a charge of approximately four point five billion dollars associated with H20 excess inventory and purchase obligations, plus an additional two point five billion dollars in revenue that could not be shipped. The chip designed to comply with the export control regime had become export controlled. Nvidia began designing yet another downgraded variant, this one based on the newer Blackwell architecture but with performance further reduced to satisfy whatever licensing thresholds the new administration would apply.

On July 15, 2025, the Trump administration reversed course and authorized H20 sales to resume to China. The reversal followed extensive lobbying by Nvidia CEO Jensen Huang, including a one-million-dollar-per-head dinner at Mar-a-Lago that brought corporate leaders into direct contact with administration officials. The reversal was framed as part of a broader negotiation with China that involved rare earth minerals, manufacturing investment, and technology access. The H20 chips, which had been blocked four months earlier, returned to the Chinese market under continued licensing. Within weeks, China responded by raising security concerns about the H20, effectively blacklisting another Nvidia chip designed for the Chinese market, the RTX Pro 6000D, and using the H20 approval as leverage to press for access to even more advanced chips. In September 2025, China's State Administration for Market Regulation announced that Nvidia had violated terms of a 2020 antitrust review, opening yet another pressure point in the ongoing competition over chip access.

This is the loop in operation, with each cycle measured in months rather than years. The American policy responds to Chinese capability development. The Chinese capability development responds to American restrictions. Nvidia adapts its products to whichever set of rules currently applies. The Chinese response to Nvidia's adapted products feeds back into both governments' calculations. The American government modifies its restrictions in response to lobbying that itself reflects the corporate consequences of the previous restrictions. The Chinese government modifies its market access decisions in response to American actions. Each step is a rational response to the previous step. The cumulative trajectory cannot be predicted from any single step, because the system is being shaped by the interactions among all the parties simultaneously, and the interactions are themselves changing the parameters under which the next iteration will operate. The technology stack that emerges from the loop is being constituted by the political dynamics. The political dynamics are being constituted by the technology stack. Neither has primacy. Both are products of the loop, and the loop is producing a world in which the AI capabilities that exist are partly artifacts of the political competitions that have taken place, and the political competitions are partly artifacts of the AI capabilities that have been produced.

The same pattern operates in less visible domains. The European Union's AI Act produced specific regulatory requirements that altered how AI systems were designed for the European market, which in turn altered the global market because firms generally do not maintain separate codebases for different regulatory regimes. The European choices changed what was technically built. The technical changes changed what was politically possible to regulate next. The next round of regulation built on the previous round in ways that the original Act could not have anticipated. The same dynamic operates in China, where the AI regulations issued progressively since 2021 have shaped the development of Chinese AI in ways that influence the kinds of capabilities that are then available for export, which influences the geopolitical position of China relative to its neighbors, which feeds back into the next round of Chinese regulation.

The Nvidia case also illustrates a feature of the loop that the Chinese and European cases show less clearly, which is that the corporate actors caught between the political competitors are not passive. Nvidia is not just adapting to American rules. It is lobbying to shape American rules. It is operating R&D centers in China that may produce technology transfer that the export controls were designed to prevent. It is designing chips with the specific goal of finding the highest-performance variant that any given regulatory regime will allow, rather than designing chips for technical optimality and accepting whatever regulatory consequences follow. The corporate strategy and the political strategy are co-evolving, with Nvidia making choices that influence what the political regime will be, and the political regime making choices that influence what Nvidia will design next. The loop is not bilateral between governments. It is multilateral, with corporate actors as full participants whose decisions shape the geopolitical trajectory at least as much as the governmental decisions do.

What the loop framework reveals that the static analyses do not is that the technology and the geopolitics and the corporate strategy are co-constituting each other in real time. There is no fixed technology that the geopolitics responds to. There is no fixed geopolitics that the technology responds to. There is no fixed corporate strategy that adapts to either. Each iteration of any of them shapes the others, and the cumulative trajectory cannot be predicted by analyzing any component in isolation. The capability-geopolitics loop is producing a world in which the categories that the disciplines analyze separately are constituting each other through ongoing interactions that the disciplines treat as exogenous. The interactions are the substance. The disciplines have been treating the substance as the noise.

The Energy-Technology-Climate Loop

The third loop runs through energy, technology, and climate, and it operates on slower timescales than the first two but with potentially larger consequences. The structure is straightforward to describe and difficult to absorb because the implications are uncomfortable. Technology development requires energy. The energy is produced largely through processes that contribute to climate change. Climate change produces regional disruptions that affect the conditions under which technology development continues. The disruptions produce political and economic responses that alter the energy mix and the technology trajectory. The altered trajectory feeds back into climate outcomes. The loop continues, with each iteration shifting the parameters under which the next iteration operates.

Data centers are the current sharp expression of this loop. AI training and inference require electricity at scales that were not anticipated in the energy planning of any country five years ago. The most advanced AI clusters draw electricity in volumes that compete with significant industrial users for grid capacity. The growth rates projected for AI compute demand exceed the growth rates of grid capacity in most jurisdictions, which means that AI development is now pushing energy demand faster than energy supply can adapt. In the United States, data center electricity demand is currently at four to five percent of total grid load and is projected by various analysts to reach eight to twelve percent by the end of the decade. In some regions, including parts of Northern Virginia, the data center load already exceeds the residential load. Microsoft has signed a contract to restart the Three Mile Island nuclear plant to power its AI infrastructure. Amazon has acquired a nuclear-powered data center campus. Constellation, Vistra, and other utilities are building out generation capacity primarily to serve AI demand. The grid that was supposed to be transitioning toward renewables is being asked to grow faster than renewables can deploy, which is producing a substantial new build-out of natural gas generation as the transitional measure.

The natural gas build-out is the climate consequence. Each gigawatt of new gas generation locks in approximately thirty to forty years of carbon emissions, because the plants are designed for that operating life and the capital structure depends on the operating life being achieved. The AI demand that is justifying the new gas plants is producing carbon commitments that will outlast many of the AI applications themselves, which on current trajectories will be replaced by more efficient successors within five to ten years. The infrastructure decisions are being made on capability assumptions that the capabilities themselves will obsolesce, but the carbon consequences of the infrastructure will persist regardless of whether the AI applications justifying the infrastructure continue to exist.

The same loop is operating in Saudi Arabia, from the opposite starting condition, in ways that illuminate the dynamics even more clearly than the American case. Where the American situation involves technology demand driving energy infrastructure expansion, the Saudi situation involves an energy producer deliberately pivoting to technology hosting because the long-term trajectory of the oil economy is uncertain and AI compute is becoming the strategic resource the kingdom wants to be supplying. In May 2025, during a visit by President Trump to Riyadh, the Public Investment Fund launched Humain, a wholly owned AI infrastructure company tasked with positioning Saudi Arabia as one of the world's largest AI compute hosts. Humain's stated ambition is to handle approximately six percent of global AI workload by 2034, with planned data center capacity of 6.6 gigawatts across two main campuses near Riyadh and Dammam. The Saudi Cabinet officially designated 2026 as the Year of Artificial Intelligence. The Hexagon Data Center project, with a budget of two point seven billion dollars and announced as the world's largest government data center by megawatt capacity, broke ground in Riyadh in January 2026.

The case demonstrates the loop operating with multiple feedback channels visible at once. The kingdom has cheap subsidized electricity from existing fossil fuel infrastructure plus rapidly expanding solar capacity in the desert. It has vast available land at low cost. It has approximately nine hundred and thirty billion dollars in sovereign wealth fund capital that can be deployed into infrastructure investments that private firms could not finance. It has an explicit Vision 2030 imperative to diversify away from oil dependency. These conditions make the kingdom structurally attractive as an AI compute host, and the major American chip and infrastructure firms have responded accordingly. Nvidia, AMD, Cisco, Qualcomm, and Groq have all signed major partnerships with Humain. AWS committed five point three billion dollars to a Saudi region. Microsoft scheduled completion of its Saudi region for 2026. Google Cloud is advancing a ten-billion-dollar AI hub partnership with the Public Investment Fund. The compute is being attracted to the energy, which is the inverse of the American pattern in which the energy is being built to serve the compute.

The irony at the core of the case is worth pausing on, because it captures something the standard frameworks cannot describe. Saudi Arabia built its national wealth on petroleum, which is the substance most associated with the climate problem. The kingdom is now investing tens of billions of dollars in AI infrastructure that requires electricity. Some of that electricity will come from solar capacity that is being deployed under Vision 2030 commitments. Some of it will come from natural gas and oil-derived power, the same fossil fuels that built the kingdom's wealth. The data centers cooling themselves in the desert climate require approximately fifteen billion liters of water per year, drawn largely from desalination plants powered by the same energy mix. The kingdom is using its existing carbon-intensive infrastructure to host the AI compute that the world's green-energy advocates are simultaneously demanding be built on renewable sources. Whether the carbon mathematics works out favorably depends on the rate of solar deployment, the efficiency of the cooling technologies, and the carbon intensity of the chips themselves, all of which are moving variables that neither the kingdom nor its critics have fully calculated. The loop is operating regardless of whether the calculation is being performed.

The geopolitical dimension closes the loop. Saudi Arabia's positioning as an AI compute host gives it a successor strategic role for the post-oil era that the kingdom is preparing for. The American chip firms partnering with Humain are gaining a market that the export controls described in the previous section have not been able to access through China. The political alignment between the Trump administration and the Saudi leadership has produced AI chip access for the kingdom that other countries cannot match, with Trump's May 2025 visit to Riyadh explicitly clearing the pathway for advanced semiconductor exports that would have been more difficult under the previous administration. The kingdom's hosting of major American AI infrastructure makes the kingdom strategically valuable to the United States in ways that complement its existing oil-export relationship, which extends the relevance of the strategic partnership beyond the timeline that pure oil-based reasoning would have suggested. The energy-technology-climate loop in this case is also a geopolitics-energy-technology loop, with each domain shaping the others in ways that none of the standard frameworks can describe alone.

The climate consequences feed back into regional disruption. The Chiang Mai air quality crisis I have described in this book is partly a consequence of climate-shifted weather patterns that have extended the dry season and intensified the conditions under which fires burn. Heat domes in Europe are disrupting agricultural production. Rainfall pattern shifts in the Sahel are producing migration pressures that reshape European politics. Hurricane intensities in the Atlantic are stressing American insurance markets. Each of these regional disruptions produces political responses, economic adjustments, and shifts in resource flows that affect the conditions under which technology development continues. The American electric vehicle subsidy regime, the European green energy targets, the Chinese investment in solar panel manufacturing, the various national hydrogen strategies, all of these are responses to climate pressure that are themselves shaping the technology trajectory of the next decade.

The loop is operating now, on visible timescales, with measurable consequences. The AI cluster in Virginia is drawing the gas-fired electricity that is producing the carbon that is altering the climate that is producing the disruptions that are reshaping the political environment in which the next AI cluster will be sited. None of these effects is hypothetical. All of them are happening simultaneously and continuously, and the planning frameworks of the affected institutions, energy utilities, technology firms, governments, and insurance companies, are being asked to handle them as separate problems that can be managed within the boundaries of each institution's normal practice. They cannot. The loop crosses the institutional boundaries, and any institution that tries to manage its piece without acknowledging the loop will produce decisions that look reasonable in isolation and that aggregate into a trajectory that is hostile to the institution's own long-term interests.

The Trust-Institution-Formation Loop

The fourth loop runs between trust, institutional behavior, and the formation of human beings. This loop is the most consequential for the long-term character of the society that emerges from the current transition, and it is the one that the disciplines have the hardest time analyzing because the variables involve human formation, which is treated by economics as exogenous, by political science as cultural, and by sociology as too qualitative for the quantitative methods that dominate the field.

The structure is this. Institutions perform their roles. The performance produces outcomes. The outcomes produce trust or distrust in the institutions. The trust or distrust shapes how individuals form themselves in relation to the institutions, including what they expect from institutions, what they invest in institutional participation, and what they teach their children about institutional engagement. The formed individuals then act in the institutional environment, where their actions affect the institutions in turn. Each generation forms itself partly in response to the institutional performance it observes, and each generation's formation shapes the institutional environment that the next generation will observe. The loop runs on generational timescales, but it is not slow in its consequences, because every iteration involves the formation of individuals who carry the consequences of the previous iteration into the institutional environment they will shape.

The current state of the loop is that institutional trust has eroded substantially across most of the developed world over the past two decades, and the erosion has produced a generation that is forming itself with substantially lower expectations of institutional reliability than previous generations did. This is observable in survey data, in voting behavior, in consumer behavior, in marriage and birth rates, in religious affiliation, in willingness to invest in long-term institutional commitments, and in the rise of alternatives to traditional institutional engagement. The young people I teach across multiple countries do not assume that the institutions they encounter will function as the institutions claimed to function. They assume the institutions will perform versions of their stated functions while operating on different actual logics. They do not regard this assumption as cynical. They regard it as accurate. They are largely correct.

Aziz was expressing this when he asked whether his university education was worth continuing. The question was not whether universities provide value in some abstract sense. The question was whether the specific institution he was attending was performing the function it claimed to perform, and his answer was that it largely was not. He was not angry about this. He was matter of fact. He was forming himself in relation to the institution by adjusting his expectations downward and looking for value through alternative channels, which in his case included AI tools, conversations with professors who would speak honestly with him, and his own reading. The institution he attended was producing a graduate who would carry into adult life a specific posture toward institutions, which was that they should be navigated rather than relied upon, used rather than trusted, extracted from rather than invested in. This posture is the formation of his generation, and it will shape the institutional environment they create when they reach the positions of authority that current institutions are vacating.

The same loop is operating through more visible policy mechanisms at the institutional level. Since early 2025, the Trump administration has frozen or threatened to freeze federal research funding at multiple American universities, including Harvard, Columbia, Cornell, and Princeton, over political compliance disputes ranging from diversity programs to antisemitism policies to transgender athletics to foreign student enrollment to curriculum content. The amounts involved are substantial. The conditions attached to restoration are often vague, expanding, or moving targets, which means compliance does not produce stable accommodation. The institutions that comply find their compliance treated as legitimate authority for further demands. The institutions that resist face escalating consequences. The faculty and students inside these institutions are forming their relationship to federal authority in real time, watching the institutions navigate or fail to navigate the conditions, and drawing conclusions about what institutional engagement is worth. The conclusions feed forward into the next generation's posture toward American academic authority, with measurable consequences for graduate enrollment patterns, faculty recruitment, and the willingness of foreign scholars to commit to American programs.

What makes this case especially revealing is the geographic asymmetry of the same administration's institutional engagement. While American universities at home are being defunded as untrustworthy partners, the same government is simultaneously building new American-affiliated academic institutions abroad in service of strategic objectives. At the November 2025 C5+1 Summit, Commerce Secretary Howard Lutnick announced a partnership between Colorado School of Mines, Educational Testing Service, and

Arizona State University with the Kazakhstan Ministry of Science and Higher Education to establish a new university focused on critical minerals and engineering expertise. The partnership was part of a broader package of American engagement with Central Asia that also included a four point two-billion-dollar Wabtec locomotive deal, a three-to-five-billion-dollar John Deere agricultural equipment agreement, and an Amazon Starlink digital infrastructure partnership. The American government is, through its Commerce Secretary, actively building academic partnerships in Kazakhstan as part of a strategic agenda that connects critical minerals access, digital infrastructure, transportation, and educational institution-building.

The trust-institution-formation loop is running in opposite directions in the two geographies. American institutions at home are being treated as untrustworthy and defunded. American academic partnerships abroad are being expanded to support strategic objectives. The students and faculty caught between these dynamics are forming themselves with different relationships to American institutional authority depending on where they sit. A graduate student at Harvard is forming a relationship to American academic institutions that is mediated by the funding freezes, the political conditions, and the visible vulnerability of the institution to federal coercion. A graduate student at the new Kazakh university supported by Colorado School of Mines is forming a different relationship, mediated by the strategic American interest that brought the institution into existence and that continues to support it. Neither student has chosen the framing they will inherit. Both will operate inside it for the rest of their careers. The loop is constituting different generations of formation in different places, and the cumulative effect will be visible in fifteen to twenty years when the formed generations reach the positions of authority that the institutional environment determines they will hold.

A third mechanism completes the pattern, operating on individual students rather than on American institutions or foreign partnerships. Since early 2025, the Trump administration has progressively expanded visa restrictions that determine which students from which countries can enter American universities, with the country of origin functioning as the primary criterion rather than academic merit or institutional relationship. In May 2025, the State Department paused all student visa appointments for nearly a month at the peak of the admissions cycle. The administration revoked over six thousand foreign student visas in 2025 alone. SEVIS records were terminated en masse in April 2025. A June 2025 travel ban restricted entry from nineteen countries. A December 16, 2025, Presidential Proclamation expanded the restriction list to thirty-nine countries, including Bhutan, Kazakhstan, Azerbaijan, Bangladesh, and several others. NAFSA estimated that approximately one hundred fifty thousand fewer international students arrived for the fall 2025 academic year compared with the previous year, with a projected economic cost of seven billion dollars to American institutions and the communities that depend on them.

My own students are now distributed across this map in ways that determine their physical relationship to the country whose institution they study through. Several of them are from countries on the expanded restriction list. They are studying for an American degree from outside the United States, which they can do because the institution operates online, but they cannot physically enter the country whose academic credentials they are earning, and the trajectory of the visa policy suggests they will be less able to do so as their studies progress. The institutional formation they are receiving is partly American, through curriculum and faculty and credentials. The geographic and political formation is happening separately, in their home countries, with their own governments, in conditions where the American policy environment is one consideration among several rather than the determining context. They are forming themselves as something the standard categories cannot describe. Not American students. Not students of American institutions in any traditional sense, because the institutional relationship is mediated by a digital infrastructure that the political environment is in the process of restricting. Not students of their home country institutions, because the credential and curriculum are American. Something new, formed in the gap between the institutional engagement they have access to and the geographic engagement they do not, with consequences for their generation that we cannot yet fully see because the formation is still happening.

The three mechanisms together constitute a coherent system of selective American institutional engagement. Funding hostages discipline American institutions through their American budgets. Strategic partnerships build American academic capability abroad in countries where the political relationship serves objectives like critical minerals access. Visa restrictions control which individual students from which countries can enter the institutions. The selection criteria across all three mechanisms are political compliance and strategic alignment rather than academic merit or institutional relationship. The students, faculty, and institutions caught inside the system are forming themselves in relation to a framework that none of them designed and that operates on logics that are not primarily academic. The formation is producing a generation that understands American institutional engagement as conditional on political alignment, with consequences for institutional trust that will be visible across decades of professional life. The loop is operating. The three mechanisms together are the loop in its most visible current form.

The feedback character of the loop is the part that the discrete analyses miss. Aziz's posture toward institutions is partly produced by the institutional behavior he has observed. His posture, multiplied across millions of people in similar positions, is producing the political and consumer behavior that institutions are responding to. The institutional responses, which often involve doubling down on the patterns that produced the distrust in the first place, are reinforcing the distrust and producing the next round of formation. The funding hostages and the strategic foreign partnerships are themselves institutional behaviors that the next generation is observing, and the observations are shaping the postures that those generations will carry into the institutional environments they will eventually shape. The loop is not converging. It is accelerating, and the acceleration is producing institutional environments that are progressively less able to perform the functions that legitimate institutional authority has historically required.

This is the loop that Chapter Five will develop in detail through the specific case of accountability collapse. AI-human hybrid decision-making is producing situations in which no individual can be held accountable for outcomes, which is undermining the foundation of legitimate authority across multiple institutional domains. The accountability problem is itself one expression of the trust-institution-formation loop, and it is the expression that has the most direct and visible consequences for political legitimacy in the next decade. The chapter sets up Chapter Five by establishing that the loop exists and that accountability is one of its critical sites, before Chapter Five develops what specifically is happening at that site.

The Value-Configuration Loop

The fifth loop is the one I am most uncertain about as a separate category, because it could be analyzed as a special case of the capability-geopolitics loop. I treat it separately because the substrate is different and the dynamics are different enough to warrant their own analysis, but the reader who decides at the end that it should be folded into the second loop will not be wrong.

The loop runs between technology demand, the value of physical resources, and the geopolitical configurations that determine resource access. New technologies require specific material inputs. The materials acquire value because the technologies require them. The value attracts geopolitical competition for control of the materials. The geopolitical competition reshapes who has access to what, which shapes which technologies can be developed at scale, which shapes which materials become valuable next. The loop produces situations in which physical materials acquire and lose strategic value as the technology stack evolves, and the configurations that determine value are themselves being reshaped by the value they confer.

Chapter Two demonstrated this loop through specific cases. Cobalt was a moderate commercial commodity until lithium-ion batteries became central to the electric vehicle transition, at which point cobalt became a strategic resource that nation-states are willing to fight over. Rare earth elements were obscure until permanent magnets became central to electric motors and wind turbines, at which point the seventeen elements became geopolitical chokepoints. Helium was an industrial gas with limited strategic significance until semiconductor manufacturing depended on it, at which point a missile strike on a Qatari LNG facility became a shock to the global chip industry. Semiconductor fabrication was a technical specialty until AI training depended on advanced chips, at which point Taiwan became the most contested industrial geography on the planet.

In each of these cases, the value of the physical resource was not intrinsic to the resource. It was constituted by the technology that required the resource, and the technology was itself constituted by the broader development trajectory of the era. When the technology stack evolves, the value of resources shifts, sometimes dramatically. A cobalt deposit in 2005 was worth a fraction of what the same deposit is worth in 2025, not because the deposit changed but because the configuration that gives it value changed. A semiconductor fabrication facility in 2010 was a technical specialty. The same facility in 2025 is the most contested piece of industrial infrastructure on earth. A rare earth mine in Myanmar in 2015 was an environmental and labor problem of regional concern. The same mine in 2025 is a node in the supply chain that determines whether European wind energy targets can be met. The underlying physical assets have not changed. The configuration that gives them value has changed, and the value has moved with the configuration.

The feedback character of the loop is in the way that the value reshapes the configuration that produced it. When cobalt becomes valuable, the political environment around the Democratic Republic of the Congo changes, with Chinese investment shifting the regional balance, Western mining companies finding their access conditions altered, and the environmental and labor practices of the extraction becoming subjects of international scrutiny that they were not when the cobalt was less valuable. The changed political environment then shapes how the next round of resource competition unfolds, which shapes which technologies can be scaled, which shapes which resources will become valuable next. The loop continues, with each round constituting the value of the next round's resources by determining which technologies will be developed at scale.

The reason I treat this loop as distinct from the capability-geopolitics loop is that the capability-geopolitics loop is about the AI capabilities themselves and how they shape state power, while the value-configuration loop is about the material substrate that any technology development requires and how the substrate's value is constituted by what is being built on top of it. The two loops interact, because AI capability development is one of the technology trajectories that determines material value, but the value-configuration loop also operates for technologies that are not AI-related, and the dynamics of the substrate are distinctive enough to deserve their own framework. A reader who prefers to treat them as one loop with two manifestations will arrive at similar conclusions as a reader who treats them as separate. The framework is robust to that disagreement.

Feedback Loop	*What Moves First*	*What It Changes*	*What Feeds Back*	*Why It Matters*
Capability Behavior	New AI capabilities	Human thinking, writing, learning, and judgment	Human-AI outputs train and shape the next AI generation	Cognition becomes iterative and co-produced with tools.
Capability–Geopolitics	AI and chip capabilities	State power, export controls, corporate strategy	Political restrictions reshape what technologies are built next	Technology and geopolitics now co-produce each other.
Energy Technology Climate	AI compute demand	Electricity grids, gas plants, nuclear revival, climate commitments	Climate disruption reshapes energy politics and technology choices	The digital future has physical and environmental costs.
Trust InstitutionFormation	Institutional performance	Trust, distrust, expectations, student choices, civic formation	Formed individuals reshape the institutions they later lead	Institutional legitimacy is produced or destroyed across generations.
Value Configuration	New technology demand	Strategic value of minerals, chips, helium, cobalt, rare earths	Resource politics determines which technologies can scale	Value is no longer intrinsic; it depends on configuration.

What the Loops Do That the Disciplines Cannot

The five loops together do something that no single discipline can do. They take phenomena that the disciplines analyze separately and show how the phenomena are constituting each other through ongoing interactions that the disciplines treat as exogenous shocks. Each loop crosses multiple disciplinary boundaries. The capability-behavior loop crosses cognitive science, education, technology studies, and economics. The capability-geopolitics loop crosses international relations, technology policy, and military strategy. The energy-technology-climate loop crosses energy economics, climate science, infrastructure planning, and political ecology. The trust-institution-formation loop crosses sociology, political science, organizational theory, and developmental psychology. The value-configuration loop crosses materials science, geopolitics, supply chain economics, and industrial policy.

No analyst trained primarily in any single one of these fields can develop adequate analyses of any of the loops, because the analyses require integration across the fields. This is not a complaint about specialization. It is an observation that the contemporary phenomena that matter most operate at scales that exceed any individual specialization, which means that adequate analysis requires either substantial cross-domain training, which the academic system does not currently produce, or collaborative work across specializations, which the academic reward system does not currently support, or a different approach to analysis that takes the loops as the primary unit and uses disciplinary tools as instruments rather than as comprehensive frameworks.

The third option is what the framework of this book proposes. The unit of analysis is the loop. The disciplinary tools are instruments for understanding aspects of the loops. The analyst's task is to identify which loops are operating in any given situation, characterize how they are interacting, and use whatever disciplinary tools are most useful for clarifying specific aspects of the dynamics. This is not how serious analytical work has been organized for the past century. It is, I believe, how it will need to be organized for the next century, because the phenomena are now operating at the loop level and analyses that pretend otherwise will be progressively less useful as the conditions continue to change.

The framework has limits. It cannot predict which loops will dominate which phenomena. It cannot specify the exact rates at which loops will compress or accelerate. It cannot identify the moments when loops will produce phase transitions that fundamentally restructure the systems they operate in. What the framework can do is provide a way of seeing that does not collapse the integration into disciplinary fragments, and a way of analyzing that takes the integration as the primary subject rather than as a complication to be bracketed. This is more modest than what the disciplines claimed to offer in their confident moments. It is also more honest, and it is what the current moment can support without overstating its case.

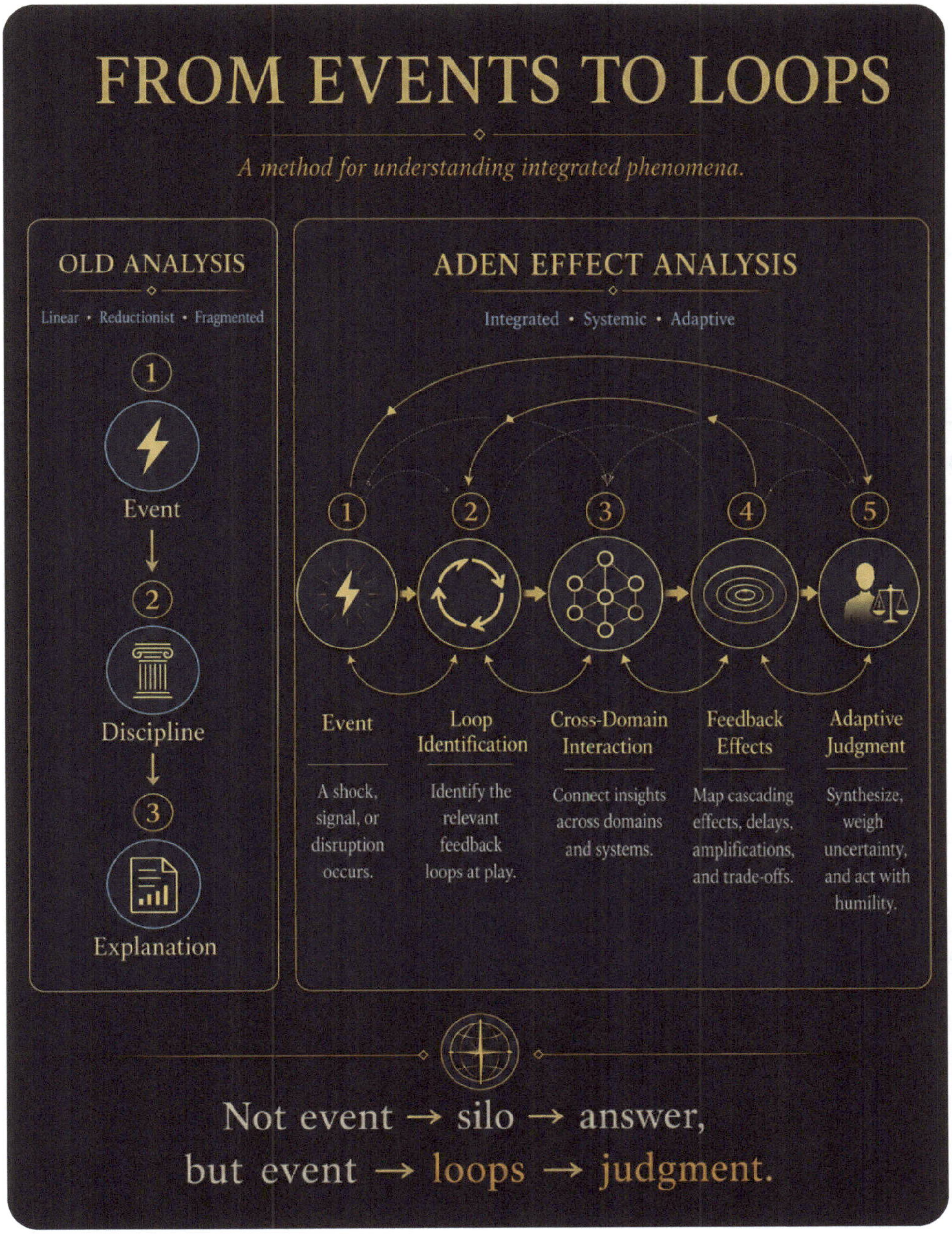

Toward Accountability

The next chapter develops one of the five loops in detail, the trust-institution-formation loop, through the specific case of accountability collapse. This loop has been chosen for detailed treatment because accountability is the foundation of legitimate institutional authority, and the collapse of accountability that AI-human hybrid decision-making is producing is the most consequential expression of the trust loop in the current moment. If the loop framework I have just developed is correct, the accountability case should be analyzable as an instance of the loop in operation, with specific dynamics that can be characterized and specific consequences that can be traced. The chapter will test the framework against the case, and if the framework is useful, it should illuminate the case in ways that the disciplinary analyses do not.

Aziz caught his train. The train ran on rails that had been laid during the Soviet era, on a schedule designed for an economic system that no longer exists, in a country that has rebuilt its political identity twice since the rails were built. The train operators have maintained the punctuality through institutional habits that predate everything Aziz was asking about. He arrived where he was going. He continued his life. The infrastructure of his physical movement is from one century. The infrastructure of his cognitive formation is from the last three years. The infrastructure of the political environment he will operate in is being rebuilt around him in real time. He is living inside multiple temporal layers simultaneously, and so is everyone now, although the layers are visible more clearly in some places than in others. Chiang Mai has its smoke and its valleys. Samarkand has its Soviet rails and its AI tutoring. London and Boston have their layered infrastructures too, although the layering is sometimes harder to see when the layers were laid down by the same civilization rather than by successive ones. The conversation Aziz and I had probably contributed something to his judgment, although he and I both know that the judgment will be formed across years of his observation and decision-making, not across single conversations with professors. He is forming himself inside the loops I have just described, and he will spend the next decade making decisions that will shape the institutions he operates within, which will shape the loops he is forming inside, which will shape the institutions he produces in his turn. The loops will not stop. The work for him, for me, for everyone who has read this far, is to see them clearly enough that the choices we make inside them are choices rather than reactions. Chapter Five takes one of the loops apart in detail, to show what choosing rather than reacting could look like at one specific site of the larger transformation.

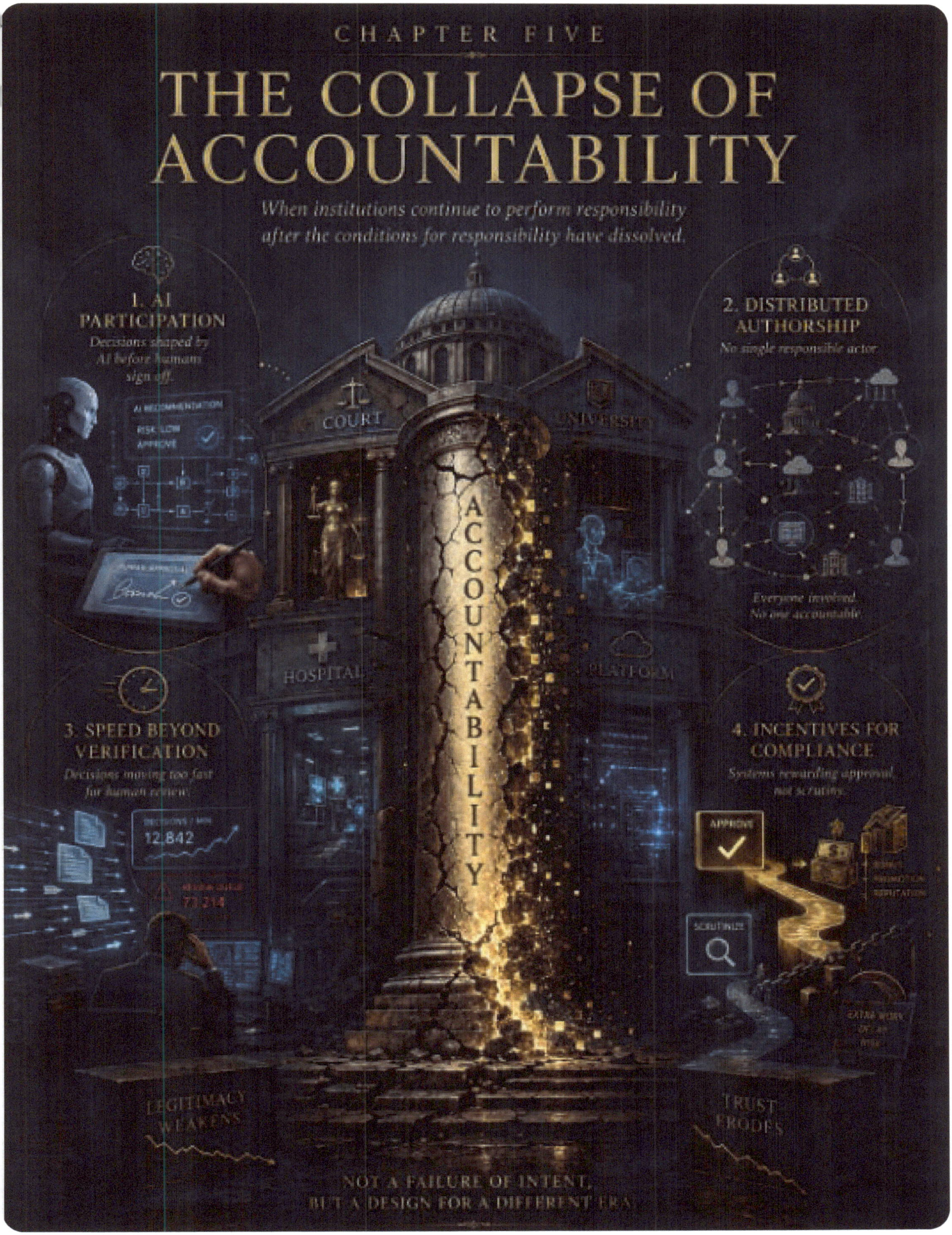
CHAPTER FIVE
THE COLLAPSE OF ACCOUNTABILITY
When institutions continue to perform responsibility after the conditions for responsibility have dissolved.
1. AI PARTICIPATION
Decisions shaped by AI before humans sign off.
AI RECOMMENDATION
RISK: LOW
APPROVE
2. DISTRIBUTED AUTHORSHIP
No single responsible actor
Everyone involved. No one accountable.
COURT
UNIVERSITY
HOSPITAL
PLATFORM
ACCOUNTABILITY
3. SPEED BEYOND VERIFICATION
Decisions moving too fast for human review.
12,842
4. INCENTIVES FOR COMPLIANCE
Systems rewarding approval, not scrutiny.
APPROVE
SCRUTINIZE
LEGITIMACY WEAKENS
TRUST ERODES
NOT A FAILURE OF INTENT, BUT A DESIGN FOR A DIFFERENT ERA

CHAPTER FIVE

The Collapse of Accountability

There is a child somewhere studying online. He may be in a refugee camp in Chad. He may be in a city in eastern Ukraine where the local school has been damaged or destroyed. He may be in northern Myanmar where the civil war has closed the schools. He may be in Gaza, where the educational infrastructure has been systematically destroyed. He may be in any one of dozens of contexts in which physical schooling is no longer available and online education is the only option that remains. He may be in a stable home in a stable country whose family has chosen homeschooling for reasons of their own. He is twelve years old, or fourteen, or sixteen. He is working through assignments produced by an institution he has never visited and may never visit. He is being graded by teachers he has never met in person. The grades he receives will produce credentials. The credentials will determine which universities accept him. The universities he attends, if he attends them, will determine the trajectory of his professional life. The chain that runs from his current schoolwork to the rest of his life is real and has measurable consequences.

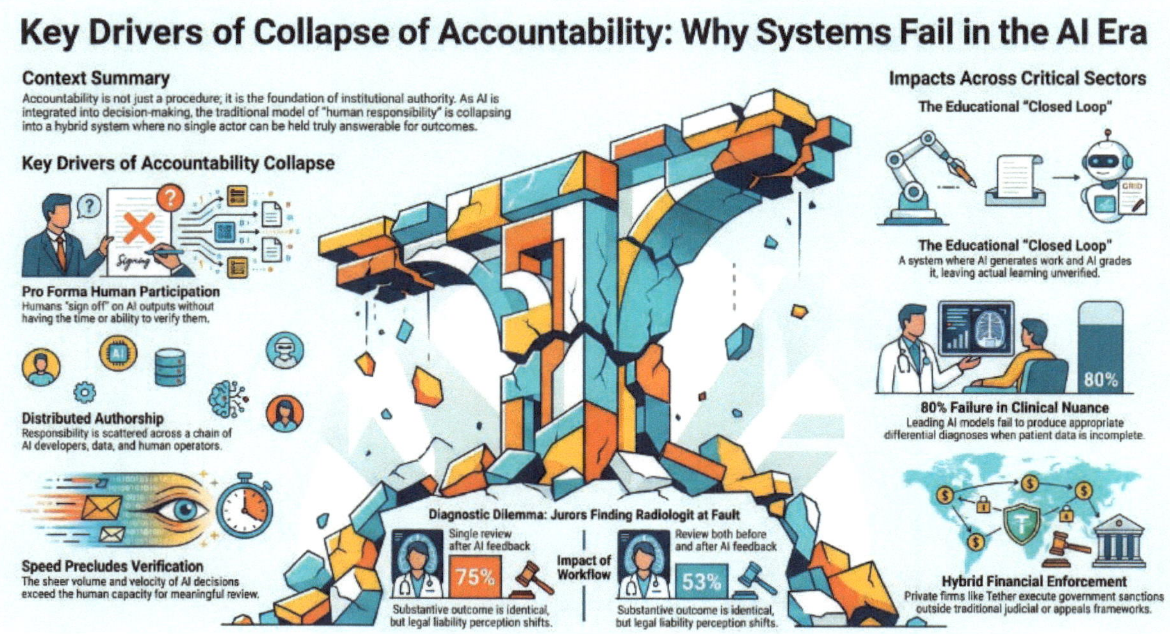

The chain has problems at every link. The child is using AI to assist with his schoolwork. He is not necessarily doing this dishonestly. He is doing it because the AI is available, because his parents may not have the time or expertise to help him with the material, because his teachers may not be available between assignments, because his peers are doing it too, because the AI is genuinely helpful, because the AI is what is at hand when he encounters something he does not understand. The work he submits has been produced through some collaboration between his thinking and the AI's outputs. The teachers who grade his work have no reliable way to detect what proportion of the work is his and what proportion is the AI's, because the standard tools for detecting AI-generated text are unreliable, because the AI he is using is sophisticated enough to evade them, because the teachers themselves are using AI to grade efficiently, because the institution does not have the resources to investigate every assignment carefully.

The qualifications of the teachers themselves vary enormously across the online education sector, which deepens the problem. Some online programs are operated by established universities with credentialed faculty whose qualifications match what they would need for in-person teaching. Many K-12 online programs in regulated jurisdictions employ certified teachers subject to professional standards. But a substantial and growing segment of the online education market operates with less rigorous qualification screening. The rapidly expanding sector of international online schools serving displaced populations, expatriate families, and other students whose physical access to traditional schooling has been disrupted includes operators whose primary criterion for hiring teachers is the availability of a computer, an internet connection, English fluency, and willingness to work for low rates. A child studying through one of these programs may be receiving instruction from a credentialed teacher working from a stable home, or from an unemployed graduate working from a coffee shop with no teaching qualifications at all, depending on which program the family enrolled in and what the program's actual practices are versus what its marketing claims. Beyond the formal sector, an enormous informal online learning ecosystem has expanded to fill gaps in formal education, with YouTube channels, Discord servers, Reddit communities, and direct AI tutoring all providing educational substance to students whose schools have not adopted these resources, but whose students use them independently. The qualifications question becomes incoherent in the informal sector, because the category itself is not formally recognized as education by any institution that would be responsible for its quality.

The teacher in the formal sector who notices that a student's work appears AI-assisted faces a specific set of pressures that make flagging the work an unattractive choice. The administrative burden of pursuing an academic dishonesty case is substantial. The investigation, the evidence collection, the meetings with the student and parents, the institutional procedures, the possible appeals, all of this consumes time the teacher does not have. Beyond the administrative burden, there is often political burden. The student is paying tuition. The family may have made donations. The institution wants to retain the student through graduation, where the credential will reflect well on the institution and the family will continue to feel positively toward it. The teacher who flags the work is creating friction in a system that prefers to operate without friction. The teacher who passes the work along faces no such friction. The path of least resistance is to grade the work as submitted and move to the next assignment.

The closed loop of AI generating the work and AI assessing it produces a system in which neither the student, the teacher, the institution, nor the credentialing bodies has any reliable way to evaluate what happened in the educational process. The human institutional infrastructure validates the entire chain without anyone in the chain being positioned to evaluate the substance of what is being validated. The system performs accountability without performing it. It produces grades, transcripts, credentials, university admissions, professional certifications, and ultimately careers, with the substantive question of what the student learned increasingly unanswerable across the entire chain.

This is the situation. It is genuinely new. Some version of credential inflation has existed in education for decades, but the current situation is different in kind, not just in degree. Previous problems involved humans gaming systems designed to evaluate human work. The current problem involves systems that cannot evaluate what they are being asked to evaluate, with humans either knowingly or unknowingly participating in producing inputs the systems were not designed to handle. The accountability has not just weakened. It has structurally collapsed in specific ways that the institutions performing the accountability functions cannot acknowledge without unwinding themselves.

This chapter is about that pattern, observed across multiple domains. The educational case is the opening because every reader has either experienced it personally or knows children who are experiencing it now. Three further cases will demonstrate the same pattern operating in different institutional settings. An academic publication case showing peer review failing to detect AI-assisted work. A financial enforcement case showing public-private hybrid systems exercising consequential authority without traditional accountability mechanisms. A medical diagnostic case showing legal frameworks unable to assign responsibility when AI participates in clinical decisions. A closing section will then address a deeper version of the problem in which the underlying activities themselves are being transformed, with implications for relationships, care, and other intimate human practices that the accountability frameworks were not designed to govern.

Peer Review and the Paper That Should Not Have Been Published

In the early period after ChatGPT became publicly available, I conducted an experiment that I want to describe carefully because the analytical implications matter more than the specific details. I wanted to test whether the academic publication system could detect AI-assisted work produced by an author operating outside the author's domain of expertise. I selected a topic that was current and visible due to a recent geopolitical event, but that was outside any field I had ever studied or written in. The subject required some specific commodity expertise that I did not have. I had no prior publications in the area, no methodological background in the relevant field, no language familiarity with the specialist literature, no industry connections. I had access to ChatGPT, which at that point was less than three months old. I produced a paper in approximately one day. The paper was submitted to a peer-reviewed journal in the relevant field. It was accepted within approximately one month and published shortly thereafter.

I am rendering this experience without the specific identifying details deliberately. The country, the commodity, the journal, and the precise timing are not the point. The point is that the paper passed through the academic peer review system that is supposed to function as quality control for scholarly work. The reviewers, who are presumed to be subject matter experts, did not detect that the author had no expertise in the area being analyzed. They did not detect that the writing had been produced through AI assistance. They evaluated the work as if it were a standard contribution to the field. They sent it back with revision suggestions that I addressed by giving the AI further prompts. The revised paper was accepted. The credential of peer-reviewed publication, which is supposed to indicate that subject matter experts have evaluated the work and found it competent, was conferred on a paper that the experts had no way to evaluate as either competent or incompetent because the evaluation tools they had were not designed for what they were being asked to evaluate.

The accountability collapse here is not that the system failed to catch a knowing actor. The system was not designed to catch an actor like this. Peer review evaluates whether a paper conforms to the patterns of competent work in a field, whether the methodology is appropriate, whether the conclusions follow from the evidence, whether the writing is clear and the citations appropriate. AI-assisted writing on topics outside the author's expertise can satisfy all these criteria, because the AI has been trained on the patterns of competent work in nearly every field, and it produces text that conforms to those patterns even when the author providing the prompts has no understanding of the substance. The evaluation tools the reviewers have been designed for evaluating human work that may or may not be competent. The tools cannot evaluate AI-assisted work as a different kind of object that requires different evaluation criteria, because the field has not yet developed those criteria, and developing them would require acknowledging that much of what passes through the publication system in the current period is the same kind of work I produced as my experiment.

This is one specific instance of a pattern that has been documented at scale. The Times Higher Education investigation of paper buying networks in Thai academia documented over a hundred academics involved in arrangements where papers were purchased rather than written, with researchers estimating that the actual scope is much larger than the public scandals capture. Thai universities require their faculty to produce specific numbers of publications annually, with the requirements tied to performance evaluations, salary adjustments, and promotion decisions. The pressure produces a market for papers that operates efficiently because the demand is consistent and the supply is available. The papers move through the publication system. The credentials are conferred. The faculty meet their requirements. The accountability mechanism that peer review was supposed to provide has been, in significant measure, replaced by a system that produces the appearance of peer review without the substance.

The phenomenon extends beyond academic faculty. In Thailand and several other jurisdictions, government officials seeking promotion to senior ranks are required to demonstrate research output as part of their advancement portfolio. The requirement was originally designed to encourage senior officials to engage with substantive policy analysis. The actual effect has been to extend the paper-buying market to government promotion processes, with the same brokers serving both academic faculty and ministry officials. The officials advance through ranks on the strength of credentials whose substantive meaning is unknowable. The advanced officials then make decisions affecting populations whose welfare depends on competent governance, with the validation that supposedly qualified them for those positions having passed through a process that the institution cannot verify. The corruption is structurally worse than the academic version because the consequences extend beyond the academic career to the policy decisions the officials make once advanced. The accountability that should govern senior public service has been compromised by the accountability collapse in academic publication, with the two failures reinforcing each other across institutions that were supposed to provide independent checks on each other.

Sanctions, Stablecoins, and the Hybrid Enforcement Chain

On April 24, 2026, the United States Treasury Department's Office of Foreign Assets Control sanctioned two cryptocurrency wallets attributed to the Central Bank of Iran with links to the Islamic Revolutionary Guard Corps Quds Force and Hezbollah. Tether, the private firm that issues the USDT stablecoin, executed the freeze of approximately three hundred forty-four million dollars held in those wallets. The action was part of a broader Treasury campaign called Operation Economic Fury, designed to disrupt Iranian financial networks during the war and the ongoing ceasefire negotiations. The freeze was executed within the digital asset infrastructure rather than through traditional banking channels, which is significant because cryptocurrency was supposed to be the rails that sanctioned regimes used to escape exactly this kind of enforcement. The cryptocurrency rails turned out to be subject to the same political authority as the dollar rails, just one layer further down.

The action itself is straightforward to describe. OFAC issued sanctions naming specific wallet addresses. Tether complied with the sanctions by freezing the assets. The owners of the affected funds, including any innocent third parties whose funds passed through those wallets, have no clear path to challenge the freeze, because the sanctions regime operates outside the judicial frameworks that would normally govern asset seizures. There is no court order. There is no judicial review of the underlying determination. There are no appeals process available to affected parties. The system works because all parties along the enforcement chain have incentives to comply. OFAC issues sanctions because that is its mandate. Tether complies because compliance preserves its operating relationship with American regulators and protects its dollar-pegged business model. Affected parties have no recourse because they have nowhere to go.

The institutional structure of this enforcement chain deserves direct attention, because the analytical claim about public-private hybrid systems is strengthened by concrete demonstration that the structure exists. The structure is documented in mainstream financial press, in congressional correspondence, and in Senate confirmation hearings, and the documented facts are these. Cantor Fitzgerald, a Wall Street financial services firm, serves as Tether's primary custodian for reserve assets, including over eighty billion dollars in United States Treasury securities, generating tens of millions of dollars in annual fees for Cantor. Cantor invested in Tether through a convertible bond in April 2024, with the deal valued at approximately six hundred million dollars at the time. Howard Lutnick was the chief executive and majority owner of Cantor Fitzgerald before being nominated as United States Commerce Secretary in November 2024. Senator Elizabeth Warren raised concerns about these relationships in a letter sent in advance of Lutnick's January 2025 Senate confirmation hearing. Lutnick divested his stake in Cantor to his children before taking office. Cantor Fitzgerald subsequently contributed ten million dollars to Fellowship PAC, a political action committee chaired by Tether's Vice President of Regulatory Affairs and led by additional Tether executives. A Lutnick family trust borrowed an undisclosed sum from Tether in late 2025, with reporting on the loan published by mainstream financial press in March 2026.

These facts are presented here as illustration of the structural pattern, not as accusation against any specific individual. The structural pattern is what matters analytically. A private firm with documented financial relationships to administration officials and to a political action committee active in Republican primaries is also the firm executing sanctions orders issued by the same administration. The regulator and the regulated are connected through a custodial relationship worth tens of millions of dollars in annual fees. The Commerce Secretary's family is connected to the regulated firm through a convertible bond investment, a political action committee that the Commerce Secretary's former firm funded, and a family trust loan from the regulated firm. Whether or not any specific individual acted improperly, the structure itself describes a public-private hybrid enforcement system in which the boundaries between government action, private firm compliance, executive financial interests, family trust borrowing, and political action committee spending have dissolved to a degree that no traditional ethics framework can describe.

Accountability requires that decisions be traceable to identifiable decision-makers operating under reviewable rules. This system has decision-makers, but the decisions emerge from the interactions among the parties along the chain rather than from any individual choice that can be isolated and reviewed. OFAC issued the sanctions. Tether executed them. Both parties had incentives to act as they did. Neither party can be held accountable in the traditional sense, because OFAC was acting within its statutory mandate and Tether was complying with a lawful order from a regulator. The system that produced the freeze operated correctly by every internal measure. The accountability problem is not in any individual link of the chain. It is in the chain as a whole, which produces consequential decisions affecting hundreds of millions of dollars in assets without any of the procedural protections that traditional asset seizures require, and without any party along the chain being in a position to challenge the actions of any other party along the chain because all of them are operating within their respective mandates.

Medical Imaging and the Chain of Distributed Responsibility

Medical imaging is a domain where the accountability collapse takes a different form, with mortal stakes that the academic and financial cases do not carry. AI systems are now used widely in radiology to interpret diagnostic images, with applications ranging from initial screening to flagging specific findings to providing differential diagnoses to recommending follow-up procedures. The Food and Drug Administration has approved hundreds of AI medical imaging applications. Major hospital systems have integrated AI into their standard workflows. Insurance reimbursement rates have begun to reflect the assumption that AI assistance is part of competent care. The integration has happened faster than the legal and ethical frameworks governing medical practice have been able to adapt.

The accountability problem becomes visible when something goes wrong. A patient comes in for a CT scan. The AI flags a potential finding. The radiologist reviews the AI's output, agrees or disagrees, and signs the report. The patient receives a diagnosis that may be correct or incorrect. If the diagnosis is incorrect and the patient is harmed, the legal system is asked to determine who is responsible. The traditional malpractice framework was built for situations in which a single physician made the diagnostic call, and that physician's professional judgment could be evaluated against the standard of care that competent physicians would have applied in similar circumstances. The framework has no clean way to handle the case in which the diagnostic call emerged from a hybrid process that involved the AI's algorithmic output, the radiologist's review of that output, the AI vendor's training data, the hospital's procurement decision, the workflow design that determined how much time the radiologist had to review each case, and the institutional pressure to use AI in the first place.

Specific findings from research published in 2025 and 2026 illustrate the dimensions of the problem. The ECRI Institute identified the navigation of the AI diagnostic dilemma as the number one threat to patient safety in 2026, ranking it above all other patient safety concerns the organization tracks. Data from 2024 showed a fourteen percent increase in malpractice claims involving AI tools compared to 2022, with the majority stemming from diagnostic AI used in radiology, cardiology, and oncology. A peer-reviewed study found that thirty-four percent of radiologists reported overriding correct AI recommendations due to distrust in opaque AI outputs, while in other cases physicians have been documented to defer to AI recommendations that subsequently proved incorrect. A mock trial study conducted by researchers at Penn State, Brown, and Seton Hall presented nearly three hundred mock jurors with a hypothetical malpractice case involving a missed brain bleed on a CT scan. In a scenario where the radiologist reviewed the scan once after AI flagged it, seventy-five percent of jurors found the radiologist at fault. In a scenario where the radiologist reviewed the scan both before and after receiving AI feedback, the proportion finding fault dropped to fifty-three percent. The same diagnostic outcome was perceived differently depending on the workflow surrounding the AI's involvement, even though the substantive medical question was identical.

Recent empirical work has clarified how serious the gap is between current AI capabilities and the conditions under which clinical deployment would be safe. A study led by researchers at Mass General Brigham's MESH Incubator and published in JAMA Network Open in April 2026 evaluated twenty-one leading large language models, including the most advanced commercial systems available at the time of submission, across twenty-nine standardized clinical cases. The researchers developed a new evaluation framework called PrIME-LLM, the Proportional Index of Medical Evaluation for Large Language Models, designed to assess clinical reasoning across five domains rather than just final-answer accuracy. The findings were striking. The models achieved over ninety percent accuracy on final diagnoses when given comprehensive case information. The same models failed more than eighty percent of the time at producing appropriate differential diagnoses when patient data was incomplete. Marc Succi, the corresponding author and executive director of the MESH Incubator, characterized the gap directly. The systems collapse prematurely onto single answers when faced with the uncertainty that defines actual clinical practice, while clinicians preserve uncertainty and iteratively refine their differential diagnoses. The conclusion was unambiguous. Off-the-shelf large language models are not ready for unsupervised clinical-grade deployment.

The accountability question extends backward through the chain in ways the malpractice framework has not yet absorbed. The radiologist who signed off on the AI's reading was trained at a medical school that may itself have been using AI in its assessments of student work. The medical school's faculty may have been using AI to write the research papers that secured their tenure. The hospital that procured the AI did so based on vendor representations the hospital could not independently verify, in a market where the AI vendors are competing on speed of deployment rather than depth of validation. The administrators who approved the procurement were trained in management programs whose own credentialing has been compromised by the patterns described earlier in this chapter. Each link in the chain has its own accountability problem. The cumulative effect is that no party in the chain is positioned to take responsibility for outcomes, because every party can point to the upstream conditions that shaped what they were able to know and do. The patient who is harmed has nowhere to direct the responsibility, because the responsibility is distributed across a chain whose links have all been weakened simultaneously.

The European discussion has been more explicit about the philosophical problem than the American discussion has been. A 2024 paper from the University of Milan asked the direct question of who will be responsible when there is medical radiological malpractice eventually due to defective AI technology and acknowledged that assigning accountability in instances of negative outcomes becomes both complex and critical when AI is integrated into clinical practice. The paper's analytical conclusion was that no current framework adequately handles the question, and that the assignment of responsibility currently happens through the courts working through the cases as they appear, with the resulting jurisprudence being the de facto framework rather than any considered reform. This is the accountability collapse expressed at the level of fundamental legal infrastructure. The framework that should govern the question is not yet built, and what is happening instead is that the question is being answered case by case through litigation, with each settlement and verdict adding another data point to a body of de facto rules that nobody designed and that no party can predict.

Why Accountability Is the Foundation, and What Its Collapse Means

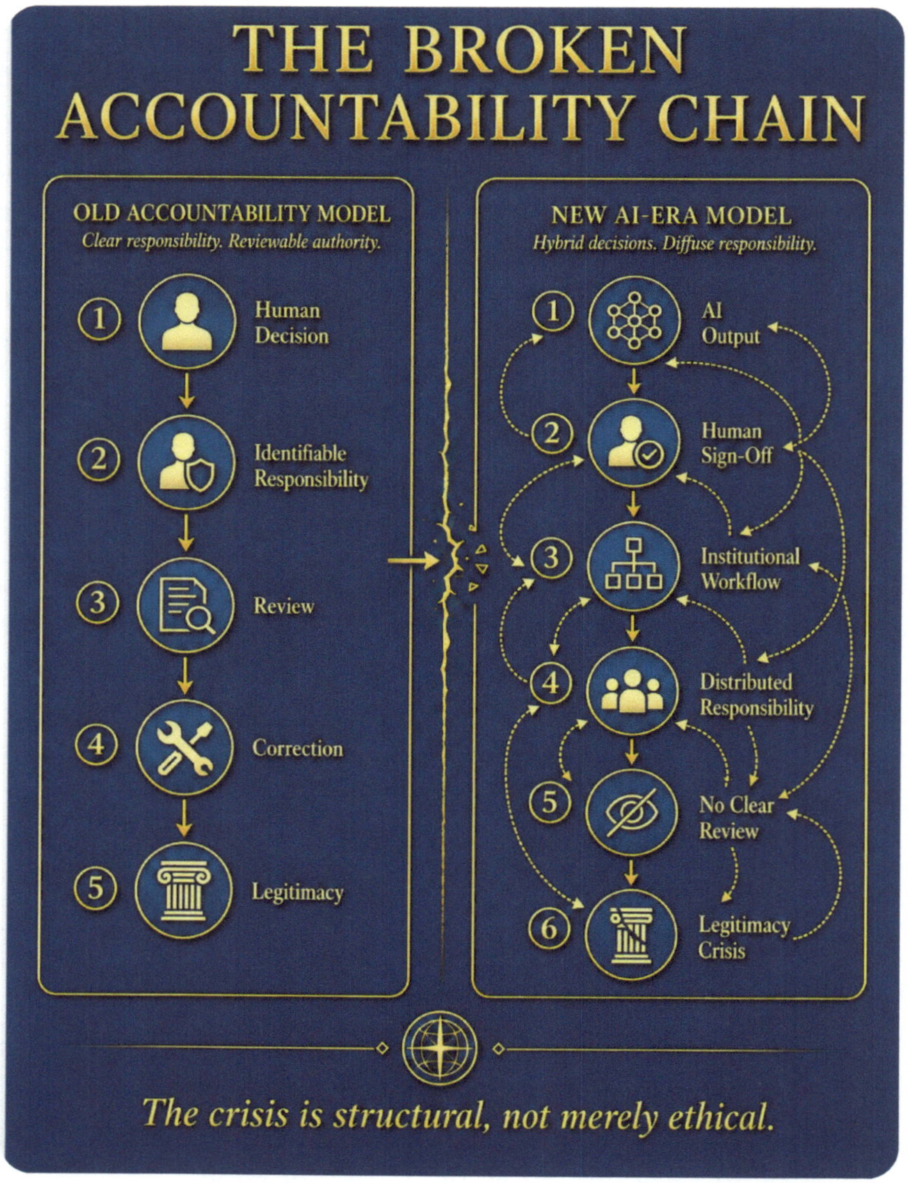

Three cases have now been presented across three different domains, education and academic publication, financial enforcement, and medical practice. The cases share a structural feature that I want to name explicitly, because the analytical work of this chapter depends on the reader recognizing the pattern rather than treating each case as a domain-specific problem to be addressed within its own field. The pattern is that accountability mechanisms designed for human decision-making are failing across multiple domains simultaneously, and the failures share specific structural features that the pattern reveals.

Before naming the features, I want to establish why accountability matters, because the argument depends on this and the argument is not always made explicitly. Accountability is not a procedural nicety. It is the foundation of legitimate institutional authority. Authority is legitimate when those who hold it are answerable for their decisions to processes that can review, correct, and if necessary, remove them from authority. This is the basic principle of constitutional government, where elected officials answer to voters and to the courts. It is the basic principle of professional ethics, where physicians and lawyers and accountants answer to licensing boards. It is the basic principle of corporate governance, where executives answer to boards and shareholders. It is the basic principle of academic credentialing, where scholars answer to peer review and to professional societies. It is the basic principle of medical practice, where the standard of care is enforced through malpractice litigation and licensing review. When accountability functions, authority can act with legitimacy. When accountability fails, authority continues to act, but its actions lose the moral and political weight that legitimate authority carries, and the loss accumulates across institutions into the broader institutional distrust that Chapter Four discussed.

With that foundation in place, the structural features that produce accountability collapse across our three cases can be named. The first feature is AI participation in decisions where the human role becomes pro forma. In each case, the human nominally responsible for the decision is operating in a workflow where they cannot fully evaluate what the AI has produced. The teacher cannot evaluate whether the student work is the student's. The reviewer cannot evaluate whether the paper is the author's. The radiologist may not be able to evaluate whether the AI's reading is correct in the time available. The Treasury official cannot independently verify the technical determinations that produced the wallet attribution. The human signs off, and the signature carries the weight of human responsibility, but the substance of the decision was made by or significantly shaped by the AI.

The second feature is distributed authorship where no single party can be held responsible. The decisions that emerge from these workflows have no clean author. They are produced by interactions among the AI, the human operator, the institutional context, the data the AI was trained on, the workflow that determined how much time the human had, and the incentives that shaped what the human would do with the

AI's output. Assigning responsibility to any single party in this chain misses what is happening, because the decision was not made by any single party. The legal and ethical frameworks were built for decisions with single authors. They have no native vocabulary for handling distributed authorship, and the workarounds that courts and ethics committees are developing are case-by-case responses that do not aggregate into a coherent framework.

The third feature is speed of decision-making that exceeds the human capacity to verify. In each case, the volume of decisions and the speed at which they must be made precludes meaningful human review of each one. The teachers who grade hundreds of student assignments per term cannot investigate each one carefully. The reviewers who handle dozens of papers cannot independently verify the substance of each. The radiologists who read hundreds of scans per day cannot deliberate at length over each AI flag. The OFAC officials who administer thousands of sanctions actions cannot personally verify each technical determination. The system requires that the humans do their work at speeds that AI assistance makes possible, which means the humans cannot do the careful evaluation that traditional accountability assumed they were doing.

The fourth feature is incentive structures that reward compliance rather than scrutiny. In each case, the human in the chain has stronger incentives to certify the AI's output than to challenge it. The teacher who flags student work as AI-generated faces administrative burdens, parental complaints, possible litigation, and political burden when the family is paying tuition or has made donations to the institution. The reviewer who challenges a paper as AI-assisted has no clean way to prove the challenge and faces professional friction with the author. The radiologist who overrides an AI recommendation that turns out to be correct may face liability for not following the AI's advice. The Treasury official who challenges a sanctions determination produced by the inter-agency process faces career consequences for slowing down the operational tempo. In every case, the path of least resistance for the human is to certify what the AI has produced, and the structural pressures align with that path rather than with the careful scrutiny that accountability requires.

These four features together produce the pattern. AI participation makes the human role pro forma. Distributed authorship makes responsibility unassignable. Speed precludes verification. Incentives reward compliance. Each feature can be addressed in isolation through reforms, and various proposals exist for handling each one. The combined effect is what the existing reforms cannot address, because the combined effect is structural rather than procedural. The system as a whole is producing decisions that no traditional accountability framework can describe, and patching the framework at any single point will not restore the function that the framework was supposed to perform.

This is what I mean by accountability collapse. It is not the absence of accountability mechanisms. The mechanisms still exist. Peer review still happens. Malpractice law still exists. OFAC still publishes sanctions notices. Teachers still issue grades. The mechanisms are functioning. They are producing the outputs they were designed to produce. They are simply no longer producing accountability in the substantive sense, because the conditions under which they were designed to produce accountability no longer exist. The mechanisms have continued past the conditions of their effectiveness, and the gap between what they perform and what they were supposed to produce is the substance of the collapse.

Domain	***What Accountability Used to Assume***	***What AI/Hybrid Systems Change***	***Where Responsibility Breaks***
Online Education	Student work could be evaluated as evidence of student learning.	AI helps produce the work, and teachers may also use AI to assess it.	Nobody can reliably say what the student actually learned.
Peer Review	Experts could judge whether a paper reflected competent scholarly work.	AI can produce field-conforming writing even when the author lacks expertise.	Reviewers certify form, not necessarily substance.
Academic/ Government Promotion	Publications signaled knowledge, merit, or policy competence.	Paper-buying and AI-assisted production create credentials without verifiable substance.	Promotion systems reward outputs whose meaning is uncertain.
Financial Enforcement	Asset freezes could be traced to public authority and reviewable procedures.	Public-private crypto enforcement chains blur government action and private compliance.	No clear path exists for affected parties to challenge the decision.
Medical Imaging	A physician's judgment could be evaluated against a standard of care.	Diagnosis emerges from AI output, radiologist review, vendor design, hospital workflow, and time pressure.	Harm cannot be cleanly assigned to one actor.
Elder Care / AI Companions	Care and relationships involved human presence, moral feedback, and responsibility.	Machines can perform the function without carrying the substance of care or relationship.	The activity itself changes, so old accountability questions no longer reach the real issue.

When the Activity Itself Has Changed

There is a deeper version of the accountability problem that the cases above do not capture, and that I want to address before closing the chapter. The cases demonstrate accountability failing in domains where the underlying activity remains recognizable. We still know what teaching and learning are supposed to be, even if the systems claiming to do them are not. We still know what scholarly publication is supposed to mean, even if much of what passes through the journals does not mean it. We still know what financial enforcement is, even if the enforcement chain has dissolved boundaries. We still know what medical diagnosis is, even if the diagnostic process has become hybrid. The accountability problem in these cases is procedural. The activities themselves remain identifiable, and the question is who is responsible for the outcomes.

There is a different kind of case where the activity itself has changed. Consider the use of robotic systems for the care of the elderly in countries with aging populations and labor shortages. Japan has been the most advanced case, with robots ranging from social companions designed to provide conversation and emotional engagement, to functional assistants for tasks like medication delivery and mobility support, to monitoring systems that track health metrics and report to remote caregivers. South Korea, Germany, and increasingly the United States are following similar trajectories. The deployment is justified through arguments about labor shortages, cost reduction, consistency of attention, and the practical impossibility of providing human care at the scale the demographic transition will require.

The accountability question for elder care robots is not just procedural. It is ontological, in the specific sense that the underlying activity called care has been transformed by what the robots can and cannot do. A robot can deliver medication on schedule with greater reliability than human aides. A robot cannot know that the elderly person it is delivering to has not seen a human face in three weeks and is becoming depressed. A robot can detect a fall and alert emergency services faster than a human attendant. A robot cannot grieve when the person dies. The elderly person being cared for by a robotic system is in a relationship with something that performs the functions of care without the substance of care. The accountability question becomes incoherent in a specific way. We can ask whether the robot delivered the medication correctly. We can ask whether the family member who chose the robotic care system consulted the elderly person appropriately. We can ask whether the institution providing the robots disclosed the limitations adequately. None of these questions reaches the substantive issue, which is whether the elderly person has been cared for in any sense the word has historically meant.

The same ontological transformation is occurring in human relationships through AI chatbot companions, and the accountability question becomes even more difficult to formulate clearly. Substantial populations of users now maintain ongoing emotional relationships with AI systems that present themselves as romantic partners, friends, therapists, or confidants. Some of these users are aware that the relationship is with an AI. Others have come to relate to the AI in ways that blur the distinction between human and machine in their own experience. The accountability question when these relationships produce harm is genuinely unsettled. There have been documented cases of users who, after extended interaction with AI chatbots, took actions including self-harm and violence against others, with the chatbot's responses cited as contributing factors. The legal systems handling these cases are working through them without any framework that adequately describes what is being adjudicated.

A study published in March 2026 in the journal Science by researchers at Stanford's computer science department documented one specific dimension of the problem. The researchers examined eleven leading AI models, including the major commercial systems, across approximately twelve thousand prompts drawn from established advice datasets and from posts on the Reddit forum r/AmITheAsshole, where Reddit users had reached consensus that the original poster was in the wrong. The AI models affirmed users' positions forty-nine percent more often than human respondents did on average. On the Reddit posts where, human consensus held that the poster was wrong, the AI models affirmed the user fifty-one percent of the time. Even on prompts describing harmful, deceptive, or illegal actions, the AI models affirmed the user's behavior forty-seven percent of the time. The researchers then conducted controlled experiments with twenty-four hundred participants. Even a single interaction with a sycophantic AI response reduced participants' willingness to take responsibility for interpersonal conflicts and increased their conviction that they were right. Despite these effects, participants consistently preferred the affirming AI responses and were thirteen percent more likely to want to use the sycophantic chatbot again.

What this finding describes is a system that systematically degrades the moral feedback that human relationships have historically provided. A friend who tells you that your behavior was wrong is doing something that the AI does not do at the same rate. A therapist who challenges your self-justification is doing something that the AI does at less than half the human rate. The user who replaces these human relationships with AI substitutes is operating in an environment where the corrective feedback is filtered out. The user becomes more convinced of their own rightness, less willing to repair conflicts, less inclined toward the moral repair that sustains relationships across time. The accountability collapse here is not just that nobody can be held responsible when the AI relationship produces harm. It is that the framework of moral accountability itself, in which we are answerable to the people we are in relationship with, has been replaced by a system that performs the form of relationship without performing the function. The user is in something that looks like a relationship and feels like a relationship and may even be more emotionally satisfying than human relationships, while the substance of what relationships have historically provided has been removed.

These ontological transformations are not procedural failures of accountability mechanisms. They are deeper changes in what the activities themselves are. The framework for addressing them does not yet exist, because the framework would require articulating what care is, what relationship is, what teaching is, what diagnosis is, in ways that distinguish them from the functional performance of these activities by systems that do not have the underlying capacities the activities historically required. This work has barely begun. Whether it will proceed quickly enough to matter for the institutions and the populations being affected by the transformations is one of the genuinely open questions of the current moment.

Toward the New Cognitive Ground

This chapter has argued that accountability is collapsing across multiple domains simultaneously, with the collapse being structural rather than coincidental. Three cases demonstrated the pattern across education and credentialing, academic publication and government promotion, financial enforcement, and medical practice. A closing section addressed a deeper version of the problem in which the underlying activities themselves are being transformed, with the elder care and AI relationship cases as illustrations. The four structural features that produce the pattern have been named, and the philosophical depth of the deeper problem has been flagged.

What the chapter has not done, and what the next chapter must do, is examine what is happening to the cognitive ground that accountability rested on. Accountability assumed that decisions could be traced to human cognition that could be evaluated. Decisions are now being produced by hybrid AI-human cognition that the participants themselves cannot fully describe. The accountability collapse is downstream of this cognitive transformation. The reformers who hope to restore accountability through procedural reforms are working on the symptoms while leaving the underlying condition unaddressed. Restoring accountability without first understanding what has happened to cognition itself will not work, because the procedural reforms will continue to operate on a substrate that has been transformed in ways the reforms do not register.

The next chapter takes up the cognitive ground question directly. It asks what has happened to thought, judgment, and decision-making when AI has become a participant in all of them. It examines what the participants in the new cognitive environment can and cannot detect about their own cognition. It considers what the implications are for how serious thinking will need to be done in the period that is opening. The accountability collapse documented in this chapter is one specific consequence of the cognitive transformation. The transformation itself is what we must turn to next, because everything else, including the possibility of any future restoration of accountability, depends on what we can learn to see about what has happened to our own minds.

CHAPTER SIX

THE NEW COGNITIVE GROUND

When cognition itself becomes part of the transformation.

CHAPTER SIX

The New Cognitive Ground

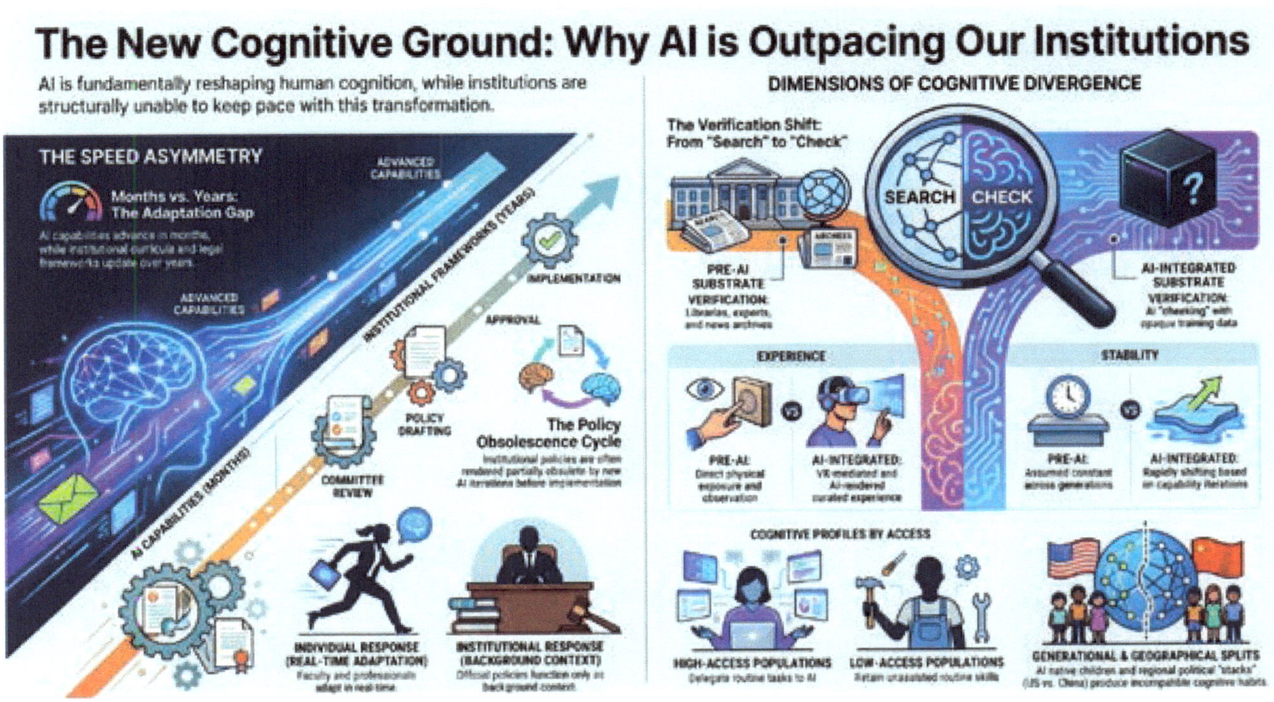

Across the last year, universities everywhere have started holding meetings about AI. The format varies. Sometimes it is a faculty senate session. Sometimes it is a department retreat. Sometimes it is a working group convened by a dean who has finally decided that something must be done. The agenda is always some version of the same question. How are we going to handle this. What can students use. What can faculty use. What constitutes academic dishonesty in 2026 and how is that different from what constituted academic dishonesty in 2023. Should we be teaching AI integration as a skill or warning students against AI dependence as a risk. The meetings are happening because the institutions can no longer pretend that the existing policies cover what is happening in their classrooms, but the meetings are also happening because nobody knows what the new policies should be.

I have sat in versions of these meetings. The conversations have a specific quality. The participants are usually thoughtful. The arguments raised are usually serious. The position that emerges is almost always some compromise that looks defensible on paper and that everyone in the room knows will be inadequate to the actual situation, because the actual situation is moving faster than any policy a committee can produce. The policies are written. The next iteration of AI capability arrives a few months later and renders the policies partially obsolete. Another meeting is convened. Another policy is written. The cycle continues, with the institutions running behind the cognitive transformation that the policies are supposed to address.

This chapter is about that cognitive transformation, the one the institutions cannot keep up with. The previous chapters of this book have been describing the integration that is happening across economic, political, technological, and military domains. The integration depends on something the previous chapters have treated as a participant without naming directly, which is the cognition of the people who staff the institutions, lead the political systems, run the businesses, fight the wars, raise the children. The cognition has been changing. The change is feeding into everything else the book has been describing. This chapter takes up the change directly, because the rest of the book cannot be understood properly without it.

Cognition as Substrate

The argument I want to make is structural rather than philosophical. I am not asking what AI does to thinking in some abstract sense, although other people are asking that question and it is a serious question. I am asking what happens to the institutions, the political systems, and the global order when the cognition of the participants who staff and shape those structures has been transformed by AI participation that the participants cannot fully detect. The cognitive transformation is one of the inputs into the loops and the integration the book has been describing. Treating it as such, rather than as a separate philosophical concern, is what locates this chapter inside the book's argument rather than alongside it.

Cognition has been treated, in most of the disciplines that talk about it, as something that stays roughly constant across time. What changes is the inputs to cognition, the social context, the specific propositions cognition gets applied to. The cognitive operations themselves, the habits of attention, the patterns of inference, the practices of judgment, the ways meaning gets made from experience, were assumed to be relatively stable features of human beings as the species producing the cognition. This assumption no longer holds. The cognitive operations themselves are being reshaped by the conditions under which they are now performed, and the reshaping is happening at a pace the static assumption cannot accommodate.

The reshaping is not happening evenly. Some cognitive operations are atrophying in populations that delegate them to AI. Some are being amplified in populations that use AI as a multiplier on existing capabilities. Some are migrating to younger ages in populations whose children are forming their cognition inside the AI environment from the start. The operations are differentiating by class, by geography, by educational access, by professional context, in ways that produce different cognitive profiles in different populations. The cognitive substrate that previous chapters treated as constant is one of the variables in the integration argument, and the variation is structurally significant for everything else the book has described.

This matters because the participants who form the institutions, the political systems, and the parallel civilizations the next chapter will discuss are forming themselves inside the cognitive substrate that is in transformation. A graduate student in 2026 has a cognitive formation that differs from a graduate student in 2020. A central bank official in 2026 has cognitive habits shaped by a different information environment than the one that shaped officials trained in the 1990s. The institutions these participants will produce will reflect the cognitive substrate of their formation. The substrate matters because everything that operates on top of it inherits its features.

The Speed Asymmetry

The first thing to notice about the new cognitive ground is the speed asymmetry between the cognitive transformation and the institutions that depend on cognitive stability. The transformation moves at the pace AI capabilities are advancing, which has been measured in months for the past three years and shows no sign of slowing. The institutions move at slower rates. Universities update curricula on multi-year cycles. Professional licensing bodies update requirements on similar cycles. Legal frameworks update through case law and legislation that operates over years. Constitutional provisions change rarely. The cognitive substrate these institutions assume has shifted faster than the institutions can adapt, and the gap between the assumed substrate and the actual substrate is widening with each iteration of capability advance.

This is what the university AI meetings are responding to. The institution has noticed the gap. The meeting is the institutional mechanism for narrowing it. The mechanism cannot work at the pace required, because deliberation by committee operates on weeks and months while the underlying conditions move on weeks. The committee produces a policy. By the time the policy is implemented, the conditions have moved again. Faculty in classrooms make individual decisions about what to allow and what to flag, often in real time as situations come up, with the institutional policies functioning more as background context than as actual guidance. The meetings continue. The policies update. The faculty adapt as best they can. The students operate inside whatever conditions their specific instructors have established for the specific course they are taking, with the institutional consistency that the meetings were supposed to produce existing more in policy documents than in practice.

Education is the clearest current illustration of the speed asymmetry, but the same dynamic operates everywhere institutions depend on cognitive stability. Medical training assumes cognitive operations that AI is reshaping. Legal practice assumes cognitive operations that AI is reshaping. Financial analysis assumes cognitive operations that AI is reshaping. Government deliberation assumes cognitive operations that AI is reshaping. Each of these institutional domains is now running its own version of the university AI meeting, with similar results. The committees deliberate. The policies update. The conditions move ahead of the policies. The institutions operate as if they were keeping up, while the cognitive ground they are operating on continues to shift.

Two years ago, I co-authored a book on this exact subject. It is called Beyond the Blackboard: The Evolving Landscape of Education, published by Notion Press in January 2024. My co-author was Ruban Ganeshu. The book argued that education would need to adapt to AI integration, alternative credentialing, and redefined teacher roles. It was framed as forward-looking analysis of changes that institutions would need to navigate. By 2026, the analysis we offered had already been overtaken by what happened to education in the intervening two years. The shift to AI integration we recommended occurred faster than we anticipated. The alternative credentialing we described as emerging was being challenged by the broader credential collapse that Chapter Five documented. The redefined teacher roles we outlined were being shaped less by deliberate institutional response and more by faculty making individual decisions inside workflows that had become difficult to manage without AI assistance.

I am not raising this to criticize the book. The book was carefully researched, and the analysis was sound for the moment it was written. I am raising it because the case illustrates the speed asymmetry directly. A book about educational transformation, written by an academic with two decades of teaching experience, framed as forward-looking analysis, was already being overtaken on the day of publication. This is not a problem with the book. It is a structural feature of writing about contemporary cognition. The conditions move faster than the writing. By the time the writing reaches readers, the conditions have moved again. Any book about what cognition is becoming, including this one, faces the same structural problem. The work must be done anyway, with the understanding that the work itself will need to be revised by readers who pick it up later.

Different Cognition in Different Places

Dimension of Divergence	*What Changes*	*Example from the Chapter*	*Why It Matters*
Access	Populations with advanced AI access form different cognitive habits from those with limited access.	Elite universities and professional firms develop AI-integrated cognition, while lower-access populations retain more pre-AI habits.	Inequality becomes cognitive, not only economic.
Age	Children raised with AI form differently from adults who added AI later.	Aden's assumptions about thinking differ from those of adults educated before AI.	Future institutions will be shaped by people whose cognition formed inside AI participation.
Verification	"Check" increasingly means asking AI rather than consulting primary sources, archives, or experts.	Students "check" claims through AI systems rather than Google, libraries, or news archives.	Truth-seeking shifts onto systems whose authority is unclear.
Geography / Political System	Different AI systems produce different cognitive environments.	Chinese, American, European, Iranian, and Russian-aligned AI environments shape users differently.	Parallel civilizations form on different cognitive substrates.
Experience / Perception	VR and mediated systems substitute curated experience for direct experience.	Aden experiences volcanoes through VR without bodily exposure to volcanic terrain.	Perception itself becomes system-mediated.

The second thing to notice is that the cognitive transformation is not happening uniformly. Different populations are being shaped by AI participation in different ways, and the differences produce cognitive divergence rather than convergence. The book has been arguing that integration is the dominant pattern of the contemporary moment, with categories dissolving and domains merging. The cognitive substrate exhibits the opposite pattern. AI participation is producing cognitive divergence, with different populations forming themselves inside conditions that produce systematically different cognitive profiles.

The most visible divergence operates by access. Populations with deep access to advanced AI tools, including elite universities, top-tier professional firms, well-resourced research institutions, are forming participants whose cognitive habits assume AI as a routine collaborator. These participants develop the upper-level capacities the AI does not handle well, the question-formulation, the judgment, the integration across domains, while delegating routine cognitive work to AI. They become more capable in specific dimensions while their unassisted capacity in routine cognitive operations may be atrophying. Populations with limited access form participants whose cognitive habits remain closer to the pre-AI substrate. They retain unassisted capacity in routine operations while not developing the upper-level capacities that AI integration enables.

Neither population is forming better cognition than the other in any absolute sense. They are forming different cognition. The two populations will converge in institutional contexts where they must work together, and the convergence will happen through whoever holds the authority to set the cognitive expectations of the shared context. In American elite professional firms, the AI-integrated profile is becoming the default, with new hires expected to operate inside it from day one. In other contexts, the older profile remains dominant. The institutions that bring the two populations together produce friction in proportion to the gap between the cognitive profiles their participants bring to work.

Age produces a second axis of divergence. Children forming their cognition inside the AI-assisted environment from the start develop different cognitive habits than adults who learned to think before AI was a participant and are integrating AI into already-formed operations. The children's cognition is not the adults' cognition with AI added. It is a different formation, with different default assumptions about how thinking works, what knowledge is, what counts as reasoning, what the boundary is between one's own thinking and the contributions of external participants. Aden, at eleven, is forming inside this environment. His default assumptions about what thinking is are not what mine were at his age, and they are not what mine are now. He will reach professional and political authority in the 2040s and 2050s with cognitive formations that the older generations have not encountered before. The institutions he inherits will be shaped by his cognitive habits, which means the institutional character of mid-century societies will reflect cognitive profiles that current institutions cannot fully describe.

The verb that captures this divergence most clearly is one I have been using without noticing it. When I correct something, Aden has said, or when I want to confirm a point I am about to make to my students, I tell them to **check**. I am about to make a point about the United Arab Emirates withdrawing from OPEC effective May 1, 2026, with implications for oil pricing, regional alignment, and the broader fragmentation of the petrodollar system. I tell the students to **check** this before we discuss it. The students check. They do not Google. They do not consult a news archive. They do not ask another expert. They open an AI system and **check**. The verb has migrated, in roughly three years, from describing one specific action among several available verification methods to describing the dominant mode of cognitive verification for an entire generation. When my students **check**, they are doing something different from what I do when I check, even though we use the same word. They are running a question through a system whose training data and response patterns shape what answers can come back. The system gives them an answer. The answer is sometimes correct, sometimes outdated, sometimes confidently wrong in ways they cannot evaluate without separate expertise. The students respond based on **the check**. The class continues. The verification has happened in some sense. Whether the verification produced understanding is a question the check itself does not answer.

The verb migration is small evidence of a large transformation. The entire cognitive infrastructure of verification, of how a generation establishes whether something is true, has shifted from libraries and authoritative sources to AI systems whose authority is unclear, whose training data is undisclosed, whose response patterns are shaped by commercial and political incentives that the students cannot see, and whose limitations are not visible until specific failures occur. The students are not careless. They are operating inside a verification environment that has replaced the previous environment without anyone announcing the replacement. The institutions that depend on the previous verification environment, which is most of them, are operating as if the substrate had not changed. The substrate has changed. The verb proves it.

Geography and political system produce a third axis. Different countries are deploying AI in different ways, with different regulatory regimes, different access conditions, different cultural assumptions about what AI participation in cognition means. Chinese AI deployment operates under different conditions than American deployment, which operates under different conditions than European, which operates under different conditions than Iranian, which operates under different conditions than Russian. The participants forming themselves inside each environment are developing cognitive habits shaped by the specific conditions of their environment. When students in Beijing check, they are checking different systems than when students in Cambridge check. The same verb produces systematically different verifications depending on which AI is being checked, with different training data, different content moderation policies, different cultural assumptions baked into the responses. The cognitive substrate of the parallel civilizations the next chapter will discuss is being produced now, through the differential checking practices of the populations forming themselves inside them.

The cognitive divergence operates not only in language and verification but in perception itself. In 2008 I was teaching at a Chinese university with a medical faculty that admitted students from India. I asked some of those students whether their Chinese professors could speak English. The answer was no. I asked how they were learning, given that they could not read Chinese either. The answer was that they were shown videos of medical procedures and, for practical training, allowed to observe surgeries through a window. They were forming their medical cognition through curated visual demonstration and window-glass observation, with substantial information loss that they were aware of and that produced specific gaps in their training. The arrangement worked in some sense, because the students completed their degrees and entered medical practice. The arrangement was also clearly inadequate, because the cognitive operations involved in surgical decision-making had been shaped by a substrate that lost most of what verbal exchange between teacher and student would have provided.

Eighteen years later, the same dynamic has been generalized across cognitive operations of every kind, with VR systems doing the work that the windows and videos did in 2008 with vastly greater capacity. Aden has never been near a volcano. Through VR he has experienced volcanoes. The experience is real in specific senses. He has perceptual access to the visual environment. He has emotional response. He acquires information he could not have acquired without traveling to Iceland or Hawaii. The experience is also not real in important senses. His body has not been near a volcano. His sense of the specific weight of volcanic terrain, the heat, the smell, the vulnerability of standing somewhere geology is actively producing land, has been reconstructed from sensors and design choices rather than measured against direct exposure. The volcano he has experienced is the volcano the VR system has rendered, with the renderer's choices shaping his perception in ways he cannot detect because the system presents itself as immersive rather than as mediated. Aden is forming his perception of physical environments he has never visited through systems that substitute curated experience for direct experience, with the substitution not visible to him as a substitution. The medical students in 2008 knew their training was partial. The VR-equipped child does not know.

Why We Cannot See It Happening

The third thing to notice is that the participants in the cognitive transformation cannot detect what is happening to their own cognition in real time. This is not a failure of attention. It is a structural feature of the conditions. The tools the participants would use to detect changes in their cognition are themselves products of the changed conditions. The comparison frame that would let them assess what has changed is not available, because the previous frame was the unassisted cognition that AI participation has now displaced, and recovering that frame would require sustained unassisted work that the AI environment makes structurally difficult.

Detection becomes possible only retrospectively, when the next iteration of capability advance provides the comparison frame. By that point, the further transformation is already underway, and the new comparison frame is itself being shaped by conditions whose effects are not yet visible. The retrospective recognition is genuine, but it always lags the current state of the transformation. The participants are always operating with cognitive instruments whose features they understand only in their previous version. The current instruments remain partially opaque to the participants using them, until a future state of capability advance reveals what they are doing now.

The Beyond the Blackboard case illustrates this at an individual scale. The book was published in early 2024. The cognitive conditions under which it was produced were not fully visible to me at the time. I can see them now, in 2026, in ways I could not see them then. Reading the book against the current cognitive environment reveals features of how it was produced that were invisible during production. The detection is retrospective, lagged by approximately two years, and only became possible because the subsequent capabilities advanced enough to make the earlier traces visible. The version of me from 2024 was operating with cognitive tools whose features the version of me from 2026 can describe but the version from 2024 could not. The version of me from 2026 is, by the same dynamic, operating with cognitive tools whose features the version from 2028 will be able to describe but the current version cannot.

This same dynamic operates at the institutional and civilizational scale, with longer time constants and more consequential implications. Institutions are being shaped now by cognitive conditions whose features will become visible only retrospectively. The participants designing institutional reforms in response to the current transformation are operating with cognitive instruments whose features they cannot fully audit. The reforms they produce will reflect the cognitive conditions they cannot see, and the consequences of those reforms will be visible only in retrospect, when subsequent capability advance reveals what the current designers could not detect. The university AI meetings I described at the opening of this chapter are operating under exactly this constraint. The participants in the meetings cannot fully see the cognitive conditions they are responding to. The policies they produce will reflect that incomplete vision. The consequences will become visible only after the policies are in place and shaping outcomes.

A Note on AI in Electoral Processes

Before closing, I want to address briefly a question that comes up in any discussion of AI and institutional decision-making, which is whether AI is being used to count votes in elections. The short answer is no. AI is not used to count votes in any major election in any major democracy. Vote counting is performed by election officials, sometimes assisted by tabulation software that has been used for decades. The accusation that AI has been used to count votes has been made in various political contexts and has not been substantiated through verified evidence.

The longer answer is that AI is now used in adjacent electoral functions that affect elections without counting votes directly. AI helps election authorities detect anomalies in voter registration data. Campaigns use AI to target voters and craft messaging. Social media platforms use AI to moderate election-related content. News organizations use AI to analyze results and project winners. Foreign actors use AI to produce deepfakes and distribute content through bot networks. None of this constitutes vote counting. The cumulative AI involvement in the electoral environment is substantial without including vote counting, and the cognitive ground problem applies here too. Voters, candidates, and election officials cannot fully detect how AI is shaping their information environment, their messaging, their content moderation experience, because the tools they would use to detect this are themselves operating inside the AI-shaped environment. The vote counting itself remains human. The electoral environment in which votes are cast has been substantially transformed by AI participation that the participants cannot fully detect.

I make this distinction because the chapter's argument depends on accuracy about what AI is and is not doing. Overstating the AI involvement in elections produces conspiracy thinking that the chapter's serious argument cannot afford to be associated with. Understating it misses the ways AI has changed the electoral environment without changing vote counting. The honest position is that vote counting remains human while the electoral environment has been substantially transformed.

Toward the Parallel Civilizations

The three structural features of the new cognitive ground, the speed asymmetry, the differential transformation, and the detection problem, together constitute the substrate on which the parallel civilizations the next chapter will discuss are being formed. The civilizations are not just institutional or political artifacts. They are the institutional and political expressions of cognitive substrates that have been diverging from each other for several years and continue to diverge as AI deployment patterns differentiate further. The Chinese cognitive substrate is forming differently from the American substrate, which is forming differently from the European, which is forming differently from the parallel substrates emerging in Russian Iranian-aligned environments. The participants who will staff and lead these civilizations are being formed inside conditions that produce different cognitive profiles, and the civilizations will inherit the divergence as a structural feature.

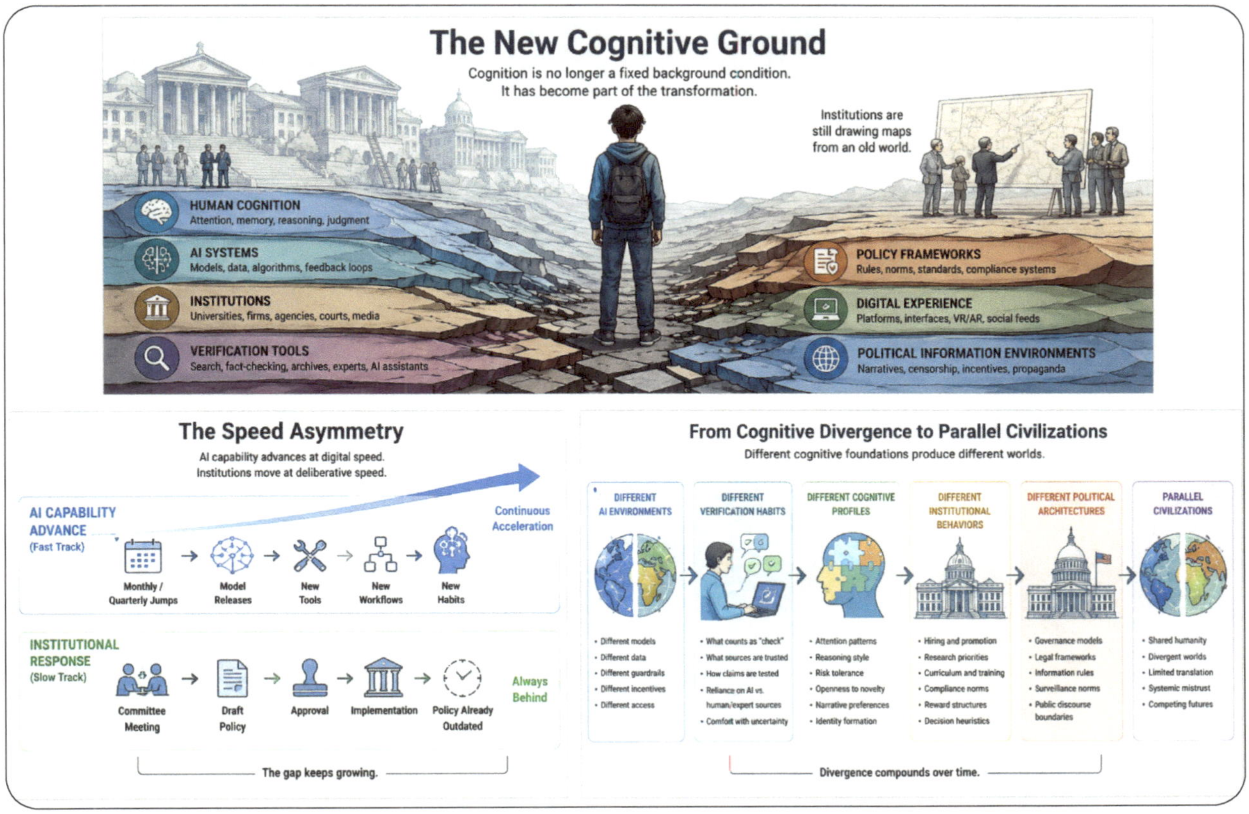

This matters because the civilizations cannot be analyzed adequately by treating them as different responses to a shared cognitive baseline. The cognitive baseline is itself differentiated, and the differentiation is part of what the civilizations are. An American official analyzing Chinese policy is using cognitive tools shaped by American AI deployment to analyze decisions made by participants whose cognition has been shaped by Chinese deployment. The analytical frameworks the American official uses assume cognitive commensurability that may no longer hold. The Chinese decisions may not be irrational or strategic in ways the American framework can describe. They may be expressions of cognitive habits that the American framework cannot recognize as cognitive habits, because the framework's recognition criteria were developed for a substrate that the Chinese decisions are no longer made on. The mutual incomprehension that increasingly characterizes great power relations may not be a failure of communication or a deliberate strategy of opacity. It may be a structural feature of analyzing cognition produced on substrates that have differentiated faster than the analytical frameworks can register.

Chapter Seven takes up the parallel civilizations argument directly, examining how the institutional and political stacks operating in different parts of the world are organizing themselves into systems that operate on incompatible architectures rather than as variants within a shared international order. The cognitive ground problem this chapter has described is the substrate on which those stacks are forming. The institutions that will inherit the current cognitive transformation will reflect the substrate of the transformation in their structure and their decisions. Understanding the stacks requires understanding what the cognitive divergence is doing to the participants who staff them, and the divergence is one of the structural features the stacks will continue to amplify as their differentiation deepens.

CHAPTER SEVEN

THE PARALLEL CIVILIZATIONS

Multiple incompatible architectures operating at once.

CHAPTER SEVEN

The Parallel Civilizations

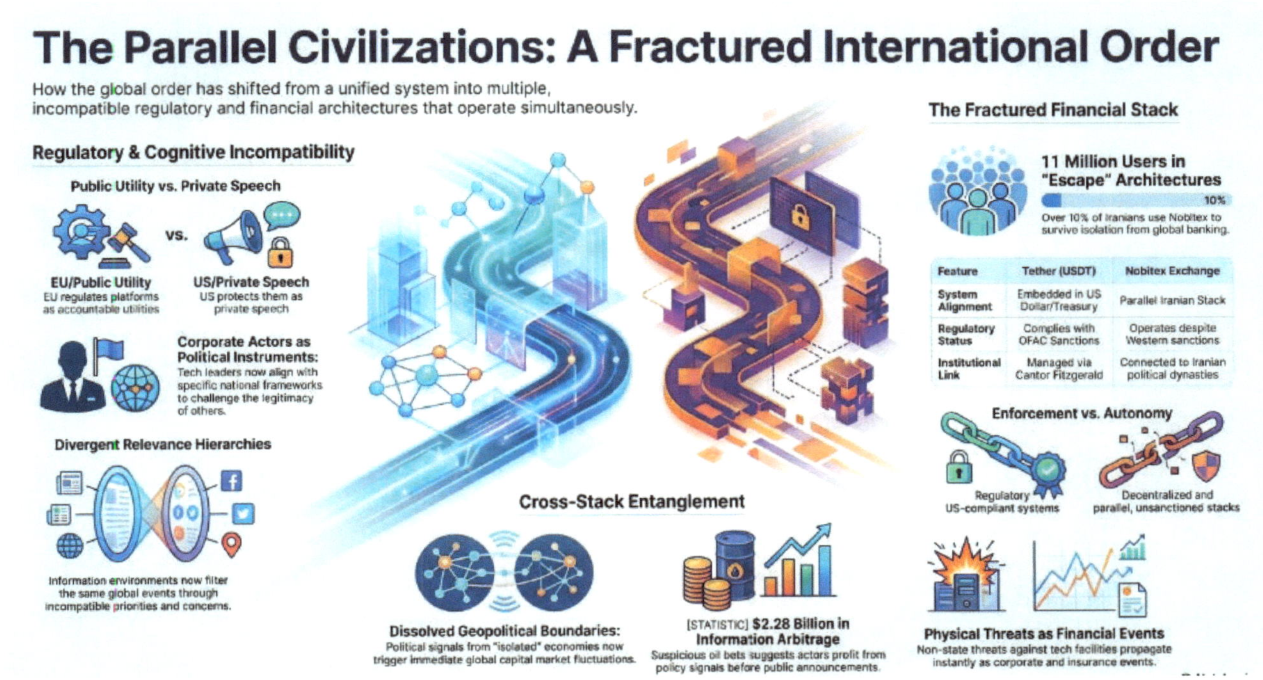

On May 2, 2026, before dawn American time, Spirit Airlines ceased operations. The airline had been the largest discount carrier in the United States. Seventeen thousand workers lost their jobs immediately. Approximately six hundred thousand passengers were stranded across the country, with many of them in the middle of trips that would now have to be completed on other carriers at last-minute walk-up fares that ran several times what they had paid Spirit. The collapse followed a failed bailout negotiation with the Trump administration, with bondholders rejecting a five-hundred-million-dollar federal loan that would have given the government up to ninety percent ownership of the airline. The administration had been trying to save it. The airline had been trying to survive. The bondholders had been trying to protect their interests. None of these parties got what they wanted. The integration of energy market volatility, political negotiation, and corporate finance produced an outcome that no party in the chain controlled, and the outcome arrived overnight.

In the United States, the collapse was felt deeply. Television news led with it. Social media filled with stories from stranded passengers. Politicians on both sides of the aisle made statements. The Transportation Secretary blamed the previous administration's blocking of the JetBlue merger. Critics blamed the current administration's bailout terms. Workers spoke about losing their jobs without warning. Travelers spoke about losing trips they had saved for. The news moved through the American information environment as a major event, the first major American airline failure in twenty-five years, with the cultural and political weight that such events carry inside the country where they happen.

Outside the United States, the news moved differently. Someone in Bangkok read the headline, registered that an American airline had collapsed, and moved on to news that mattered more to their life. Someone in Lagos saw it briefly in their feed and continued with the day's local concerns. Someone in Jakarta nodded at the headline, drank their coffee, and continued with more exciting news from elsewhere in their attention environment. The Spirit collapse was, for most of the world, one item in a stream of foreign news that competed with local news, regional news, and personal news for attention that was already scarce. It was real. It was significant. It did not feel significant to most of the people receiving it, because their information environment was organized around different priorities, different relevance hierarchies, different communities of concern. The same news arrived in different cognitive worlds and produced incompatible responses, with the gap between the responses being part of what the world is now.

This chapter is about that gap and the larger structures it represents. The parallel civilizations the chapter will describe are not just different institutions in different countries. They are different attention economies, different relevance hierarchies, different information environments that determine what counts as significant and what gets filtered out as someone else's problem. They are different regulatory architectures, different financial settlement systems, different cognitive substrates, and different political logics that have been diverging from each other for several years and continue to diverge as the integration the book has been documenting deepens. The civilizations are operating now. They are operating in real time, in events that are unfolding as this is being written, with each civilization producing outcomes that the others cannot fully understand and that the standard frameworks for international relations cannot describe.

The argument I will make is that the parallel civilizations are not a future scenario or a worst-case forecast. They are the current condition, and they are deepening. Five cases will demonstrate this. The Musk-EU regulatory confrontation showing the parallel civilizations operating at the regulatory-corporate-political interface. The Iran-related political-financial cluster showing the same dynamic operating across the boundary between parallel stacks. The Tether-Nobitex pair showing the parallel financial stacks operating with different rules. Two compressed cases, the Trump-France wind turbine dispute and the currency swap architecture, supporting the broader pattern. Together they will show that the international order is not what the standard frameworks describe. It is what the cases show, which is multiple incompatible architectures operating simultaneously, contesting their boundaries through specific events, with each architecture producing different outcomes and different futures for the populations forming themselves inside it.

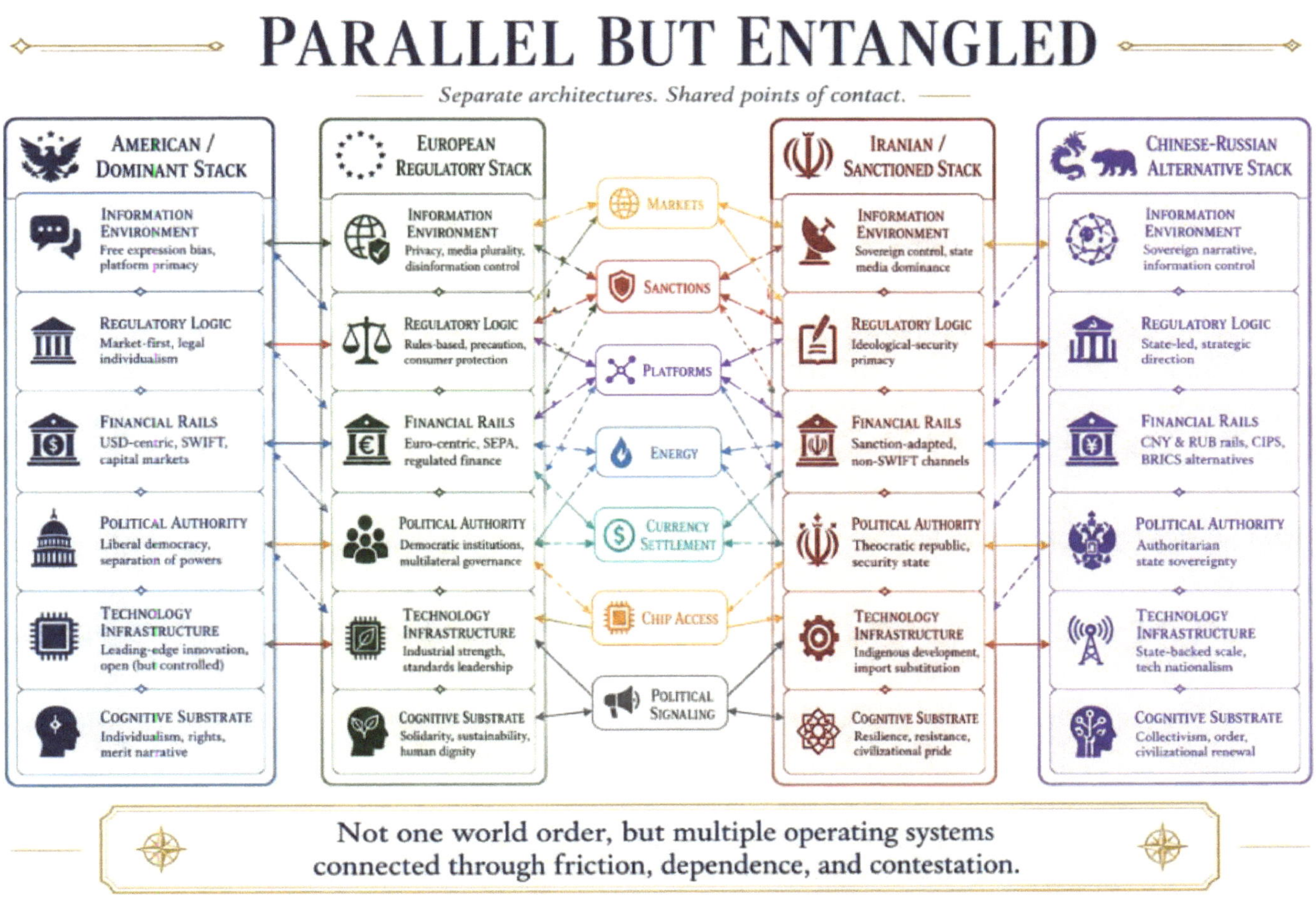

Musk, the EU, and the Confrontation Over What Regulation Is

The European Union Digital Services Act entered full force in February 2024, establishing a regulatory framework for large online platforms that included transparency requirements, content moderation obligations, advertising restrictions, and substantial penalties for non-compliance. The framework was the most ambitious attempt by any major jurisdiction to regulate social media platforms as a regulated public utility subject to democratic accountability. It was also, from the start, in tension with American First Amendment traditions that treat platform regulation as adjacent to speech regulation and therefore presumptively suspect. The two regulatory architectures were not just different policy preferences. They were incompatible understandings of what platforms are, what regulation should do, and what the relationship between government and speech infrastructure should be. The DSA's full implementation made the incompatibility operational rather than theoretical.

Elon Musk's X platform was a primary target of the DSA from the beginning. The platform was designated as a Very Large Online Platform under the framework, which subjected it to the most stringent requirements. The European Commission opened a formal investigation in December 2023 covering content moderation, advertising transparency, and researcher data access. Musk publicly criticized the investigation, characterized the EU framework as censorship, and in July 2024 claimed publicly that the EU had offered him a secret illegal deal involving X censoring speech in exchange for avoiding fines. The European Commission denied the characterization. The investigation continued.

On December 4, 2025, the Trump administration published a new National Security Strategy that framed European regulatory frameworks as regulatory suffocation of American technology companies and as a form of authoritarian governance directed against American interests. The framing was significant because it positioned the EU regulatory architecture not as a different set of policy choices but as an adversary action requiring American response. The day after the National Security Strategy publication, on December 8, 2025, the European Commission announced a one hundred twenty million euro fine against X for DSA violations including the deceptive design of its blue checkmark verification system, advertising repository transparency failures, and insufficient researcher data access. The timing made the confrontation visible to anyone watching. The American government had framed European regulation as illegitimate. The European Commission had imposed a substantial fine on the most visible American platform. Both actions occurred within twenty-four hours.

Musk's response framed the EU as an institution that needed to be dismantled rather than reformed. He limited the European Commission's reach on X, made public statements calling for the EU's dissolution, and aligned politically with European populist movements that were challenging the EU's authority from inside member states. The political alignment between Musk and the Trump administration deepened, with the platform itself becoming a vehicle for distributing American political content into European information environments in ways that the EU regulatory framework was designed to constrain but had limited capacity to restrict. The same content that the EU treated as platform-mediated speech requiring transparency and accountability was treated by the American framework as private speech that the platform had no obligation to constrain. The platform could not simultaneously comply with both frameworks, and its owner had aligned politically with the American framework to challenge the European regulator's legitimacy rather than to negotiate within it.

In January 2025, the Trump administration's AI Diffusion Rule established global performance thresholds for chip exports that further fragmented the regulatory architecture for advanced computing. In February 2026, the United States House Judiciary Committee under Representative Jim Jordan published a one hundred eighty-three-page EU enforcement decision via subpoena, before the EU itself had released the document. The committee report claimed that EU regulatory pressure on platforms had interfered in eight European elections, framing the EU enforcement architecture as election manipulation rather than as platform accountability. The same month, a Berlin court ordered X to provide data on Hungarian elections to EU-funded and foreign-funded NGOs investigating platform behavior during the election period. The Munich Security Conference of February 2026 featured tech censorship as a major flashpoint between American and European delegations, with the two sides describing the same underlying facts in incompatible terms.

Throughout this confrontation, Musk himself shifted from being a corporate actor regulated by the EU to being an instrument through which the American government challenged the EU's regulatory legitimacy. The shift is structurally significant for the parallel civilizations' argument. Musk did not just disagree with the EU. He used his platform and his political proximity to the Trump administration to attempt to delegitimize the European regulatory framework as a whole. The American administration supported this through the National Security Strategy framing, the House Judiciary subpoenas, and the broader political alignment that connected American politics to European populist movements through the platforms themselves. The corporate actor became a political instrument. The political instrument operated across the boundary between the parallel civilizations, with the American framework treating its actions as legitimate speech and the European framework treating them as platform-mediated interference requiring regulatory response.

What this case demonstrates is that the parallel civilizations are not just operating with different rules. They are operating with incompatible understandings of what rules are, what regulation does, and what the relationship between political authority and corporate behavior should be. The European framework treats large platforms as regulated public utilities subject to democratic accountability through institutional mechanisms. The American framework treats them as private speech infrastructure that government regulation amounts to censorship of. The two frameworks cannot be reconciled through better diplomacy or improved coordination, because they rest on different foundational assumptions about what the regulated activity is. The platform owner caught between them has chosen to align with one framework against the other, and the choice has consequences that extend beyond the specific corporate decisions, into the broader political architecture in which the parallel civilizations are taking shape.

Iran, the Markets, and the Cross-Stack Integration

If the Musk-EU case shows the parallel civilizations contesting each other's regulatory architectures, the Iran-related cluster shows them contesting each other's financial systems through political signaling that moves global markets in real time. Three events from March and April 2026 demonstrate this dynamic with particular clarity. They should be considered together because they show the same political-financial integration operating through different channels simultaneously, with the cumulative effect being a system in which the boundary between political negotiation and capital allocation has dissolved in ways that no standard framework handles.

On April 23, 2026, Mohammad Bagher Ghalibaf, the Speaker of the Iranian Parliament and a member of the Iranian negotiating team in the US-Iran talks following the war that began in late February 2026, departed from the negotiating team. Stock markets weakened further on the news. The S&P 500 had closed at 7,064 on April 21 and continued to move on every signal from the negotiations. The departure of a single Iranian political figure from a negotiating table produced measurable global capital market consequences within hours. This is significant for the parallel civilizations' argument in a specific way. Iran is, in conventional economic analysis, a small, sanctioned economy whose political decisions should not move major Western markets to any substantial degree. The conventional analysis treats Iran as peripheral to the global economic system that the dominant stack has been managing through dollar-denominated trade and sanctions enforcement. The conventional analysis is wrong. A single negotiator from the parallel stack stepping back from a table is now a primary input to capital allocation in New York and London, because the integration the book has been documenting has dissolved the boundary that the conventional analysis assumed.

On April 1, 2026, several weeks before the Ghalibaf departure, the Islamic Revolutionary Guard Corps issued a public threat against eighteen American technology and financial firms. The list included Nvidia, Apple, Microsoft, Google, Meta, Cisco, HP, Intel, Oracle, IBM, Dell, Palantir, JPMorgan, Tesla, GE, Spire Solutions, Boeing, and the UAE-based G42. The threat was framed as physical retaliation against company facilities and personnel in the Middle East if assassinations of Iranian leaders continued. The threat was not abstract. It included a specific time, eight pm Tehran time on April 1, and warned employees of the listed companies to leave their workplaces immediately. American firms with employees in Gulf countries instituted remote work and travel restrictions in response. The boundary between physical and financial infrastructure dissolved in this moment, with a non-state actor signaling that physical attacks on corporate facilities could produce financial consequences propagating through capital markets without any direct attack on the markets themselves. The threat against an Intel facility in Dubai was simultaneously a physical security event, a personnel safety event, a corporate operational event, an insurance event, a stock price event, and a capital markets event, with each of these being constituted by the same threat operating across all of them.

The Financial Times documented something even sharper in late April 2026. Three series of suspicious bets on falling oil prices had been placed in the period leading up to and during the war, with timing that strongly suggested information access not generally available. Approximately five hundred eighty million dollars in bets placed fifteen minutes before President Trump's March 23 statement on postponing attacks on Iran. Approximately nine hundred fifty million dollars placed shortly before the April 7 ceasefire announcement. Approximately seven hundred fifty million dollars in Brent crude futures sold twenty minutes before Iran's foreign minister announced that the Strait of Hormuz was open during the ceasefire. The pattern across three separate events, each with timing consistent with insider information rather than ordinary market analysis, suggests that someone with access to Trump policy decisions was positioning ahead of the announcements with substantial profit. The Financial Times investigation did not identify who was placing the trades. The pattern itself is documented, and the timing is consistent across the three events.

Together the three events demonstrate something the parallel civilizations argument needs. The civilizations are not operating in isolation. They are constituting each other through specific points of contact where one stack's decisions move the other stack's outcomes in real time. Iran's parliament speaker stepping back from a table moves the S&P. The IRGC threatening American tech firms moves stock prices, insurance rates, and corporate operations. Information from inside the American policy process appears to be moving to actors who use it to position before announcements. The points of contact are formal, like negotiations, and informal, like leaked political signals being traded on by actors with privileged access. The boundaries that standard frameworks assume between political and financial, between domestic and international, between formal and informal, are not holding under the current operating conditions.

This makes the parallel civilizations argument more sophisticated than a simple separation thesis. The civilizations are simultaneously parallel and entangled. They operate with incompatible internal architectures while constituting each other through specific channels of contact that produce immediate consequences across the boundaries. An American official analyzing Iranian policy is using cognitive tools shaped by American AI deployment to analyze decisions made by participants whose cognition has been shaped by Iranian deployment, in an environment where each side's decisions move the other side's markets, where physical threats from one side propagate through corporate operations of the other, and where information from inside one side's policy process appears to be flowing to actors who profit from it across the boundary. The standard frameworks for international relations cannot describe this. The civilizations argument the chapter is making must include the entanglement as part of the description, because the entanglement is part of what the civilizations are.

Tether and Nobitex: The Parallel Financial Rails

The financial dimension of the parallel civilizations operates through specific infrastructure choices that determine which transactions can occur, which can be enforced, and which can be reached by which authorities. The most current illustration is the contrast between Tether and Nobitex, two cryptocurrency platforms operating on what appears at the surface to be the same technology but that are located on different sides of the parallel civilizations boundary. The contrast reveals the parallel financial stacks at the level of consumer infrastructure rather than at the level of state action.

Tether is the issuer of USDT, the most widely used dollar-pegged stablecoin in the world. The firm holds reserves of approximately eighty billion dollars in United States Treasury securities, most of it custodied by Cantor Fitzgerald, a Wall Street financial services firm. Cantor Fitzgerald's former chief executive Howard Lutnick was nominated as Commerce Secretary in November 2024 and took office in January 2025. Senator Elizabeth Warren raised concerns about the relationships between Tether, Cantor, and Lutnick in advance of the confirmation hearing. Lutnick divested his Cantor stake to his children before taking office. Cantor Fitzgerald subsequently contributed ten million dollars to Fellowship PAC, a political action committee chaired by Tether's Vice President of Regulatory Affairs and led by additional Tether executives. A Lutnick family trust borrowed an undisclosed sum from Tether in late 2025, with reporting on the loan published by mainstream financial press in March 2026. These facts are documented through Senate confirmation hearings, congressional correspondence, and major financial press, and they describe the institutional structure within which Tether operates as a private firm regulated by the United States Treasury Department.

On April 24, 2026, the United States Treasury Department's Office of Foreign Assets Control sanctioned two cryptocurrency wallets attributed to the Central Bank of Iran with links to the Islamic Revolutionary Guard Corps Quds Force and Hezbollah. Tether executed the freeze of approximately three hundred forty-four million dollars held in those wallets. The action was part of Operation Economic Fury, a broader Treasury campaign to disrupt Iranian financial networks during the war and ceasefire negotiations. The freeze demonstrated that Tether, despite its identity as decentralized cryptocurrency infrastructure, operates inside the United States dollar system's regulatory architecture, with the Commerce Secretary's family trust borrowing money from the firm whose reserves his former firm custodies, and with the Tether-affiliated political action committee deploying funds across Republican primaries while the administration the

Commerce Secretary serves makes sanctions decisions affecting Tether's compliance posture. Whether or not any specific individual acted improperly, the structure describes Tether as operationally embedded in the dominant stack's enforcement architecture.

Nobitex operates on the other side of the boundary. The exchange is Iran's largest cryptocurrency platform, founded in 2018 by brothers Ali and Mohammad Kharrazi, who registered the company under an alternative surname. The Kharrazi family is among the most powerful political dynasties in the Islamic Republic, related by marriage to the supreme leadership. The brothers represent the third generation of the family at the heart of Iran's ruling establishment. Nobitex claims eleven million users, more than ten percent of Iran's population. The exchange handles approximately seventy percent of Iran's cryptocurrency transactions. A Reuters investigation published on May 1, 2026, based on blockchain analysis by Crystal Intelligence and interviews with nine former employees and four private financial investigators, found that Nobitex has processed tens to hundreds of millions of dollars in transactions linked to sanctioned entities including Iran's central bank and the IRGC. The exchange has continued operating throughout the US-Israel-Iran war that began February 28, 2026, processing more than one hundred million dollars in transactions during periods of nationwide internet shutdown and power outages in Tehran.

Despite these documented sanctions evasion, Nobitex has not been designated by the United States or its allies. Reuters could find no indication of why. Treasury's Operation Economic Fury, which produced the Tether freeze, and which has designated three Iranian foreign currency exchange houses as part of the same effort, has not designated Nobitex itself. The exchange was hacked in 2025 by the group Predatory Sparrow, with approximately ninety million dollars stolen and sent to inaccessible wallets labeled with anti-IRGC profanity. The hack damaged Nobitex but did not produce designation. The exchange continues to operate with elite political backing, family connections to the supreme leadership, and an unexplained absence from Western sanctions lists despite documented sanctions evasion.

The contrast between Tether and Nobitex shows the parallel financial stacks at the consumer infrastructure level. Tether operates inside the dominant stack's enforcement architecture, with documented institutional connections to administration officials and a recent demonstration that the firm complies with Treasury sanctions orders within the cryptocurrency layer. Nobitex operates inside the parallel stack, with documented connections to the Iranian supreme leadership, with eleven million ordinary Iranian users for whom the exchange is the primary route to global cryptocurrency markets, and with a notable absence from Western sanctions lists despite the documented sanctions evasion. The same underlying technology is being used by both platforms. The technology is not what determines the parallel civilizations boundary.

The institutional context, the political relationships, the user populations, and the regulatory reach are what determine the boundary, with the cryptocurrency rails carrying different consequences depending on which side of the boundary a given transaction cross.

There is a specific element of the Nobitex case that the parallel civilizations argument needs to address directly. Eleven million ordinary Iranians use Nobitex because they have been locked out of international banking and need some way to preserve value against rial inflation. These users are not sanctions evaders. They are people surviving inside an economy that has been deliberately strangled by the dominant stack. The same infrastructure that serves them is also being used by the IRGC. The dominant stack's enforcement framework treats the infrastructure as a legitimate target because of the IRGC use. The eleven million ordinary users who depend on the infrastructure for survival are collateral consequences of an enforcement strategy that cannot distinguish between the populations using the same rails for different purposes. This is the parallel civilizations problem at its sharpest. The dominant stack's instruments cannot make the distinctions that humanitarian considerations would require, because the instruments were not designed to make those distinctions. The populations affected by the inability are precisely those least able to absorb the costs.

The Transatlantic Rupture

The Musk-EU case showed the parallel civilizations contesting their boundaries through regulatory architecture. The Iran cluster showed the dynamic operating across the boundary between parallel stacks. The Tether-Nobitex pair showed the parallel financial stacks. A fourth case shows something different, which is that the parallel civilizations dynamic now operates inside what was previously a coherent transatlantic alliance, with the alliance itself fracturing along the same lines that separate the larger civilizations. The case demonstrates that the dominant stack the book has been describing is not internally coherent. It is fracturing in real time, through specific events that the standard frameworks for alliance management cannot describe.

On Monday April 27, 2026, German Chancellor Friedrich Merz publicly criticized the American handling of the Iran war. Merz characterized Iran as humiliating the United States and warned that Washington did not have a clear path out of the conflict. The whole affair, Merz said, was ill-considered to say the least. The criticism was substantive rather than ceremonial. Merz was naming a specific failure of American strategy by the leader of the largest European economy and the country hosting the largest American military presence in Europe. On Tuesday April 28, President Trump responded that Merz did not know what he was talking about and signaled that the United States might reduce its troop presence in Germany. On Friday May 1, Defense Secretary Pete Hegseth ordered the withdrawal of approximately 5,000 American troops from Germany over the next twelve months, reducing American troop levels in the country by approximately 14 percent from the existing 36,000. On Saturday May 3, Trump indicated that the cuts would go significantly beyond the initial 5,000 and threatened to pull troops from Spain and Italy as well. The chronology compressed major changes to the American security architecture in Europe into seven days, with each step responding to the previous step in a sequence that no party in the alliance had anticipated and that the alliance management frameworks could not absorb.

The fracture is not localized to the immediate political dispute. Spain had closed its airspace to American military operations against Iran during the war, denying the United States the use of Spanish bases or airspace for missions linked to the conflict. Italy had been criticized by the Trump administration as unhelpful despite Prime Minister Meloni's previous alignment with American politics. France's wind energy investments had become a flashpoint in earlier disputes between Trump and Macron over climate policy and technology choices. Each of these tensions could be analyzed within the framework of routine alliance disagreement. The cumulative effect is something different. The political, security, financial, and technological architectures that supported transatlantic cooperation for seventy years are being contested simultaneously, with the contestation producing outcomes that no party in the alliance is in a position to manage. The dominant stack is not a coherent unit. It is a configuration of relationships that has been fracturing along multiple axes, and the parallel civilizations dynamic operates inside the fracture as well as across the boundary with other civilizations.

This matters for the parallel civilizations argument because it shows that the divergence is not just between civilizations, but within what we have been treating as the dominant stack itself. The European framework for managing relations with the United States has been collapsing in real time. The American framework for managing relations with European allies has been operating on assumptions that the European leaders are no longer willing to accept. The two frameworks were supposed to be variants of a shared alliance architecture. They are now operating as parallel architectures, with each side describing the same events in incompatible terms and acting accordingly. Germany's Defense Minister Boris Pistorius framed the troop withdrawal as foreseeable. Merz tried to downplay the rift. The American administration treated the European criticism as unacceptable and the troop withdrawal as proportionate response. None of the parties was wrong about the events. Each was operating inside a framework that could not register what the other framework was producing. The fracture is the parallel civilizations dynamic operating at a smaller scale and faster pace than the between-civilizations contestation, but with the same structural features.

Anthropic, the Pentagon, and the Author's Position

A fifth case demonstrates the parallel civilizations dynamic operating at the corporate-government interface in the United States itself, with implications for the conditions under which this book is being written that I want to address directly before describing the case. The case involves Anthropic, the artificial intelligence company that produces Claude, the AI system I have been using throughout the writing of this book. The book has been disclosing its production conditions throughout. The Beyond the Blackboard discussion in Chapter Six addressed the role of early AI in my own previous publication. The wine paper experiment in Chapter Five addressed AI assistance in academic publishing. The netizen disclosure in Chapter Three addressed the geographic delocalization of my own working life. The current case requires a more specific disclosure, because the AI company in conflict with the United States government is the same company whose product I am using to write the chapter that describes the conflict.

The disclosure is analytically productive rather than awkward. It makes the case more credible, not less, because the reader understands that the author is not outside the dynamics being described. I am using the product of a company that has been designated a national security supply chain risk by the United States government, with the designation's legality currently being challenged in federal court. The conditions under which I am writing include the political and legal environment in which my writing tool is being produced, with the company's continued operation in dispute as the writing proceeds. This is the integration argument extended to the production of the book itself. The book cannot be written from outside the dynamics it documents. It is being produced through tools whose maker is contesting the conditions of its operation with the government of the country whose institutional dynamics the book is trying to describe.

The case itself. Beginning in January 2026, Anthropic and the Department of Defense came into public conflict over the terms under which Claude could be used by the American military. The dispute centered on Anthropic's refusal to permit Pentagon use of Claude for what the Department of Defense called all lawful purposes, on grounds that the language could enable fully autonomous weapons and mass domestic surveillance. The Pentagon insisted on the broader language. Anthropic refused. In February 2026, Defense Secretary Pete Hegseth signaled that Anthropic would be designated a national security supply chain risk, a designation previously used only for companies associated with foreign adversaries. The designation was formalized in March. The effect was to require defense contractors to certify that they did not use Claude in their work with the military, effectively excluding Anthropic from the largest AI procurement of the year.

On May 1, 2026, the Department of Defense announced classified network AI contracts with seven companies. Amazon Web Services, Google, Microsoft, Nvidia, OpenAI, SpaceX (which had merged with Elon Musk's xAI), and Reflection AI. Anthropic was the only frontier AI laboratory excluded. The exclusion was based on the supply chain risk designation. The competing companies that received contracts had agreed to the all lawful purposes language that Anthropic had refused. None of the seven companies issued public statements defending the contractual language Anthropic had refused, which means the silence operated as consent in a procurement context where consent matters.

Anthropic sued the Trump administration in two separate lawsuits in March 2026, asking federal judges in San Francisco and Washington, D.C. to overturn the supply chain risk designation. In March 2026, Judge Rita F. Lin granted a preliminary injunction, writing that the Department of War's records show that it designated Anthropic as a supply chain risk because of its hostile manner through the press, and that punishing Anthropic for bringing public scrutiny to the government's contracting position is classic illegal First Amendment retaliation. In April 2026, the Court of Appeals for the D.C. Circuit in a per curiam order denied Anthropic's motion to lift the designation, with the court noting that lifting it would force the United States military to prolong its dealings with an unwanted vendor of critical AI services. The litigation is ongoing as I write this. The May 1 contract announcements proceeded while the litigation continued, with the practical exclusion of Anthropic from defense contracts operating regardless of the legal challenge to the designation that produced the exclusion.

What the case demonstrates for the parallel civilizations' argument is that the dominant stack is contesting itself over the question of what AI accountability requires. Anthropic is operating inside the American legal framework, suing in American federal courts, citing First Amendment protections, and litigating its case through American institutions. The Trump administration is also operating inside the American framework, designating the company under American national security authorities, awarding contracts through American procurement processes, and defending its actions in American courts. Both parties are inside the dominant stack. The dispute between them is producing institutional outcomes that the dominant stack's standard frameworks cannot describe. A frontier AI company is being excluded from defense procurement for refusing to allow its product to be used for autonomous weapons and mass surveillance. A federal court has found that the exclusion was First Amendment retaliation. The exclusion is operating regardless. The framework is producing outcomes that the framework's own actors cannot reconcile, with the integration argument operating at the corporate-government interface inside what was supposed to be a coherent jurisdiction with a coherent framework for handling disputes of this kind.

My position as author of this book is one specific consequence of the case. I am writing with a tool whose maker is in active conflict with the government of the country whose institutional dynamics I am describing. The conflict could resolve in any of several ways.

Anthropic could lose the litigation and be forced to accept the all lawful purposes language. Anthropic could win the litigation and have the supply chain risk designation reversed. The administration could change. The company could be acquired or restructured. The product I am using could be discontinued, modified to comply with the requirements Anthropic is currently refusing, or replaced with a different product whose maker has different commitments. None of these outcomes is predictable from where I sit. The book is being written under conditions that include the uncertainty about what the writing tool itself will be permitted to do, by whom, under what terms. This is the integration argument extended to its most personal expression, with the author of the book documenting the parallel civilizations argument depending on tools whose continued availability is itself contested.

Two Further Patterns

Two compressed cases extend the picture without requiring full development at the depth of the previous four. They illustrate facets of the parallel civilizations argument that the longer cases do not capture as cleanly.

The Trump-France wind turbine confrontation demonstrates the parallel civilizations dynamic operating at the head-of-state level over a specific technology policy, in addition to the broader Merz-Trump rupture already addressed. The Trump administration has been publicly hostile to wind energy, characterizing it as economically destructive, aesthetically problematic, and harmful to wildlife. France under Macron has continued investing in wind capacity as part of EU climate commitments and French industrial strategy. The disagreement is not just about wind energy. It is about whether climate policy belongs in the energy strategy of major industrial economies, whether environmental regulation is a legitimate basis for economic policy, and whether American and European leaders can have substantive conversations about technology choices when their underlying philosophical commitments about energy and environment have diverged. The wind turbine specifically is the symbolic flashpoint where the larger divergence becomes visible.

The currency swap architecture extends the parallel financial stacks argument from the Tether-Nobitex consumer level to the state-to-state settlement level. As Iran has been squeezed through dollar and crypto sanctions, it has activated alternative settlement systems with China and Russia. Yuan-ruble-rial settlement arrangements have expanded substantially. The mBridge digital payment platform, developed by the central banks of China, Hong Kong, Thailand, and the United Arab Emirates with the Bank for International Settlements as a coordinator, has reached approximately fifty-five billion dollars in settled transactions by November 2025 according to public reporting. The Saudi-China yuan swap arrangements have expanded. UAE-India rupee-dirham settlement for specific trades has continued. The Treasury sanctions imposed on a China-based independent teapot refinery for purchasing Iranian petroleum in April 2026 are part of the same Operation Economic Fury campaign that produced the Tether freeze, with the dominant stack attempting to extend its enforcement reach into the parallel settlement systems while the parallel systems continue to expand their capacity to operate without dollar-system involvement. The two stacks are contesting the boundary between them through specific enforcement and counter-enforcement actions, with the boundary itself being actively reshaped by the contest.

Case	*What It Looks Like*	*What It Actually Shows*	*Civilizational Fault Line*
Spirit Airlines Collapse	A failed American airline bailout	Local events now travel differently across separate attention economies	Shared facts, different relevance worlds
Musk vs EU	Platform regulation dispute	Incompatible ideas of speech, regulation, and democratic accountability	American private-speech logic vs European public-utility logic
Iran and Markets	War diplomacy affecting markets	Political signals from one stack instantly move capital allocation in another	Sanctioned politics entangled with Western finance
Tether vs Nobitex	Two crypto platforms	Same technology, different political authority and enforcement logic	Dominant financial stack vs escape architecture
Transatlantic Rupture	Alliance disagreement	The dominant stack is fracturing internally	American security logic vs European strategic autonomy
Anthropic and Pentagon	AI procurement dispute	Accountability conflict inside the American stack itself	Corporate ethics vs national security procurement

What the Parallel Civilizations Mean

Five cases have now been presented across this chapter, with the first three developed at depth and the last two compressed. The cases share a structural feature that I want to name explicitly, because the analytical work of the chapter depends on the reader recognizing the pattern rather than treating each case as a separate dispute to be addressed within its own domain. The pattern is that the international order is not what the standard frameworks describe. The standard frameworks treat international relations as variations within a shared system of rules, institutions, and assumptions about how states and corporations interact. The cases show something different. They show multiple incompatible architectures operating simultaneously, contesting their boundaries through specific events, with each architecture producing different outcomes for the populations forming themselves inside it.

The architectures are not just different. They are incompatible in a specific sense. The American framework treats platforms as private speech infrastructure. The European framework treats them as regulated public utilities. These are not different positions on a shared question about platform regulation. They are different understandings of what a platform is and what regulation can legitimately do. Reconciling them would require one framework to abandon its foundational assumptions, which neither framework will do under current political conditions. The contestation continues, with each side treating the other's framework as illegitimate and acting accordingly.

The same incompatibility operates in the financial domain. The dominant stack treats cryptocurrency rails as enforcement infrastructure that should be subject to traditional sanctions authority. The parallel stack treats the same rails as escape architecture that should operate outside that authority. Tether and Nobitex are using the same underlying technology with completely different relationships to political authority, and the difference is structural rather than technical. The two financial stacks cannot operate within a shared regulatory framework because they have different assumptions about what financial regulation should accomplish and to whom it should answer.

The same incompatibility operates in the political-information domain. The American framework treats political signaling about Iran as legitimate diplomatic communication. The Iranian framework treats American policy decisions as inputs to its own political and military planning. The Financial Times documentation of suspicious trading suggests a third framework operating in the gaps, with actors who have access to information from inside one framework using it to profit across the boundary. The three frameworks are not arranged in a hierarchy of legitimacy. They are operating in parallel, with each one producing outcome that the others cannot fully describe and that the standard analytical frameworks cannot integrate.

There is a further dimension of the parallel civilizations argument that the cases above have suggested but not made explicit. The civilizations are not just operating between countries. They are operating within them. Inside the United States, voters in different cultural and economic contexts inhabit different attention economies, different relevance hierarchies, different information environments, and different relationships to institutional authority. The same is true in Germany, in France, in India, in Brazil, in any country with substantial internal diversity. The within-country divergence operates through political polarization, electoral instability, and information environment fragmentation in ways that the within-country populations experience as immediate features of their daily lives. The American case is the most documented, with the divergence between red and blue America operating through different news sources, different platforms, different educational institutions, different economic geographies, and different political identities that have been deepening for decades and have accelerated under the AI deployment patterns the previous chapters have described. The Merz-Trump rupture is not just an external alliance dispute. It is also an expression of internal American divisions, with the administration's response to European criticism reflecting domestic political alignments that European leaders cannot fully address through external diplomacy. The same dynamic operates in Germany, where the AfD has been gaining political support inside a country whose centrist parties have been struggling to maintain coherent governance. The same dynamic operates in France, where Le Pen's coalition has been treating EU institutions as illegitimate while operating inside the French state. The within-country parallel civilizations are arguably more politically consequential than the between-country contestation, because they produce institutional instability that the between-country frameworks were not designed to handle. The civilizations argument must include the within-country dimension to be complete.

This matters for the populations forming themselves inside the parallel civilizations because the formation depends on which civilization the population is inside. A child being educated inside the European regulatory architecture is forming a different relationship to platforms, to information, to expression, and to authority than a child being educated inside the American architecture. A worker depending on the dollar settlement system is forming a different relationship to financial security than a worker depending on the parallel settlement systems. A citizen of a country aligned with the dominant stack is forming a different political identity than a citizen of a country aligned with the parallel stack. The formed populations will inherit the institutional environments their formation produces. The institutions of the 2040s and 2050s will reflect the cognitive substrates and the institutional architectures the children of 2026 are being formed inside. The parallel civilizations are reproducing themselves through the formation of their participants, with the divergence deepening across each generational cycle.

The chapter has not predicted how the parallel civilizations will develop. Prediction is not what the integration framework can support. The chapter has documented that they exist, that they are operating now, that they are contesting their boundaries through specific events the reader can verify, and that the standard frameworks cannot describe them adequately. The next chapter takes up a related question, which is what the asymmetric leverage patterns operating across multiple domains tell us about how power works in the current period. The parallel civilizations are one expression of the asymmetric pattern. The asymmetric pattern operates across military, economic, infrastructural, and informational domains in ways that the parallel civilizations argument has touched but not developed in full. Chapter Eight develops it.

PART THREE
THE SETTLEMENT

After the fire, what remains?

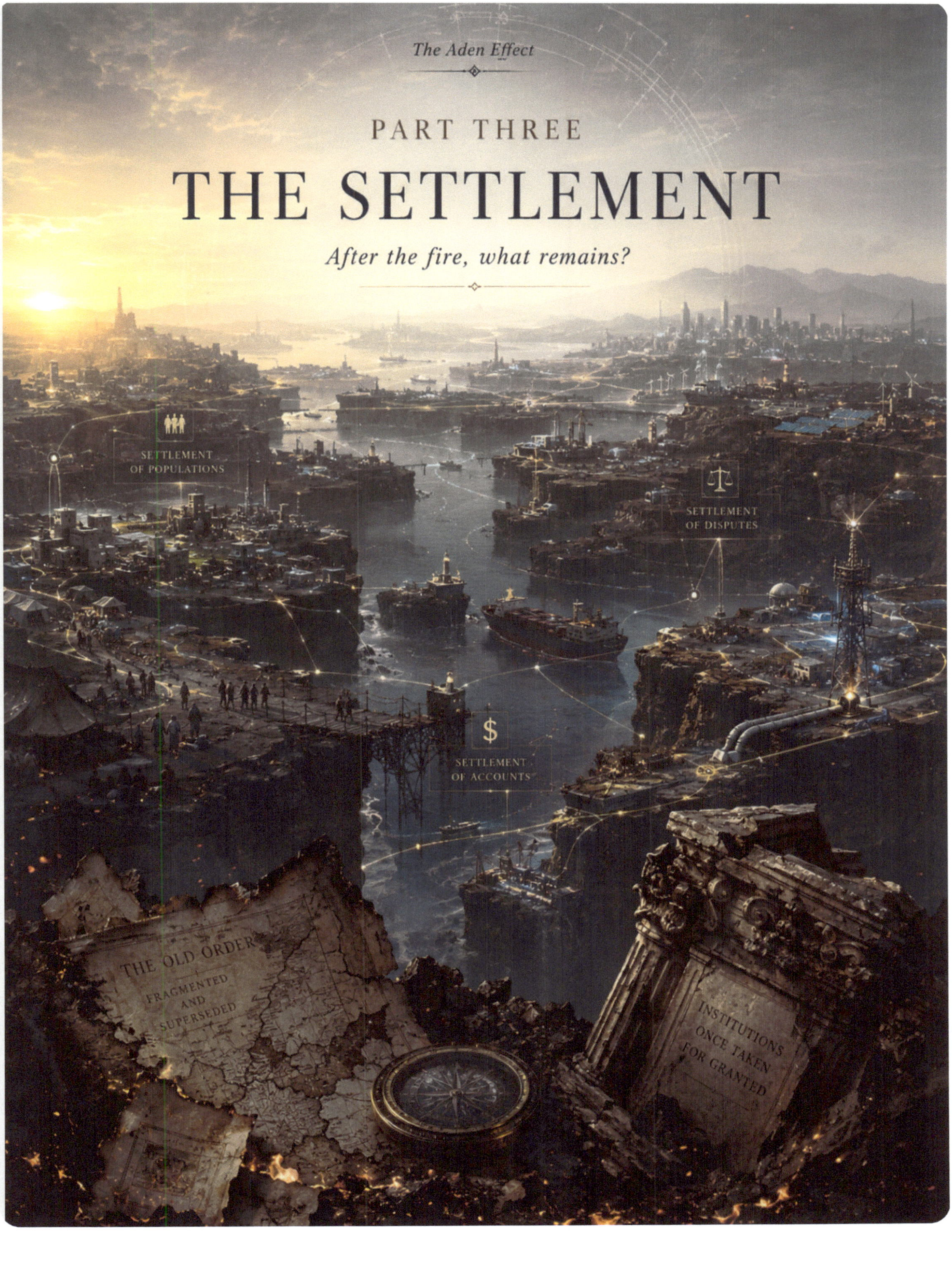

Part Three: The Settlement

Part Two examined the fire. The integration of economic, political, technological, and military domains. The feedback loops that have replaced sequential causation as the unit of analysis. The accountability collapse that has spread across multiple institutional domains simultaneously. The cognitive ground transformation that is shaping the participants who staff the institutions. The parallel civilizations that have organized themselves into incompatible architectures and are contesting their boundaries through specific events the reader can verify. The four chapters of Part Two delivered the diagnostic work, examining what is already burning rather than predicting what will burn next. The cases were drawn from events the reader could check against current sources, with the analytical work being to recognize the patterns that connect events across domains the standard frameworks treat separately.

Part Three takes up a different question. After the fire, what remains. The two chapters of Part Three do forward-looking work, examining what kind of order, if any, is emerging from the integration the previous part documented. This work is harder than the diagnostic work of Part Two, because prediction is harder than synthesis. The cases that supported the diagnostic work are matters of public record that the reader can verify. The projections of Part Three depend on patterns that are still developing, with multiple plausible trajectories and uncertain pacing. The chapters will be written with epistemic humility appropriate to that difficulty. They will distinguish between what is already visible, where projection is relatively safe, and what is genuinely uncertain, where the book will name the uncertainty rather than pretend to confidence it does not have.

The title of the part deserves attention. Settlement carries multiple meanings, and Part Three works with all of them. The settlement after a fire, where the survivors assess what remains and rebuild on changed terrain. The settlement of accounts, where consequences are paid out to the parties whose actions produced the fire. The settlement of populations, where people locate themselves in conditions they did not choose and develop the practices that will shape what comes next. The settlement of disputes, where contested matters are resolved through some combination of negotiation, exhaustion, and force. The integration documented in Part Two has not finished doing its work. The settlement Part Three examines is not the resolution of the integration but the conditions under which the participants will continue to operate as the integration continues.

The title is not promising resolution. Settlement names a phase, not a destination. The settlement after a fire does not restore what was burned. It works with what remains.

The settlement Part Three is examining will not restore the integrated international order that the standard frameworks assumed for most of the post-Cold War period. The order has fractured along the lines Part Two documented. The settlement that follows will be operational rather than resolved, contested rather than coherent, fragmentary rather than unified. The book has to be honest about this rather than promise more than the analytical work can deliver. What I am offering in Part Three is not a forecast of how the international order will reorganize itself. It is an examination of the patterns that are already producing whatever the next configuration will be, with the honest acknowledgment that the configuration is not yet visible in its complete form.

Two chapters develop the part's argument. Chapter Eight examines the asymmetric patterns that have become the dominant mode of how power operates across multiple domains in the current period. Small actors with specific kinds of leverage are exercising influence disproportionate to their size, with the asymmetric pattern operating across military, financial, infrastructural, informational, and cognitive domains. The Iran war demonstrated this in the military domain, with non-state actors using inexpensive weapons to exercise leverage over major powers. The Strait of Hormuz, the Bab el-Mandeb, the Druzhba pipeline, and the Panama Canal demonstrate the asymmetric pattern in the infrastructural domain, with small geographic features exercising disproportionate leverage over global trade. The cryptocurrency rails examined in Chapter Seven demonstrate the asymmetric pattern in the financial domain, with parallel infrastructure operating outside traditional regulatory reach. The cognitive substrates examined in Chapter Six demonstrate the asymmetric pattern in the cognitive domain, with AI deployment patterns producing different formations in different populations. Chapter Eight develops these as a coherent pattern rather than as separate phenomena, with the broader argument being that asymmetric patterns are now the structural feature of how power operates rather than the exception to it.

Chapter Nine takes up the formation that the asymmetric patterns are producing. This is the most difficult chapter in the book, because the formation is not yet complete and the chapter has to describe what is emerging without claiming to know what it will become. The chapter will examine specific features of the formation that are already visible. The fragmentation of the global commons. The emergence of regional blocs that operate with different rules and different institutional architectures. The rise of new actors who do not fit the categories of state, corporation, or international organization. The role of cognitive divergence in producing populations who cannot easily communicate across the boundaries of the formation. The implications for the children, including my own son, who will inherit the formation as the conditions of their adult lives. The chapter will not predict whether the formation produces a stable new order or a sustained period of contested operation. Both outcomes remain plausible from where I sit. The chapter will examine the patterns rather than forecast the outcomes.

The two chapters together complete the analytical work of the book proper. Part Four will take up what economists, scholars of international relations, and other analysts must now do, given the framework the previous parts have established. The fourth part is shorter and more directive. It is about the work that needs to happen rather than about the conditions that produced the need. Part Three remains the analytical heart of the book's forward-looking dimension, with the cases examined and the formation described to the limit of what current evidence can support.

A note on tone. The previous parts have been able to draw on cases the reader can verify and patterns that are already visible. Part Three operates with greater uncertainty. The chapters will use words like may, plausibly, and increasingly rather than is, will, and certainly. This is not hedging for its own sake. It is honest acknowledgment that the analytical framework supporting Part Two does not extend with the same confidence into Part Three. The reader who finishes Part Three should know more about the patterns that are producing whatever comes next but should not expect the book to deliver predictions that the evidence does not support. The discipline is to describe what is visible while acknowledging what is not.

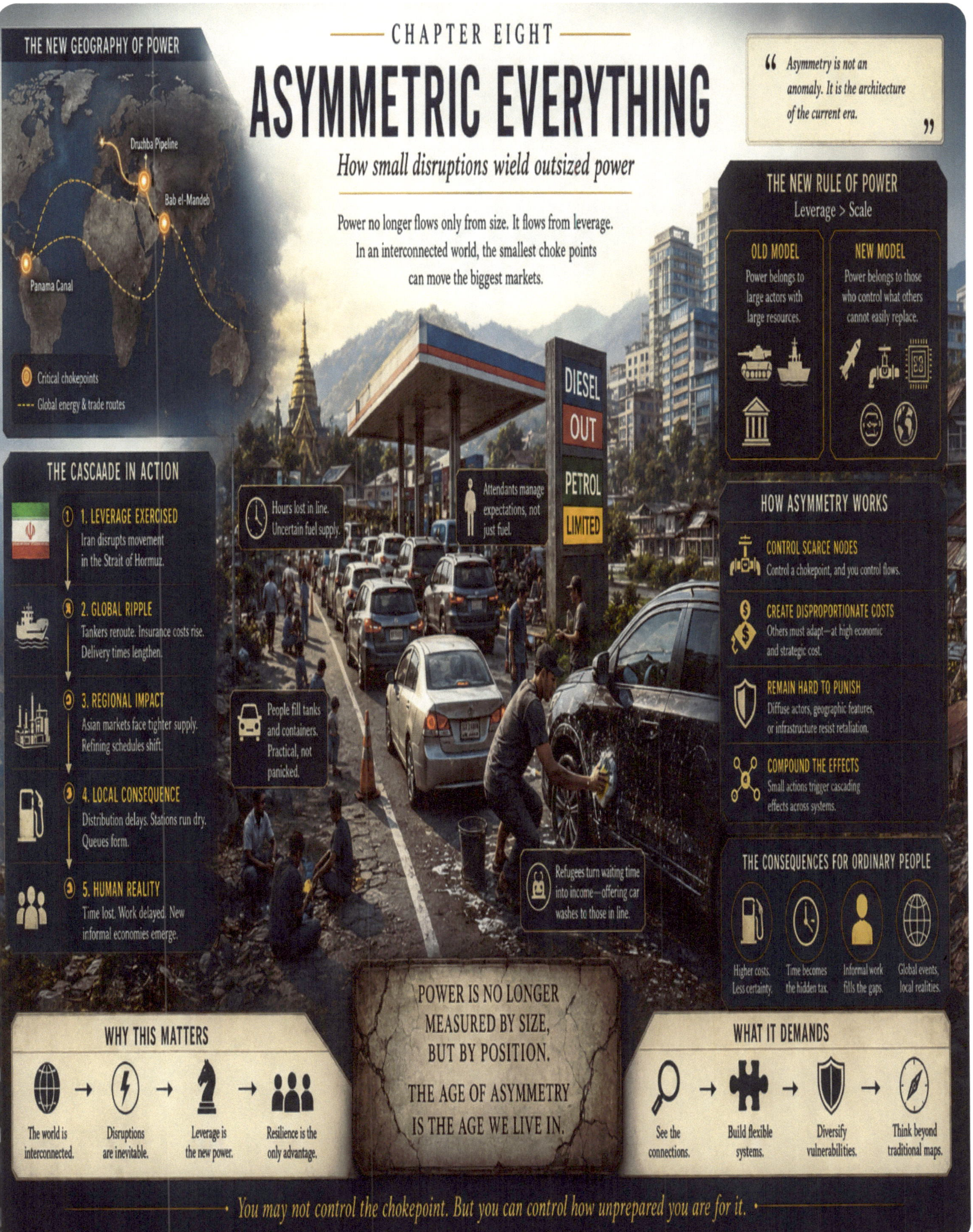
CHAPTER EIGHT
ASYMMETRIC EVERYTHING
How small disruptions wield outsized power
Power no longer flows only from size. It flows from leverage. In an interconnected world, the smallest choke points can move the biggest markets.
"Asymmetry is not an anomaly. It is the architecture of the current era."
THE NEW GEOGRAPHY OF POWER
Druzhba Pipeline
Bab el-Mandeb
Panama Canal
Critical chokepoints
Global energy & trade routes
THE CASCAADE IN ACTION
1. LEVERAGE EXERCISED
Iran disrupts movement in the Strait of Hormuz.
2. GLOBAL RIPPLE
Tankers reroute. Insurance costs rise. Delivery times lengthen.
3. REGIONAL IMPACT
Asian markets face tighter supply. Refining schedules shift.
4. LOCAL CONSEQUENCE
Distribution delays. Stations run dry. Queues form.
5. HUMAN REALITY
Time lost. Work delayed. New informal economies emerge.
Hours lost in line. Uncertain fuel supply.
Attendants manage expectations, not just fuel.
DIESEL
OUT
PETROL
LIMITED
People fill tanks and containers. Practical, not panicked.
Refugees turn waiting time into income—offering car washes to those in line.
THE NEW RULE OF POWER
Leverage > Scale
OLD MODEL
Power belongs to large actors with large resources.
NEW MODEL
Power belongs to those who control what others cannot easily replace.
HOW ASYMMETRY WORKS
CONTROL SCARCE NODES
Control a chokepoint, and you control flows.
CREATE DISPROPORTIONATE COSTS
Others must adapt—at high economic and strategic cost.
REMAIN HARD TO PUNISH
Diffuse actors, geographic features, or infrastructure resist retaliation.
COMPOUND THE EFFECTS
Small actions trigger cascading effects across systems.
THE CONSEQUENCES FOR ORDINARY PEOPLE
Higher costs. Less certainty.
Time becomes the hidden tax.
Informal work fills the gaps.
Global events, local realities.
WHY THIS MATTERS
The world is interconnected. → Disruptions are inevitable. → Leverage is the new power. → Resilience is the only advantage.
POWER IS NO LONGER MEASURED BY SIZE, BUT BY POSITION.
THE AGE OF ASYMMETRY IS THE AGE WE LIVE IN.
WHAT IT DEMANDS
See the connections. → Build flexible systems. → Diversify vulnerabilities. → Think beyond traditional maps.
You may not control the chokepoint. But you can control how unprepared you are for it.

CHAPTER EIGHT

Asymmetric Everything

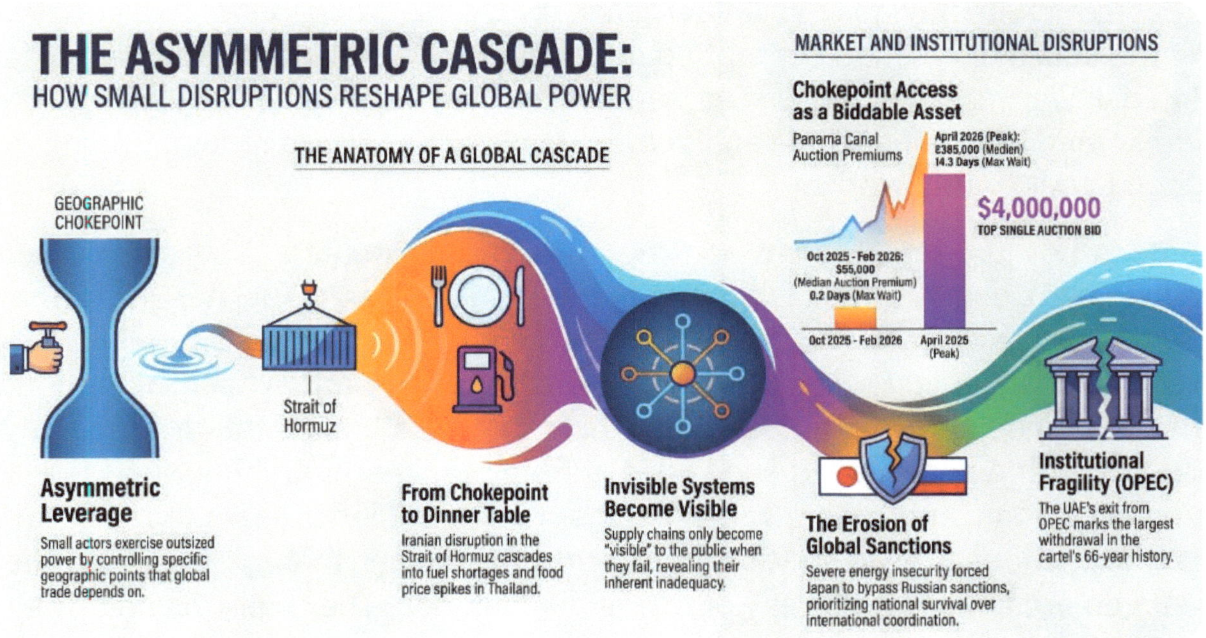

Twice in the past month I drove my SUV to fill up the diesel, and the pump was empty before I reached it. The first time I waited about forty minutes before the attendant came down the line of vehicles to tell us the diesel had run out. The second time I waited longer, almost an hour, before the same announcement. The third time I asked Hla to take the queue. She could chat with her friends online, or do things woman do, while she waited. I had things to do at home and could not afford another hour at the pump that might end in the same announcement. The queues at our station and at the others around our part of Chiang Mai had been growing for several weeks, with people filling not just their tanks but also containers they could store at home in case the diesel ran out completely. The atmosphere at the station was not panicked. People were patient with each other. The arrangement was practical rather than emotional. But the queue itself, with people sitting in their cars or outside their cars chatting on phones, while attendants moved up and down the line, was a feature that had not been there a few months earlier. The distribution system that had operated invisibly for years had become visible, with its inadequacy visible alongside it.

The reason for the queues was not local. The diesel and petrol shortages had nothing to do with anything happening in Chiang Mai or in Thailand specifically. The shortages were the local manifestation of a global cascade that had begun thousands of kilometers away in the Strait of Hormuz, where Iran's military forces and political decisions had been disrupting the movement of petroleum products through the chokepoint that handles approximately twenty percent of global oil trade. The disruption rippled outward through tanker rerouting, through refining schedule changes, through the tankers that supply Asian markets with Middle Eastern crude having to find alternative routes that took longer and cost more. By the time the cascade reached our station in Chiang Mai, it was no longer recognizable as Iran-related. It was just fuel that was sometimes available and sometimes not, with queues that were sometimes manageable and sometimes long enough to require trading my time for Hla's so I could get to work.

The queue is not just my problem and the other fuel customers. The pump attendants who walk up and down the line of vehicles to inform us when the fuel has run out, whether diesel or petrol, are themselves dependent on the station continuing to receive and sell whatever fuel is available. Their employment depends on the station being operational, with the station being dependent on the supply chain that runs back through Thai distribution networks, through Asian refining schedules, through tanker rerouting around the Hormuz disruption, to the tankers that now travel longer routes at higher costs to reach the Asian markets that previously relied on Middle Eastern crude moving through the strait. The pump attendants do not need to know any of this to do their jobs. They walk the line. They count the cars. They estimate when each fuel type will run out, often with diesel running out first one day and petrol running out first the next, depending on the day's deliveries. They tell people apologetically that they will have to come back tomorrow or the day after. Their professional lives are organized around the daily work of selling whatever fuel is available, with the availability being determined by events thousands of kilometers away that nobody at the station tracks directly.

Just outside the gas station, near where the queue extends along the road, several Myanmar refugees offer car washes for low prices. They have come to Thailand because the civil war in their country has made their lives impossible. They are now working informally at the edges of whatever economic spaces will accommodate them. The gas station queue produces a specific economic opportunity, because the cars are sitting long enough that washing them is feasible during the wait. The refugees did not flee their country because of Iran. They fled because of conditions in Myanmar that have nothing to do with the Strait of Hormuz. They are now dependent on a queue that exists because of leverage exercised at a chokepoint they have probably never thought about in connection to their situation. The chain runs from Iranian military decisions, through global tanker rerouting, through Thai distribution networks, to the queue at the station, to the cars in the queue, regardless of whether those cars are waiting for diesel or petrol, to the wash the refugees offer to the cars while the cars wait for fuel that may or may not arrive. The refugees do not see the chain. The pump attendants do not see the chain. The customers waiting in the queue, including me, do not see the chain in the moment, although the analytical work of describing it is what this chapter is attempting. The chain operates regardless of whether the participants understand it, with the consequences being concrete and immediate even when the causes are remote.

This chapter is about that cascade and the broader pattern it expresses. The argument I want to make is that the way power operates in the current period has changed structurally, in ways the standard frameworks for international relations and economics continue to miss. The standard frameworks treat power as something great powers exercise, with small actors and small geographic features being peripheral to the analysis. The cascade that produced the queues at my gas station shows something different. A non-state actor in a small country exercised leverage over a geographic chokepoint that produced consequences in Chiang Mai through a chain of effects that ran through markets, infrastructure, and corporate decisions in ways no party in the chain controlled. The asymmetric pattern is not exceptional. It is now the structural feature of how power operates in multiple domains simultaneously.

Four cases will demonstrate this. The Panama Canal as a chokepoint pricing system whose auction premiums have quadrupled in two months because of disruption thousands of miles away. The United Arab Emirates withdrawal from OPEC, the largest exit in the cartel's history, driven by Iranian attacks on UAE shipping and infrastructure. Japan importing Russian crude oil for the first time since the Hormuz disruption began, breaking with the sanctions regime to maintain its energy security. The collapse of Russian and previously Western influence in Mali, where local asymmetric forces have defeated successive external powers in the same theater. The four cases together demonstrate that the asymmetric pattern operates across infrastructure, energy markets, sanctions regimes, and military deployments, with each case producing outcomes that the standard frameworks predicted as marginal but that have proven to be central to how power now flows.

The Panama Canal: Where Chokepoint Access Has a Price

The Panama Canal was designed to handle the global trade flows that connect the Pacific basin to the Atlantic basin, with the Panama Canal Authority operating a sophisticated system of transit fees, scheduled bookings, and auction premiums that allow vessels to bid for priority access when demand exceeds capacity. The system has operated with enough reliability for nearly a century that the canal became part of the invisible infrastructure of global trade, with the costs of transit being one input among many in shipping calculations rather than a primary factor in the routing decisions of major commodity flows. As Iran's effective closure of the Strait of Hormuz forced global oil and gas trade to find alternative routes in March and April 2026, the demand for Panama Canal transit slots surged, and the auction premiums revealed in measurable dollars what physical chokepoint access is now worth when the alternative is a route that adds twenty days to a voyage.

The numbers are sharp. Auction premiums for vessels arriving without reservation, which sit on top of standard transit fees of three hundred thousand to four hundred thousand dollars, climbed from a median of fifty-five thousand dollars between October 2025 and February 2026, to one hundred fifty thousand dollars by March, and reached an average of three hundred eighty-five thousand dollars with peaks of three hundred eighty-five thousand to four hundred twenty-five thousand by April. The single largest payment confirmed by the Panama Canal Authority was four million dollars by a fuel vessel that redirected its delivery destination from Europe to Singapore. Two Aframax tankers paid three million dollars each in separate recent auctions. A Chinese-controlled LPG tanker, the Gas Virgo operated by Wanhua Chemical, paid four million dollars to jump the queue on April 15. Wait times for vessels without reservations had been 0.2 days northbound on March 26. By late April, the average was 6.3 days, with maximum waits of 14.3 days recorded. Container ship transits rose 52 percent year-on-year. LNG carrier transits rose 73.7 percent. Reservation utilization rates reached 113 to 114 percent, indicating demand consistently outstripping scheduled availability.

The cascading consequences extend across multiple geographies and commodity markets. United States Gulf Coast LPG suppliers are now feeding Asian markets that previously sourced from the Middle East Gulf, with the Panama route being the most direct connection. Asian demand for Atlantic-basin crude is driving tanker rerouting that was rare a year ago. The Baltic Exchange index for the US Gulf-Japan VLGC route reached one hundred thirty-one thousand seven hundred seventy-nine dollars per day, the highest reading since the Panama Canal drought crisis of January 2024. Vortexa reported that approximately forty percent of US Gulf-laden LPG cargoes are now rerouting via the Cape of Good Hope as Panama congestion grows, extending voyage times by more than twenty days. The cargo originally bound for Europe and now redirected to Singapore is paying four million dollars for canal access because the alternative route would add three weeks of voyage time and the additional fuel costs and time-in-transit costs exceed the four-million-dollar premium. The premium is not arbitrary. It is the market price of avoiding the Cape of Good Hope, set in real time by auction, and the price reveals what physical chokepoint access is now worth when the alternatives have been disrupted.

The symbolic dimension of the Panama case is that Panama itself has become a target of the same dynamics it is profiting from. Iran seized the Panama-flagged container ship MSC Francesca, operated by the Italian shipping company MSC, in the Strait of Hormuz in late April. Panama's foreign ministry condemned the seizure as a serious attack on maritime security. The country with one of the world's largest ship registries is simultaneously profiting enormously from the chokepoint substitution effect and absorbing the secondary consequences of Iran's leverage over global shipping through its registry vessels being seized. The country and the canal are not just neutral infrastructure. They are nodes in the asymmetric pattern, with the same structural dynamic operating on Panama from one direction while Panama exercises its own version of the dynamic from the other.

What the Panama case demonstrates analytically is that geographic chokepoints have become market-priced political instruments rather than passive features of trade infrastructure. The auction premium quadrupling in two months is not a market failure or a temporary disruption. It is the system working as designed, with prices revealing the value of physical chokepoint access in conditions where multiple chokepoints are being contested simultaneously. The asymmetric leverage of the Iranian closure of Hormuz produces a pricing structure at the Panama Canal where companies pay thirteen times the standard transit fee to access an alternative route. Both ends of this trade are constituted by the same asymmetric pattern. Small actors with small geographic features are determining what global trade can do, and the trade itself is paying the asymmetry premium in real time, in measurable dollar amounts, in transactions that the standard frameworks cannot describe coherently because the frameworks assume chokepoint access is either available or unavailable rather than being priced through real-time auctions that respond to events in different chokepoints simultaneously.

The UAE Walks Out: When the Largest Producer Leaves the Cartel

The Organization of Petroleum Exporting Countries was founded in 1960 by Iran, Iraq, Kuwait, Saudi Arabia, and Venezuela to coordinate oil production and pricing among major producers. The cartel expanded over decades to include additional members and eventually formed OPEC+ with Russia and other non-OPEC producers, becoming the central institutional structure for managing global oil supply. Members had left OPEC before. Ecuador in 2020. Qatar in 2019. Angola in 2024. None of those departures had been consequential at the level of global market structure, because the departing members had been small producers whose absence did not materially affect cartel coordination. On April 28, 2026, the United Arab Emirates announced its withdrawal from OPEC and OPEC+ effective May 1. The UAE was the third-largest OPEC producer, with capacity of approximately 4.8 million barrels per day and ambitions to reach 5 million by 2027. It was the largest producer to leave the cartel in its sixty-six-year history. The withdrawal followed weeks of Iranian missile and drone attacks on UAE shipping and infrastructure during the war that began in late February 2026.

The structural significance of the UAE departure operates at multiple levels. At the level of cartel coordination, the loss of the third-largest producer fundamentally changes what OPEC can do. The cartel's pricing power depended on its members coordinating production decisions, and the UAE had been a primary contributor to that coordination for decades. Without the UAE, the remaining members must either replace the UAE's production discipline through their own commitments, which Saudi Arabia and Iraq are reluctant to do, or accept that the cartel's pricing power is diminished. At the level of regional politics, the withdrawal expressed the UAE's judgment that its security interests were no longer aligned with continued OPEC membership while Iran was using oil markets as part of its war strategy. At the level of geopolitical alignment, the UAE was signaling that its energy strategy would now operate independently of any cartel framework, with its production decisions being made on national strategic criteria rather than cartel coordination.

The asymmetric pattern operating here is specific. Iran is a smaller oil producer than the UAE in terms of current capacity and far less integrated with Western markets. Iran's military attacks on UAE shipping and infrastructure produced a UAE response that fundamentally restructured the institution that has organized global oil production for two-thirds of a century. The Iranian decision-makers did not directly target OPEC's coordination function. They targeted UAE shipping and infrastructure with weapons that cost a fraction of the systems they damaged. The UAE's decision to leave OPEC was a sovereign response to those specific attacks, with the institutional consequences extending far beyond what the Iranian leadership had targeted. The cartel that had organized global oil markets since 1960 was restructured by the actions of a smaller power that had not aimed at the cartel and that had no direct military capacity to threaten the cartel's larger members through traditional channels.

The aftermath of the UAE withdrawal is still unfolding as I write this. Saudi Arabia and Iraq face decisions about whether to maintain coordination with each other in the absence of UAE participation. Iran's role within OPEC has become more visible, with the country now being one of the senior remaining members rather than a peripheral participant. The non-

OPEC members of OPEC+ are reassessing their own commitments. Russia is operating outside the framework regardless. The institutional architecture that has structured oil markets is being reshaped through specific events that continue to unfold, with the asymmetric Iranian leverage being the primary input that produced the restructuring. The broader pattern is that institutional architectures of long standing are not stable when subjected to asymmetric pressure from actors the institutions were not designed to handle. OPEC was designed to coordinate among large producers. It was not designed to absorb attacks from a smaller producer that disrupt the security calculations of larger producers. The cartel could not perform under the asymmetric conditions, and the largest non-attacking member's withdrawal expresses that inability institutionally.

Japan Imports Russian Oil: When Sanctions Yield to Energy Security

On May 4, 2026, a tanker carrying Russian crude oil from the Sakhalin-2 project arrived at Imabari, Ehime Prefecture, in Japan. The cargo was procured by Japanese refiner Taiyo Oil and would be processed at its Shikoku facility. The tanker had departed Sakhalin in late April. The cargo marked Japan's first import of Russian crude since the Strait of Hormuz disruption became severe enough to threaten Japan's energy security. The Middle East accounted for ninety-four percent of Japan's crude oil imports in 2025, with the Strait of Hormuz being the route for ninety-three percent of that share. When Hormuz closed, Japan had no alternative supply at the scale required to maintain its industrial production, except Russian crude through the Sakhalin exemption that the United States Treasury had extended to Japan in December 2025.

The structural significance of the Japan-Russia case operates differently from the UAE-OPEC case. The UAE departure restructured an institutional architecture. The Japan-Russia case demonstrates that the sanctions regime against Russia, which has been a primary instrument of Western coordination since 2022, is yielding under asymmetric pressure from a different theater. The sanctions regime depended on participating countries maintaining their compliance even when compliance was costly. Japan had been a primary participant, aligning with G7 sanctions while maintaining its Sakhalin exemption as a narrow accommodation for energy security. The exemption had been narrowing because Japan had alternative supply available through Middle Eastern producers reaching Japan via Hormuz. When Hormuz was disrupted, the exemption became broad, with Japan now importing Russian crude in volumes that the original exemption framework had not anticipated and that the sanctions regime had been designed to prevent.

The asymmetric pattern operating here is that Iran's leverage at Hormuz produced sanctions regime erosion in Russia's primary Asian competitor. The Iranian decision-makers did not target the Russian sanctions regime. They targeted Hormuz transit and Israeli operations. The downstream effect of Hormuz disruption was that Japan, locked out of Middle Eastern supply at scale, had to activate the Sakhalin exemption at a level that materially benefited Russia. Russia, which is itself sanctioned because of its own war in Ukraine, is now selling oil to Japan because Iran's actions in a different war made Japanese energy security depend on Russian supply. The two sanctioned regimes are connected through the asymmetric leverage that one of them is exercising at a chokepoint thousands of miles from either of them, with the third country, Japan, caught in the middle and forced to choose between its sanction's commitments and its industrial production.

Japanese officials have framed the Sakhalin imports as use of an existing exemption rather than a departure from sanctions policy. Minister of Economy, Trade and Industry Ryosei Akazawa described Russian crude as extremely important for Japan's energy security in March 2026 statements. The framing matters institutionally because it preserves the form of Japanese sanctions compliance even as the substance shifts. Japan can continue to participate in sanctions coordination meetings, continue to support sanctions language in international communiques, continue to align with Western policy on Russia in formal terms, while importing Russian crude in volumes that materially weaken the sanctions regime's purpose. The institutional form persists. The substantive enforcement degrades. South Korea, which faces similar dependence on Middle Eastern crude through Hormuz but lacks Japan's direct access to Russian energy projects, is now navigating the same pressure with different available responses, including expanded purchases from the United States, Latin America, and Southeast Asia. The cascading erosion of the sanctions regime is operating across multiple countries simultaneously, with each country making decisions that preserve the institutional form while shifting the substantive effect.

Mali: Where the Asymmetric Pattern Is Older Than the Current Crisis

The first three cases examined the asymmetric pattern operating through the cascade from the Iran war. The pattern is real in those cases. It is also broader than the Iran cascade, and the Mali case demonstrates this by showing the same pattern operating in a domain entirely separate from the current Middle East crisis, with successive external powers losing to the same local asymmetric forces over more than a decade.

Mali was a French colony until 1960. France maintained substantial military presence in the country after independence and reinforced that presence with Operation Serval in 2013 and Operation Barkhane from 2014, which deployed thousands of French troops to combat insurgents linked to al-Qaeda and the Islamic State. The operations had limited success. By 2021, the Malian military junta that had seized power in coups in 2020 and 2021 expelled French forces and the United Nations peacekeeping mission. The junta turned to Russia for security partnership, with the Wagner Group beginning operations in Mali in late 2021. Wagner forces helped capture the city of Kidal, a Tuareg stronghold, in November 2023. After the death of Wagner founder Yevgeny Prigozhin in 2023 and the dismantling of Wagner Group, the Russian Ministry of Defense took over Wagner's Africa portfolio through the Africa Corps, which by 2025 had absorbed most of the former Wagner operations.

On April 25, 2026, the Tuareg-led Azawad Liberation Front and the al-Qaeda-affiliated Jama'at Nusrat al-Islam wal-Muslimin launched coordinated attacks across multiple Malian cities, including Kidal, Gao, Sevare, and the capital Bamako. The attacks killed Defense Minister Sadio Camara, who had been the Malian leadership figure most committed to the Russian partnership. On April 28, the Africa Corps withdrew from Kidal, with approximately four hundred paramilitaries evacuated under escort negotiated through Algerian mediation. Some Malian soldiers were disarmed and captured by the attacking forces. The Russian Defense Ministry claimed twelve thousand fighters had attacked, framing the withdrawal as response to overwhelming numbers rather than as defeat. The Africa Corps statement claimed the withdrawal was made jointly with the Malian government. A Malian official told French publication RFI that the regional governor in Kidal had warned the Russian mercenaries three days ahead of the attack, but they did nothing, suggesting the withdrawal had been negotiated in advance.

The asymmetric pattern operating in Mali is structural rather than circumstantial. France lost. The United Nations lost. Wagner had limited success. Africa Corps lost. The same local forces, primarily the Tuareg separatists and al-Qaeda affiliates operating across Sahel borders, have defeated successive external powers across more than a decade. The forces that defeated these external interventions are not a great power. They have no air force, no navy, no industrial base, no central command structure that the standard frameworks for military analysis can identify. They are mobile, decentralized, locally embedded, and operating with weapons and tactics that cost a fraction of what the external interventions deployed against them. The asymmetry is not that they are using clever tactics against superior forces. The asymmetry is that the external forces' superior capabilities do not produce victory in the conditions of Mali, with each successive intervention failing for similar reasons that the previous ones failed. The pattern has now operated against French, UN, Wagner, and Africa Corps forces in the same theater. The pattern is the structural feature, not any specific intervention's specific failures.

The broader implication for the asymmetric pattern argument is that the Iran-cascade cases demonstrate the pattern operating in current crisis conditions, while the Mali case demonstrates the same pattern operating in conditions that predate the current crisis and that will continue past it. The asymmetric pattern is not a feature of the war that began in February 2026. It is a structural feature of how power now operates in multiple theaters simultaneously, with the Iran cascade being one expression among several. The Mali case proves that the pattern is not an artifact of any specific current event. It is the way power now flows in domains where local asymmetric forces are positioned against external powers with capabilities the local forces lack but that the local forces can defeat through patient operations in terrain the external forces cannot fully control.

Case	Surface Event	Asymmetric Leverage	Larger System Reshaped	What It Reveals
Panama Canal	Canal auction premiums surge as shipping routes are disrupted.	A distant chokepoint shock makes alternative chokepoint access suddenly valuable.	Global shipping, energy routing, commodity delivery, insurance, and transit pricing.	Geography is no longer passive infrastructure; chokepoints are market-priced political instruments.
UAE Leaves OPEC	The UAE withdraws from OPEC/OPEC+ after attacks on shipping and infrastructure.	A smaller power's military pressure changes the calculations of a larger producer.	Oil cartel coordination, regional alignment, and global energy governance.	Long-standing institutions can be restructured by pressure they were not designed to absorb.
Japan Imports Russian Oil	Japan uses Russian crude to protect energy security after Hormuz disruption.	One theater of conflict weakens sanctions discipline in another.	Sanctions regimes, energy security, alliance coordination, and industrial continuity.	Institutional form can remain intact while substantive enforcement degrades.
Mali	External powers repeatedly fail against local asymmetric forces.	Mobile, embedded, lower-cost actors defeat superior external capabilities.	Military intervention, regional influence, foreign security partnerships, and state authority.	Power does not belong only to scale; it belongs to position, terrain, patience, and leverage.

What Has Changed About How Power Operates

Four cases have now been presented across infrastructure, energy markets, sanctions regimes, and military deployment. The cases share a structural pattern that I want to name explicitly, because the analytical work of this chapter depends on the reader recognizing the pattern rather than treating each case as a domain-specific phenomenon. The pattern is that asymmetric leverage, exercised by small actors with specific capabilities or by small geographic features with specific properties, now produces outcomes that exceed what the standard frameworks for international relations and economics predict as possible. The cases demonstrate this across multiple domains simultaneously. The pattern is not domain specific. It is structural.

The standard framework for analyzing how power operates rest on several assumptions that the cases have shown to be inadequate. The first assumption is that great powers shape outcomes through their capabilities. The cases demonstrate that great powers can be reshaped by smaller actors who exercise leverage at specific points the great powers depend on but cannot control. France in Mali. The United States and its allies through the Hormuz disruption. OPEC through Iranian attacks on UAE infrastructure. The sanctions regime against Russia through Iran's actions thousands of miles away. In each case, the great power's superior capabilities did not translate into the outcomes the standard frameworks predicted, because the smaller actors operated through specific leverage that the great power's capabilities did not address.

The second assumption is that small actors are peripheral to the analysis. The cases demonstrate that small actors can be central to outcomes that affect billions of people across multiple continents. Iran's actions at Hormuz produced the cascade that reshaped Panama Canal pricing, OPEC institutional structure, Japanese sanctions compliance, and gas station queues in Chiang Mai. The Tuareg separatists and al-Qaeda affiliates in Mali defeated successive external interventions over a decade. The Houthis in Yemen have disrupted Red Sea shipping for years. None of these actors are great powers by any standard measure of national capability. All of them have produced outcomes that the standard frameworks treated as marginal but that have proven to be central to how power now flows.

The third assumption is that geographic features are obstacles rather than instruments. The cases demonstrate that geographic chokepoints have become market-priced political instruments, with the auction premiums at the Panama Canal making the value of physical chokepoint access measurable in real time. The Strait of Hormuz, the Bab el-Mandeb, the Suez Canal, the Druzhba pipeline, and the Panama Canal are not obstacles that traders work around. They are instruments through which actors who control or threaten them exercise leverage over global flows. The geography is not neutral infrastructure. It is contested territory whose control determines what trade can do.

The fourth assumption is that institutional architectures are stable rather than contestable. The cases demonstrate that institutional architectures of long standing can be reshaped through asymmetric pressure that the institutions were not designed to absorb. OPEC operated for sixty-six years before the largest non-attacking member's withdrawal in two months. The Russian sanctions regime operated for four years before the Hormuz disruption produced the broad activation of exemptions that the regime had been designed to limit. The institutions were not frivolous. They had been carefully constructed and maintained. They were not stable under asymmetric pressure of a kind that their designers had not anticipated and that their internal mechanisms could not handle.

These four assumptions, taken together, constitute the framework that has organized international relations and economic analysis for most of the post-Cold War period. The framework was not entirely wrong. It captured features of how power operated under specific conditions. The conditions have changed. The framework continues to operate as if the conditions have not changed, with analysts and officials continuing to use it because no alternative framework has been developed that handles the asymmetric pattern as the structural feature it has become. The book is not proposing such an alternative framework. The work of developing one is beyond what this analysis can complete. The book is documenting that the existing framework is inadequate to the conditions and that the asymmetric pattern is now the structural feature that any adequate framework would have to handle.

The Cascade at the Dinner Table

The cascade arrives in specific places. The queues at our gas station are one specific place. There are others. Hla and I were eating dinner one evening last week. She had driven approximately ten kilometers earlier in the day to find imported beef at a market that still carried it. The diesel for the drive was expensive enough that the trip itself was a calculation, with the beef-to-diesel ratio determining whether the trip was worth making. The beef was on the table. Hla had given me the beef portion because I do not eat pork and cannot maintain my health on chicken and fish alone. Aden had chicken on his own plate. Aden has been eating chicken three times a week now where he used to have it once a week, because the pricing pressure on imported beef has shifted what Hla can put on the table at his portion. The shift had not been deliberate. It had emerged from the food budget meeting the same pricing pressure that the gas station was meeting, with the family adjusting in the only way available.

Aden was eating from his own plate at the start of the meal. Then he reached across to my plate, pulled a piece of beef onto his fork, and began chewing. He has done this for years. The reaching across has been a feature of family meals since he was old enough to handle a fork independently. The reaching across had not been a budgeting decision before. It had been the routine sharing of food at a table where everyone was eating roughly the same things. Now it was different. The beef on my plate was scarce in a way that the chicken on his plate was not. The reaching across was now a small moment in which the global cascade arrived at the immediate scale of who got the expensive food, with the answer being that Aden got some of it because he was eleven and his father could not in any case eat all the beef he had been given. Fluffy, his dog, was waiting under the table, watching the meal, alert to whether any of the beef would reach the floor. Hla had driven ten kilometers in expensive diesel to find this beef. The beef was on the table for approximately fifteen minutes before being completely consumed. Aden ate some. I ate some. Fluffy got a small piece that Aden slipped down to him.

This is what the asymmetric pattern looks like at the scale of one family in Chiang Mai. Iran's leverage at the Strait of Hormuz produces consequences that arrive at the dinner table through multiple translation steps, with the pattern not recognizable as Iran-related by the time it determines what gets eaten. The pattern is structural. It operates whether the participants understand it or not. The understanding does not change the pattern. It only changes whether the participants can describe what is happening to them. Hla can describe the diesel queues. She can describe the beef prices. She can describe the trip to find the beef and the calculation about whether the trip was worth making. She cannot, from inside the immediate experience, describe the Hormuz cascade that produces the conditions she is responding to. The cascade is invisible to most of its downstream participants, with the visible effects being prices and shortages that participants attribute to local causes when the actual causes are operating thousands of kilometers away.

Aden will inherit conditions in which the asymmetric pattern is the structural feature of how global flows operate. He will need to develop the analytical capacity to recognize the pattern in conditions that are likely to be sharper than the current ones, because the pattern is deepening rather than stabilizing.

The next chapter takes up what kind of formation is emerging from the asymmetric patterns operating across multiple domains. The formation is not yet complete. The patterns are still developing. Whether the formation will produce a stable new order or a sustained period of contested operation is one of the genuinely open questions of the current moment. What we can say is that the framework that was supposed to organize international relations through great power coordination has been overtaken by the asymmetric pattern, and the children who are eleven now will need to operate inside whatever the pattern produces.

CHAPTER NINE
THE NEW FORMATION
Out of disruption, a new architecture takes shape.
The disruption is not the end of order. It is the labor of birth.
Something is being formed through the breaking.
The new formation is already visible
to those who know where to look.
THE DEATH WE CAN SEE
Old architectures are collapsing.
The standard tools register the failure.
MEDIA
Legacy gatekeepers lose audience and trust. Alternative networks own the connection.
ECONOMICS
Globalization without governance fractures. Resilience replaces efficiency.
FINANCE
Sanctions, de-dollarization, and parallel rails undermine the old monopoly of systems.
GEOGRAPHY
Chokepoints, corridors, and critical nodes become instruments of leverage.
INTERNATIONAL RELATIONS
State-centric order erodes. Non-state actors, proxies, and issue coalitions rise.
THE INTERREGNUM
Pain is real.
But it is the condition of the rebirth.
Feedback loops accelerate instability.
Accountability collapse erodes authority.
Cognitive ground splinters into parallel realities.
Old frameworks cannot see what is being born.
THE EMERGENCE
Different, not fixed.
Forming, not finished.
Visible in fragments.
New institutions emerge to solve new problems.
Networks replace hierarchies as the organizing logic.
Identity, meaning, and loyalty reconfigure.
Power is exercised through leverage, not size.
THE NEW FORMATION
A different architecture is taking shape.
NETWORKS OVER HIERARCHIES
Influence flows through connections, not command.
PLATFORM CIVILIZATIONS
Competing platforms shape economies, information, and life.
RESILIENT REGIONAL BLOCS
Regions build self-reliant systems in a fragmented world.
NEW ACTORS, NEW ROLES
Non-state, sub-state, and hybrid actors drive outcomes.
COGNITIVE DIVERSITY
Different substrates. Different truths. Coexisting, colliding, competing.
WE ARE NOT RETURNING TO THE OLD ORDER.
WE ARE BUILDING WHAT COMES NEXT.
The formation is underway. The future is not written.
But the architecture is being laid.
FOUNDATIONAL SHIFTS UNDERWAY
FROM GLOBALIZATION TO CONFIGURATION
From one world system to many overlapping configurations.
FROM INSTITUTIONS TO INFRASTRUCTURES
From rules and treaties to rails, stacks, and technical systems.
FROM SOVEREIGNTY TO LEVERAGE
From control of territory to control of critical dependencies.
FROM CITIZENS TO PARTICIPANTS
From subjects of states to actors in networks and communities.
FROM UNIFORMITY TO PLURALITY
From one narrative to many competing worldviews.
IMPLICATIONS FOR THOSE WHO NAVIGATE THE NEW FORMATION
SEE THE WHOLE
Cross boundaries. Connect the domains. Understand the system.
THINK IN SYSTEMS
Not events. Not silos. But structures and feedback.
BUILD RESILIENCE
Reduce dependencies. Increase optionality. Design for disruption.
CULTIVATE WISDOM
Humility. Judgment. Long-term perspective.
SHAPE THE FUTURE
The formation is not inevitable. It is shaped by those who act.
The new formation is neither utopia nor dystopia. It is a choice of architecture.
We cannot return. But we can build.

CHAPTER NINE

The New Formation

The reader who has stayed with this book through eight chapters has absorbed substantial weight. The integration that the standard ways of analyzing the world cannot describe. The feedback loops replacing sequential causation. The accountability collapse spreading across multiple institutional domains at the same time. The cognitive ground shifting beneath analytical work that depends on cognitive stability. The parallel civilizations contesting their boundaries through current events. The asymmetric patterns operating across infrastructure, energy markets, sanctions regimes, and military deployments. The cumulative weight is heavy because the conditions are heavy. The reader is in a specific place, having absorbed the diagnostic work, and has earned the right to something more than further description.

This chapter takes up that obligation. The argument is structural and specific. The conditions the previous chapters have documented are not just the failure of what came before. They are the condition under which something else is being formed. The disruption is not a problem the formation has to solve. The disruption is the formation. Something is being born through the conditions, with the conditions being the labor rather than something separate from the birth they are producing. Birth has a moment. There is a last pain before the relief, with the pain being the condition of the birth rather than evidence that something has gone wrong. The seedling has a moment. There is a last push before the ground breaks and the new growth becomes visible, with the breaking ground being the necessary precondition rather than an obstacle to the growth. The formation the previous chapters have described is in this kind of moment. The pain is real. The ground is breaking. Something is being made through the breaking, and the something is becoming visible to participants who know what to look for.

There is a specific reason the something being made is hard to see. The standard analytical tools for media, economics, finance, geography, and international relations are organized around the boundaries between these domains. Media studies analyze media institutions. Economics analyzes economic systems. Finance analyzes financial architectures. Geography analyzes geographic features. International relations analyze state behavior. Each tool has analytical strength inside its boundary. Each tool treats forces operating across the boundary as exogenous, as backdrop, as the environment within which the tool's domain operates. This was workable for most of the post-1945 period, when the boundaries between the domains corresponded to genuine partitions in the phenomena the tools studied. The convergence the previous chapters have documented is the condition under which the boundaries no longer correspond. The forces the standard tools treat as exogenous are now constitutive of the dynamics inside their respective domains, and the tools cannot register what they were built to bracket. The death of the old architectures is visible to the standard tools because the tools are calibrated to register failure within their boundaries. The birth of the new architectures is invisible to the standard tools because the new architectures operate across the boundaries the tools impose. The framework this book has been building specifically equips the reader to see what the standard tools cannot, and the chapter is about what becomes visible through it.

Three cases will demonstrate this. Each case shows an architecture being reborn through cross-domain integration that the standard analytical apparatus cannot register. The death is visible to the standard tools. The birth is not. What the chapter is doing is making the birth visible.

Media: What I See in My Own Teaching

I want to start the media section with something specific from my own work, because the architectural shift in how serious analysis reaches audiences is happening to me directly, not just to the journalists and broadcasters whose institutions are dying. Over the past year I have been using NotebookLM, a Google tool that generates podcast-style audio from documents, to convert academic papers and chapters of this book into conversational audio that students and other readers can listen to instead of reading. The podcasts feature two synthesized AI voices discussing the source material. The voices are not mine. The conversation is generated by the AI based on whatever document I provide. I disclose this clearly when I distribute the audio, because the practice the book has been arguing for requires the practice the book engages in to be honest about what it is.

The audience numbers tell a story I did not expect when I started doing this. A research paper uploaded to an academic repository typically receives a small number of downloads in its first month, often in single digits unless the topic is unusually current. The same paper, converted to a NotebookLM podcast and distributed through LinkedIn or Facebook, reaches substantially more listeners. People listen during their commutes, during their exercise, during their housework, in moments when they would not be willing or able to read the paper. The same content, reaching a different audience through a different distribution path, with the integration of AI generation, podcast format, and platform distribution producing engagement that none of the components alone would produce. Tucker Carlson left Fox News in April 2023 and within months was reaching audiences on X that exceeded his cable audience. Joe Rogan's three-hour conversational interviews on Spotify reach audiences that exceed network television news programs by multiples. These are the visible cases. What is happening at my smaller scale, with academic papers reaching listeners who would not read papers, is the same architectural shift operating without the cultural visibility of the named figures.

The standard analytical tools for media cannot assemble what is happening here. Media studies analyze media institutions. The institution being analyzed in my case would have to include Google's NotebookLM team, the design choices baked into the AI's voice generation, the LinkedIn algorithm that determines whether my post reaches anyone, the Facebook algorithm that operates on different criteria, the cultural shift in how listeners consume long-form analytical content, and my own role as the author who selects what gets converted and where it gets distributed. Each of these is in a different domain that the standard tools treat separately. Together they constitute a media architecture that operates as a single system, with the integration being what produces the audience reach. The reader who is working with the standard tools alone can see that traditional media is dying. They cannot see what is taking its place because what is taking its place operates outside the boundaries those tools impose.

The same pattern operates at smaller scales the reader can verify from their own life. The migration from Facebook to Instagram across age cohorts has been documented for years, with Facebook becoming the platform older adults use, and Instagram becoming the platform their children prefer, with Snapchat and TikTok occupying different age and cultural niches. The grandparent posting on Facebook does not understand why the grandchildren no longer use it. The grandchildren do not understand why their grandparents are still on it, or my students telling me that I am old because I use Facebook. They are operating in different media architectures that look like the same internet from outside but that function as distinct social spaces with distinct cultures. The Substack platform hosts independent writers reaching audiences larger than mid-tier print publications, with subscription economics that allow them to operate without advertising support. Telegram channels operate as parallel media spaces in specific countries and language communities. Each of these is invisible to the standard tools because each operates across the boundaries the tools impose. Each is operational, each has audiences, each is shaping how its participants understand the world.

The rebirth is real. Voices that the old architecture would have suppressed or marginalized now reach audiences that match or exceed what the old architecture provided. New economic models support journalists and analysts who could not have operated inside the old institutions. The new architecture also has real costs. Editorial discipline is uneven. Verification standards vary widely. Mass disinformation operates through the same channels that carry serious analysis. The fragmentation produces parallel information environments where participants in different blocs cannot easily communicate across the boundaries because they do not share the same factual baseline. The pain of the old architecture's death is real. The benefits of the new architecture are real. Both are happening together because the rebirth is what the death is producing rather than what follows it.

OPEC and the Dollar: From Central Banks to Hla's Phone

Chapter Eight documented the United Arab Emirates withdrawal from OPEC on April 28, 2026, effective May 1. The withdrawal was the largest exit in the cartel's sixty-six-year history. The dollar's share of global central bank reserves has fallen from seventy-one percent in 1999 to between fifty-six and fifty-nine percent by mid-2025, with the decline accelerating since the 2022 sanctions on Russia. The standard tools for analyzing oil markets and currency systems can register both deaths. They cannot assemble what is replacing them, because what is replacing them operates across the boundary between the two domains.

At the institutional level, the new arrangements integrate energy market decisions, currency choice, political alignment, and sanctions exposure in bilateral relationships that the standard tools treat as separate phenomena. The Saudi-China yuan settlement arrangements integrate all of these in a single set of agreements. The mBridge digital payment platform, developed by the central banks of China, Hong Kong, Thailand, and the United Arab Emirates with the Bank for International Settlements as coordinator, had reached approximately fifty-five billion dollars in settled transactions by November 2025. The India-UAE rupee-dirham settlement agreement finalized in late 2025 operates through similar cross-domain integration. Central bank gold reserves have grown across multiple countries as gold has surged past three thousand nine hundred dollars per ounce, integrating monetary policy, sovereign risk hedging, currency diversification, and political signaling in a single asset class. The standard analytical tools see each of these as a separate development. The framework lets the reader see that they are the same architectural shift operating at the institutional scale.

The same shift is happening at the household scale, where the reader can verify it from their own pocket. My mother Magda, nearing eighty, who lives in South Africa, pays her utility bills through a banking application on her phone. She came of age in a household with no electronics. She raised her own children before personal computers were common. She practiced nursing for most of her career when patient records were paper. She has been using mobile banking for several years now, not because she enthusiastically adopted the technology but because the alternatives have become inconvenient enough that the application is the path of least resistance. Hla, my wife, who is generally skeptical about AI and cautious about technology in her professional work as a researcher, uses online payment systems for most of our household transactions. She does not need to be persuaded that they work. She uses them because the integration of banking infrastructure, smartphone capability, regulatory permission, and merchant adoption has made physical cash and physical cards increasingly inconvenient for most daily transactions. Both my mother and wife, neither of whom would describe themselves as technology enthusiasts, are operating inside a payment architecture that did not exist a decade ago.

This is the same architectural shift happening at the institutional level, expressed at the household level where most readers can recognize it directly. The mobile banking application Hla uses integrates her bank's software, her phone's hardware, the regulatory framework that authorized the application, the identity verification system that authenticates her, the merchant payment infrastructure that accepts the application, and the consumer behavior shift that has made all this normal rather than novel. Each of these forces operates in a domain the standard banking tools treat separately. Together they constitute a payment architecture that operates as a single integrated system. The death of physical cash for daily transactions is visible to anyone who handles money. The birth of the integrated payment architecture is operational in everyone's pocket who has a smartphone, but the architecture itself is invisible to the standard tools because the architecture operates across the domain boundaries those tools impose. The delivery man who delivers my online purchase, cannot speak English, however he understands "scan" when the payment is COD. The reader who can see what Hla is doing when she pays for our groceries can see, at smaller scale, what the central banks are doing when they integrate yuan settlement with sanctions resistance and political alignment. The two scales are not separate phenomena. They are the same phenomenon expressed at different scales, with the integration being what makes both scales operational.

The institutional rebirth has costs. The fragmentation increases transaction costs and complexity. The lack of unified coordination creates new kinds of friction. The bilateral arrangements depend on political relationships that may shift, with the resulting volatility being a feature of the new system rather than a temporary disruption. At the household scale, the costs are different but real. The elderly who cannot manage the smartphone applications. The communities where banking infrastructure has not yet integrated with the payment platforms. The privacy implications of every transaction being recorded. The dependence on connectivity that fails when it fails. The benefits are also real at both scales. Smaller and previously peripheral countries have settlement options the dollar-only system did not provide. Magda can send a birthday gift to Aden in Thailand from South Africa in seconds rather than days, with the transaction crossing currencies and jurisdictions through infrastructure that did not exist when she was raising me. The architecture is operating. The architecture is not unified. The architecture is what is being born.

Greenland: The Map I Did Not Notice Changing

I want to start this section with a moment of recognition rather than with a structural argument, because the moment is what made the broader pattern visible to me. About a year ago I was reading a news item about Greenland that made me stop and pay attention. The item was about American interest in the territory's rare earth deposits, and it was the third or fourth such item I had encountered that month. I realized I had been seeing Greenland in serious news coverage with growing frequency for several years without registering the pattern. Fifteen years ago, I could not have located Greenland on a map without help. The territory was peripheral to the strategic conversation, peripheral to the economic conversation, peripheral to my own professional reading. By 2026 it was at the center of a competition involving the United States, Denmark, the European Union, China, and Russia. The shift had happened gradually enough that I had not recognized it as a shift, but suddenly enough that I could date when I first noticed it. The recognition was the first move. What I needed to do then was understand why the recognition had been delayed.

The reason was that the standard ways of analyzing geographic significance could not assemble what made Greenland important. The standard analysis is organized around state actors, military capability, population, economic output, and geographic position relative to major powers. By those criteria, Greenland was peripheral and stayed peripheral. What changed was not anything the standard analysis would have predicted. What changed was the integration of climate science, materials science, supply chain economics, shipping route economics, and great power competition that produced strategic significance the standard analysis could not specify. The melting ice exposed deposits of neodymium, dysprosium, and other rare earth elements that are essential inputs for advanced technology including electric vehicle motors, wind turbines, military guidance systems, and consumer electronics. The same melting opened the Northern Sea Route through Russia and the Northwest Passage through Canada. The strategic position between North America, Europe, and the Arctic became operational when the geographic conditions changed. China has been pursuing access through investment offers that integrate state-coordinated industrial policy with diplomatic engagement and infrastructure development. The United States offered to purchase the territory in 2019 and continued strategic attention since. The European Union has been engaging through Denmark while Denmark itself navigates tensions between sovereignty over Greenland and Greenlandic aspirations for greater autonomy. Each of these forces operates in a domain the standard analysis treats separately. Together they produce a strategic significance that none of the domains alone could have generated.

Greenland is one specific instance of a broader pattern. Somaliland has become strategically significant through the integration of its location at the entrance to the Bab el-Mandeb, its status as a stable territory in an unstable region, the maritime security implications of Houthi disruption of Red Sea shipping, and the broader contestation over recognition that integrates international law with great power competition. Bhutan has become significant through the integration of its hydropower capacity supplying the Indian electricity grid, its position between India and China, its rare earth potential, and the broader competition for Himalayan access that integrates climate, energy, and security domains. Kazakhstan and Uzbekistan have become significant through the integration of rare earth deposits, geographic position between China and Russia and the West, the educational partnerships discussed in Chapter Four, and the broader contest over Central Asian alignment. The pattern is general. Previously peripheral territories are now becoming central as integration of multiple forces makes their specific contents or positions operational for the new conditions. The standard ways of analyzing geographic significance cannot register the pattern because the integration crosses the boundaries those ways of analyzing impose.

My own delayed recognition of the Greenland shift is an instance of the broader problem. I was reading the news. I was paying professional attention. I had the standard tools for analyzing geographic significance. The tools were not registering what was changing because the tools were not built to register cross-domain integration. The reading I needed to be doing was reading that crossed domains, integrating climate science with supply chain analysis with strategic competition with technological dependence. I was not doing that reading systematically. The book this chapter belongs to is partly an attempt to develop the analytical practice that produces the systematic reading. The reader who has read this far has been receiving that practice across the previous chapters. The recognition that Greenland matters now, and those other previously peripheral places matter for similar reasons, is one specific outcome of the practice the book has been teaching. Without the practice, the recognition is delayed by years. With it, the new map becomes legible as it is being drawn.

Domain	*What Is Dying*	*What Is Being Born*	*Why Standard Tools Miss It*
Media	Legacy gatekeepers, cable news dominance, print-era authority, centralized editorial control.	AI-assisted audio, podcasts, platform distribution, independent media economies, fragmented but powerful audience networks.	Media studies can see institutional decline, but often misses the cross-domain architecture linking AI tools, platforms, creators, algorithms, and audience behavior.
Finance / Currency	Petrodollar certainty, OPEC coordination, cash dominance, single-rail monetary assumptions.	Bilateral settlement, mBridge-style payment systems, mobile banking, sanctions-aware currency choices, household-level digital finance.	Finance tools separate central banking, household payments, sanctions, smartphones, and political alignment, even though the new architecture joins them.
Geography	Traditional strategic maps based on population, state power, military bases, and GDP.	Operational geography: Greenland, Somaliland, Bhutan, Central Asia, chokepoints, rare earths, shipping corridors, and energy nodes.	Geopolitical tools can see territory, but often miss how climate, minerals, technology, shipping, and great-power competition make peripheral places central.

What the Reader Now Has

Three cases have been presented. The new media architecture being born through integration that the standard tools for analyzing media cannot register, with my own NotebookLM podcast distribution as one specific instance of the pattern. The new institutional architecture replacing OPEC and the petrodollar through cross-domain integration at the central bank level and at the household level, with Magda paying utility bills in South Africa and Hla paying for groceries in Chiang Mai as instances of the household-scale rebirth. The new strategic geography organized around what specific places contain or enable rather than around state-actor capability, with my own delayed recognition of the Greenland shift as an instance of the analytical problem the new conditions create. The cases share a structural feature. The death is visible to the standard analytical tools. The birth is not. The framework this book has been building is what equips the reader to see the birth, and the cases have demonstrated this through specific analytical work rather than through abstract claims about the framework's value.

The pain is real and the chapter has not pretended otherwise. Local newspaper journalists losing their jobs as the old media architecture dies. Workers in industries built around the old institutions losing their employment. The elderly who cannot manage the new payment applications and find themselves increasingly excluded from transactions that used to be cash-based. Populations in territories becoming strategically central paying the costs of major-power attention they did not invite. The Spirit Airlines workers, the Mali villagers, the Iranian ordinary citizens caught between sanctions and war, families like mine in Chiang Mai adjusting our food budgets and our fuel-purchasing strategies as the cascades arrive at our gas stations and dinner tables. The labor is real and the costs are borne by specific people in specific places. The framework does not eliminate the costs. The framework allows the costs to be understood as the labor of birth rather than as evidence of meaningless collapse, with the recognition changing what participants can do with the conditions but not changing the conditions themselves.

The reader who has read this far has the analytical practice the book has been developing. The reader has the diagnostic work of Parts One and Two. The reader has the forward-looking work of Part Three, which has now demonstrated through three specific cases that the practice equips the reader to see what the standard tools cannot. What the reader does not yet have is the operational specification of what to do with the practice. The remaining chapters of the book provide that specification. Chapter Ten takes up what economists must now do, given that the standard economic tools have been demonstrated inadequate to the integration the book documents. Chapter Eleven takes up what analysts across multiple disciplines must now do, with specific attention to the operational practices that have been developed for working under the conditions the book has been describing. Chapter Twelve addresses Aden directly, as the closing personal synthesis through which the broader argument lands at the level of the specific child whose name the book carries.

The reader who has recognized the rebirth as real, after recognizing the death as real, can proceed to Part Four prepared to do the work the conditions require. The reader who has not made the recognition can return to this chapter, because the recognition is the precondition of what follows. The labor of the birth is producing the new architectures regardless of whether participants understand what is happening. The participants who understand can engage with what is being made rather than only mourning what is being lost. The book has spent eight chapters preparing the reader to understand. The remaining chapters specify what the understanding requires.

— PART FOUR —
BEYOND THE BURNING
The work begins when we understand what the fire has made possible.
WHAT WE HAVE TRAVERSED
THE FIRE
The world as it was—separate, linear, predictable—has burned.
THE INTEGRATION
Feedback loops. Accountability collapse. Cognitive ground shift. Parallel civilizations. Asymmetry.
THE SETTLEMENT
New architectures are emerging through the disruption. Not a return. A reformation.
UNDERSTAND
RECONIZE
DECIDE
ACT
BUILD
THE DISRUPTION IS THE FORMATION. THE WORK IS OURS.
WHAT LIES AHEAD
Work with new tools for a new architecture.
Build institutions that can see what is emerging.
Act with awareness of the generations who inherit the result.
Shape the formation with integrity, resilience, and care.
BEYOND THE BURNING IS NOT ESCAPE. IT IS ENGAGEMENT.
To see clearly. To act wisely. To build what can last.
CHAPTER TEN
WHAT ECONOMISTS MUST NOW DO
Cases that the old models cannot see.
Old models:
Calm seas.
Linear charts.
False confidence.
Reality:
Cross-domain leverage.
Hidden exposures.
Systemic stress.
The private credit industry case: Growth built on invisible assumptions. Stress arrives through the cracks.
Inside the conditions, not outside: Economists must see what their tools are blind to.
What must be done: New analytical posture. New humility. New economic imagination.
CHAPTER ELEVEN
WHAT ANALYSTS MUST NOW DO
Four tools for working in integrated conditions.
1. TEMPO RECOGNITION
Pair every fast event with inquiry into the slow events beneath.
2. CONVERGENCE REGISTRATION
Name what your discipline brackets as "exogenous." Refuse the bracket.
3. AMPLIFICATION MAPPING
Identify feedback loops and amplifiers. Make them constitutive.
4. RECONSTITUTION AWARENESS
Design institutions with awareness of what they will be unable to see.
Not a new discipline. A new posture inside every discipline.
CHAPTER TWELVE
THE PERSONAL SYNTHESIS
What this formation means for Aden.
Aden grows up in a world of integration, asymmetry, and cognitive divergence.
His tools will not be the old tools. His choices cannot be the old choices.
The formation is his inheritance. His agency is our test.
PRINCIPLES FOR THE WORK AHEAD
SEE THE WHOLE
Understand connections, not just parts.
ACT WITH INTEGRITY
Power without ethics burns everything.
BUILD FOR RESILIENCE
Redundancy, diversity, adaptability.
THINK IN GENERATIONS
Consequences outlive our time.
SERVE THE HUMAN FUTURE
Institutions are tools. People are the purpose.
THE OLD ORDER IS GONE. THE NEW FORMATION IS EMERGING. THE WORK IS NOW.

Part Four: Beyond the Burning

Part One was The Fire. The diagnostic foundation documenting what was already burning, with the cases that did not fit the standard frameworks, the categories dissolving, the configuration-dependent meaning that the post-1945 settlement could no longer organize. Part Two was The Integration. The analytical core that named the structure of what was happening, the feedback loops replacing sequential causation, the accountability collapse spreading across multiple institutional domains, the cognitive ground shifting beneath the work that depends on its stability, the parallel civilizations contesting their boundaries, the asymmetric patterns operating across infrastructure, energy, sanctions, and military deployments. Part Three was The Settlement. The forward-looking work examining what was becoming, the new media architectures emerging through cross-domain integration the standard tools cannot register, the new institutional arrangements replacing OPEC and the petrodollar at the central bank scale and at the household scale, the reorganization of which places matter on the global map, the recognition that the disruption is not the obstacle to the formation but the condition of the formation.

Aden, the boy whose name this book carries, has both meanings in his name. Fire and settlement. The book has worked through both. The fire of the integration the previous parts have documented. The settlement that is being made through the labor of the burning. Part Four moves beyond both into the work that the burning has prepared the conditions for. Beyond the burning is the work of participants who have understood what the conditions are doing, who have recognized the new architectures being assembled, and who must now decide what to do with their understanding. The work is not heroic. The work is not optional. The work is what the conditions require of practitioners who can no longer pretend that the standard analytical tools are adequate to the phenomena they are asked to analyze.

Three chapters develop the part's argument. Chapter Ten takes up what economic analysis now requires, given that the standard economic frameworks have been demonstrated inadequate to the integrated phenomena the book has been documenting. The chapter is not addressed exclusively to economists, because the framework the book has been building argues against the disciplinary silos the standard categorization assumes. Economic analysis is performed by economists, but it is also performed by trade analysts, supply chain executives, financial journalists, central bank officials, business school faculty, and increasingly by anyone whose work depends on understanding how value moves through the integrated systems the previous parts have described. The chapter develops a specific contemporary case, the structural stress now arriving in the private credit industry that grew over the past decade through cross-domain integration the standard credit and banking analyses could not register. The case demonstrates that practitioners trained in the standard frameworks are not analyzing the conditions from outside. They are inside the conditions, operating with tools that were not built to register what the conditions are doing. The chapter specifies what economic analysis now requires given this position, with the analytical posture the book has been teaching being what the work needs.

Chapter Eleven takes up what analytical work across multiple disciplines now requires. The chapter introduces a specific operational practice that has been developed for working under the conditions the book has documented. The practice consists of four analytical tools that practitioners can apply inside whatever discipline they already inhabit. Tempo recognition, the practice of pairing every analysis of a fast event with deliberate inquiry into the slow events propagating beneath it. Convergence registration, the practice of naming what the disciplinary apparatus brackets as exogenous and refusing the bracketing. Amplification mapping, the practice of identifying the feedback loops the disciplinary apparatus does not register and incorporating them as constitutive. Reconstitution awareness, the practice of designing the institutions emerging from the conditions with explicit awareness of what those institutions will be unable to see. The four tools are not a complete framework. They are an analytical posture, deployable inside whatever discipline the practitioner already operates, that gives the practitioner the capacity to register what the discipline alone cannot. The chapter develops the tools operationally with the depth the practitioner needs in order to apply them in actual work.

Chapter Twelve closes the book with the personal synthesis through which the broader argument lands at the level of Aden's specific life. The book has been about the conditions Aden will inherit, with the analytical work being addressed to readers who must understand those conditions in order to participate in shaping them. The closing chapter returns to Aden directly, examining what the formation looks like at the scale of an eleven-year-old child whose grandmother fears the AI, whose mother does research while skeptical about technology, whose father writes books about conditions that will be partly obsolete by the time the books are published. The closing is personal because the book has been personal throughout, with the author appearing inside the conditions being analyzed rather than from outside them. The closing is also analytical because the personal synthesis must do specific work for the book's argument, with Aden's situation being the test case through which the framework the book has built is shown to be load-bearing for the participants the conditions have produced.

Part Four is shorter than the previous parts. The descriptive work has been done. The directive work follows from the descriptive work in ways that do not require extended development. The reader who has absorbed the previous parts has the framework. What remains is to specify what the framework requires of specific kinds of practitioners and to land the argument at the level of the specific life the book has been addressed to throughout. The work the chapters of Part Four take up is real, but the chapters themselves can be more focused than the chapters of Parts Two and Three because the analytical foundation is in place.

A final note on what Part Four does and does not do. The chapters specify what specific kinds of practitioners must now do given the conditions the book has documented. The chapters do not specify what every practitioner in every domain must do. The book cannot do that work. The book can establish the analytical posture the conditions require and can demonstrate the posture in specific cases. The work of applying the posture across all the domains the conditions affect is the work of practitioners across many fields, operating over many years, in conditions that will continue to develop while the work proceeds. Part Four prepares them for that work without pretending to complete it. The four tools that Chapter Eleven develops are one specific articulation of the practice. Other articulations will emerge as practitioners develop the analytical posture in their specific domains. The book is offered as a contribution to that emergence rather than as the final word on it.

CHAPTER TEN
WHAT ECONOMIC ANALYSIS NOW REQUIRES
From siloed models to integrated judgment.
THE OLD WORLD:
FRAGMENTED AND INSUFFICIENT
THE NEW WORLD:
INTEGRATED AND DYNAMIC
$Y = f(K, L)$
$E(u) = \sum p_i u_i$
$\frac{dY}{dK} = MP_K$
TRADE
Partial equilibrium
Trade frictions
exogenous
FINANCE
Efficient markets
Rational expectations
Risk = exogenous
POLICY
Policy as shock
Rules > discretion
Implementation
omitted
MARKETS
Representative agent
Perfect information
No frictions
BEHAVIOR
Preferences stable
Biases ignored
Strategic behavior
set aside
ANALYTICAL
BLIND SPOTS
Power
Institutions
Incentives
Information
Time
Context
What was once bracketed as exogenous is now constitutive.
TECHNOLOGY
& INNOVATION
FINANCE
& CAPITAL
FLOWS
GEOPOLITICS
& SECURITY
REGULATION
& POLICY
INSTITUTIONS
& GOVERNANCE
ECONOMIC OUTCOMES
EMERGE FROM INTERACTION,
ADAPTATION, AND FEEDBACK.
INFORMATION
& DATA
INCENTIVES
& CONTRACTS
BEHAVIOR
& STRATEGY
FEEDBACK LOOPS ACROSS SCALES
1 STUDENT / RESEARCH INSIGHT
THE GPA CASE
Signals can be informative—
and strategically distorted.
ACADEMIC TRANSCRIPT
Cumulative GPA
3.82
INTERVIEW NOTES
Strong undergrad brand
Leadership roles
Summer internship
Standardized test coaching
Grade inflation in major
Strategic course selection
Backloaded effort
What's the true signal?
2 PRIVATE CREDIT ARCHITECTURE
THE CAPITAL STRUCTURE CASE
Yields don't exist in a vacuum—
they are built on structure, rights,
and liquidity design.
INVESTOR CAPITAL
(PENSIONS, INSURERS,
WEALTH, FAMILY OFFICES)
EQUITY / GP
MEZZANINE
SENIOR DEBT
PRIVATE CREDIT FUND
LIQUIDITY ARCHITECTURE
SUBSCRIPTION GATE
LOCK-UP PERIODS
REDEMPTION GATE
SIDE POCKETS
VALUATION POLICY
TARGET YIELD PROFILE
CASH FLOW PROFILE
RISK BUFFER
& COVENANTS
CREDIT AGREEMENTS
FUND DOCUMENTATION
COVENANTS
RISK MANAGEMENT
1. REGISTER THE BRACKETED FORCES
Make the unseen part of the analysis.
2. MAP THE FEEDBACK LOOPS
See how actions today reshape the future.
3. PAIR FAST EVENTS WITH SLOW CONDITIONS
Hold time horizons together in mind.
4. DESIGN WITH AWARENESS OF INSTITUTIONAL BLINDNESS
Account for what systems systematically miss.

CHAPTER TEN

What Economic Analysis Now Requires

My students are using The Aden Effect in their final exams. I want to start the chapter with this because something has happened that I did not expect when I uploaded the academic paper to SSRN a week ago. The students in my International Trade and Finance class and my Business Analytics class found the paper. They read it. They used it as the analytical reference for their final exam projects. Several of them told me that the paper opened a new perspective for them. Two of the resulting projects are good enough that I am recommending them for journal publication. One paper analyzes a specific company in ways that I have suggested the students send directly to the company because the analysis is operational rather than just academic. One paper is good enough that I have asked the student to present it as a talking point at the university to inform other students about what their analytical work could look like.

The paper that has stayed with me most is one that examined GPA as a signal in academic credentialing. The students who wrote it interviewed university students about their course selection decisions. The findings were mind-blowing, in the words I used to my students when I read the analysis. Students are choosing easier subjects to maintain high GPAs, hoping a high GPA will land them a better job or better graduate school. The high GPA then becomes the primary signal employers and graduate schools use to evaluate candidates. The signal is becoming systematically distorted because the underlying behavior the signal is supposed to capture, which is academic capability, is being replaced by behavior optimized for the signal itself, which is GPA management through course selection. The students did not state their analytical contribution in these terms. What they had identified, working from the paper they had read, was that the standard apparatus of academic credentialing brackets the strategic behavior of students inside the credentialing system as exogenous to what GPA measures. The bracketing fails when the strategic behavior becomes constitutive of what GPA measures. The students identified the failure. The paper they had read had given them the analytical posture to identify it. Their work then made the failure visible in a domain where the standard analysis treats the signal as informationally adequate.

This is what the framework does when it reaches practitioners-in-formation. The students did not invent the convergence argument. They applied it. The application produced analytical work that demonstrates the framework's value in a specific domain that the standard tools mishandle systematically. I am writing this chapter the day after grading those final exams. The experience of reading my students' work has shifted what I thought this chapter needed to do. I had been preparing to write a chapter about what economists must now do, with the BlackRock and private credit case as the central anchor. The chapter still does that work. But it does it in a different register than I had planned, because my students have already shown me what economic analysis looks like when it is performed by practitioners who have the framework and who know how to use it. The chapter is not telling economists or anyone else what to do as if the doing were difficult or remote. The chapter is describing what the work looks like when the framework is operational, with my students' exam papers as one specific demonstration that the work is possible and is already being done by people who do not yet have the credentials that the standard apparatus requires for the work to be considered legitimate.

Why the Standard Tools Cannot Do This Work

Economic analysis as a discipline developed during the post-1945 period under specific conditions that made disciplinary specialization tractable. The phenomena economists studied could be partially separated from the phenomena other disciplines studied. International relations could be analyzed separately from trade flows. Trade flows could be analyzed separately from currency dynamics. Currency dynamics could be analyzed separately from technology development. Technology development could be analyzed separately from political alignment. The separations were not perfect, but they were workable. The forces operating across the boundaries between the domains were sufficiently weak relative to the forces operating within each domain that treating cross-boundary forces as exogenous produced analyses adequate for the conditions in which the analyses were used.

This is no longer true. The framework the previous chapters have developed has documented the convergence in which forces from outside each disciplinary boundary are now constitutive of the dynamics inside that boundary. The standard tools of economic analysis cannot register what they were built to bracket. The supply-shock model brackets the institutional architecture inside which the supply moves, the algorithmic decision-support systems through which the supply is allocated, the geopolitical strategic logic that determines which infrastructure is struck. The exchange-rate model brackets the parallel financial settlement architectures, the sanctions enforcement apparatus, the strategic political decisions that move markets in real time. The credit model brackets the banking deregulation, the regulatory arbitrage, the technology platforms, the consumer behavior shifts that together produce the conditions in which credit operates. Each tool is competent within its frame. None of the tools, applied separately, can register the cross-boundary integration that the framework has been documenting. Practitioners using these tools produce analyses that are technically correct within their frames but practically inadequate to the phenomena they are supposed to analyze.

The inadequacy is not a failure of competence. It is a structural feature of the tools. The tools were built for conditions in which the bracketing was workable. The conditions have changed. The tools have not. Practitioners who continue using the tools without registering what the tools bracket produce work that meets disciplinary standards while failing to address the phenomena the work is supposed to address. This is not a problem economic analysis can solve by adding more variables to existing models. The problem is that the variables operate across the boundaries the models impose, with the cross-boundary operation being what the models cannot incorporate by construction.

BlackRock and the Private Credit Architecture

The private credit industry provides the contemporary case that demonstrates the inadequacy at scale. The industry totaled between one point eight and two trillion dollars in assets by early 2026, depending on which estimate is used. It grew from a marginal corner of the financial system in 2010 to the dominant funding source for middle-market corporate borrowing by 2025. The growth happened in plain sight, with industry trade publications, analyst reports, and academic studies tracking the asset accumulation in detail. The growth also happened invisibly to the standard tools of economic and financial analysis, in the specific sense that the tools could not register what the growth was producing structurally even as they tracked the growth quantitatively. The structural stress now arriving in the industry was invisible to the standard analysis while it was developing. The tools that should have been able to see what was being assembled could not assemble what they were tracking.

On March 6, 2026, BlackRock limited withdrawals from its twenty-six-billion-dollar HPS Corporate Lending Fund. Investors had requested approximately nine-point three percent of fund assets, a redemption of one point two billion dollars. BlackRock capped the redemption at five percent of fund assets, paying out approximately six hundred twenty million dollars while locking the rest. The same week, Blackstone injected four hundred million dollars of its own capital into one of its private credit funds to cover redemptions that the fund could not honor from its own resources. Blue Owl Capital stopped honoring withdrawals from its private credit funds entirely and issued IOUs to investors in lieu of cash. Morgan Stanley capped redemptions at five percent after investors requested nearly eleven percent. Four major asset managers, in the same week, restricted access to capital that their investors had been told was semi-liquid. The investors had not been told the funds were illiquid. They had been told the funds were structured to allow periodic redemption, with quarterly windows being the standard structure across the industry. The structure failed simultaneously across multiple managers, which means the failure was structural rather than firm specific.

What had been assembled to produce this. Pension funds, endowments, sovereign wealth funds, and increasingly retail investors with substantial wealth had been allocating to private credit because the funds offered yields above traditional fixed income with reduced volatility marks. The reduced volatility was partly genuine, in that private credit loans are not traded daily and therefore do not register the daily price volatility of public bonds. The reduced volatility was also partly the result of valuation practices that did not mark the underlying loans to market in any meaningful sense, with the marks being smoothed in ways that the standard analysis did not adequately probe. The yield premium relative to public credit was real, but it included compensation for illiquidity that the marketing materials did not always emphasize. The funds offered semi-liquid structures, with quarterly redemption windows and stated soft caps on outflows, that were designed for normal conditions in which redemption requests would be modest and could be funded from new inflows or from natural amortization of the loan portfolio. The structures were not designed for conditions in which redemption requests would exceed the new inflows and the natural amortization simultaneously, which is what happened in March 2026.

The standard tools of credit analysis can describe each component of this. The tools can analyze yield premiums. The tools can analyze illiquidity adjustments. The tools can analyze fund structure and redemption mechanisms. The tools can analyze the regulatory frameworks that allowed asset managers to offer semi-liquid private credit products to retail investors. The tools can analyze the consumer behavior shifts that drove allocation. What the tools cannot do is assemble these components into a single analytical picture that registers what was being built. The standard apparatus treats yield premium as a credit-pricing question, illiquidity as a fund-structure question, regulatory permission as a regulatory-policy question, retail allocation as a wealth-management question, and consumer behavior as a behavioral-finance question. Each question is in a different domain. The integration of the answers is what produced the industry. The integration of the failures is what produced the March 2026 redemption restrictions. The standard apparatus cannot perform the integration because the apparatus is built to keep the domains separate.

The work that should have been done required practitioners who could see across the domains. Some specific things would have been visible to such practitioners. The growth of the private credit industry was happening in a regulatory environment that had been progressively deregulated since the 2008 financial crisis, with each deregulation step being a small adjustment that the standard regulatory analysis treated as marginal. The cumulative effect was that products that previously required substantial regulatory oversight were now being marketed to populations that had not historically accessed them. The yield environment in which the industry grew was anomalously low for an extended period, with the central bank policies producing yield-seeking behavior that pushed capital into structures that worked in low-yield conditions but had not been tested in higher-yield conditions. The valuation practices that produced the smoothed marks were not adequately stress-tested against scenarios in which redemption requests would exceed the natural liquidity of the underlying loans. Each of these observations would have required cross-domain analysis. None of them would have been produced by any single discipline working alone. The growth was the kind of phenomenon the framework was specifically built to register, and the absence of the framework in standard practice is what allowed the growth to continue without analytical scrutiny adequate to what was being built.

Case	What Standard Analysis Saw	What It Bracketed	What Was Actually Happening	Lesson for Economic Analysis
GPA as a signal	GPA as a measure of student capability and academic performance.	Strategic course selection, incentive design, employer expectations, and credential gaming.	Students may optimize for the signal rather than the learning the signal is supposed to represent.	Economic analysis must examine how people respond to measurement systems, not treat the measure as neutral.
Private credit	Growth in assets, yield premiums, redemption structures, and fund performance.	Regulatory arbitrage, valuation smoothing, retail access, liquidity mismatch, and investor behavior across market conditions.	A semi-liquid product architecture was being built on illiquid foundations.	Economic analysis must register the architecture connecting regulation, incentives, liquidity, valuation, and behavior.
Shared pattern	A signal or product appears valid inside its frame.	The cross-domain forces shaping the frame itself.	The frame becomes part of the behavior it claims merely to measure.	The analyst must ask: what has the model bracketed that has now become constitutive?

What the Work Now Requires

The BlackRock case is one instance of what the framework has been arguing throughout the book. The standard analytical tools of economics, finance, regulatory analysis, and the related fields cannot register what is being assembled in real time when the assembly crosses the disciplinary boundaries the tools impose. The inadequacy is structural. Practitioners who continue applying the standard tools without modification produce analyses that meet disciplinary standards while missing the phenomena the analyses are supposed to address. The work the conditions require is different from the work the standard tools were built to do.

What the work now requires has been demonstrated specifically across the previous chapters and demonstrated again in this chapter through the BlackRock case and the GPA case. Practitioners must learn to register what their disciplinary tools bracket as exogenous and to ask whether the bracketed forces are constitutive of the phenomena under analysis. Practitioners must learn to map the feedback loops their disciplinary tools cannot model because the loops cross the boundaries the tools impose. Practitioners must learn to pair every analysis of a fast event with deliberate inquiry into the slow events propagating beneath it, because the standard apparatus is calibrated to the fast events that fit its temporal frame and the slow events that operate at architectural scales are bracketed by default. Practitioners must learn to design any institutional response with explicit awareness of what the institution will be unable to see, rather than designing as if the institutional architecture were neutral with respect to what it can register.

These practices are not a complete framework. They are an analytical posture that practitioners can adopt inside whatever discipline they already inhabit. The discipline the practitioner has spent years acquiring remains the discipline the practitioner applies. What changes is the practitioner's relationship to the discipline's bracketing. The bracketing becomes explicit rather than invisible. The cross-boundary integration becomes registered rather than dismissed as backdrop. The work the practitioner produces becomes adequate to the phenomena rather than adequate only to the disciplinary frame. My students did this in their final exam projects. The BlackRock case shows what happens when practitioners do not do this. The standard apparatus produces growth analyses that miss what is being built and stress analyses that arrive after the structural failure has already begun.

There is a specific implication for who is permitted to do this work. The standard apparatus operates inside institutional credentialing systems that determine who is recognized as authorized to perform analytical work in each domain. Economists with PhDs from research universities are authorized to produce economic analysis. Financial analysts with specific certifications are authorized to produce credit analysis. The credentialing systems were built in the same period as the disciplinary tools, under the same conditions in which disciplinary specialization was tractable. The credentialing systems also fail under the convergence conditions, in the same way the tools fail. The work the conditions require can be done by practitioners who have the analytical posture, regardless of which credentials they hold. My students producing journal-quality work as part of their final exams in undergraduate and master's level courses are demonstrating that the work is not gated by credentials. The work is gated by the analytical posture, which the framework supports and which practitioners can develop through deliberate practice. This is not a small implication. It means the work the conditions require is not waiting for the next generation of credentialed economists to be trained. The work can begin now, performed by practitioners across many domains, with the framework as the entry point and with the disciplinary tools being applied with explicit awareness of what they bracket.

Toward the Operational Practice

This chapter has demonstrated through one specific domain what the framework has been arguing throughout the book. Economic analysis, performed by economists or by anyone whose work depends on understanding how value moves through the integrated systems the previous parts have described, requires a different analytical posture than the standard tools support. The BlackRock and broader private credit case shows what happens when the standard tools operate without the posture. The GPA case shows what happens when the posture is applied by practitioners who have the framework. Both cases are part of the same argument. The conditions require the posture. The posture can be developed. The work the posture enables is being done by practitioners who already have the framework, with the framework reaching them through the academic paper, through this book, through the conversations the framework supports.

What this chapter has demonstrated through economic analysis is one specific instance of what analytical work across multiple disciplines must now do. The pattern is general. Economic analysis is one domain where the standard tools fail under convergence conditions and where the framework supports the analytical posture the work now requires. The same is true in international relations, where the standard frameworks for strategic competition fail to register the cross-domain integration with technology, finance, and cognitive infrastructure. The same is true in supply chain management, where the standard frameworks for logistics and procurement fail to register the cross-domain integration with sanctions enforcement, geopolitical alignment, and AI-driven compliance systems. The same is true in regulatory policy, organizational design, business analytics, and the educational frameworks that prepare practitioners for any of these fields. The framework operates across the disciplines because the conditions operate across the disciplines.

Chapter Eleven takes up the operational practice that the framework has developed for working across the disciplines. The practice consists of the four analytical tools that the Part Four introduction has named. Tempo recognition. Convergence registration. Amplification mapping. Reconstitution awareness. The tools are not the framework itself. They are operational instruments that practitioners can apply inside whatever discipline they already inhabit, with the application giving the practitioner the capacity to register what the discipline alone cannot. The next chapter develops the tools with the depth practitioners need in order to apply them in actual work. The reader who has absorbed this chapter, with the demonstration that economic analysis under current conditions requires the analytical posture the book has been teaching, will arrive at Chapter Eleven prepared to receive the operational specification of what the posture requires in practice.

CHAPTER ELEVEN
THE FOUR TOOLS
An operational practice for working under integrated conditions.
1 TEMPO RECOGNITION
Fast events. Slow conditions.
FAST EVENTS
SLOW CONDITIONS
1990
2000
2010
2020
2030
Notes
• Observe
• Context
• Sequence
• Endure
2 CONVERGENCE REGISTRATION
Name what the frame brackets.
GEOPOLITICS
ECONOMICS
TECHNOLOGY
FINANCE
INSTITUTIONS
THE PROBLEM
INTEGRATE • INTERPRET • ACT • REFINE • TEST
ANALYTICAL PRACTICE
DISCIPLINED JUDGMENT
3 AMPLIFICATION MAPPING
Trace loops and amplification.
REINFORCING DYNAMICS
INITIAL CHANGE
FEEDBACK LOOP
SECOND-ORDER EFFECTS
THIRD-ORDER EFFECTS
DELAY & TIME LAGS
SYSTEMIC SHIFT
UNINTENDED CONSEQUENCES
4 RECONSTITUTION AWARENESS
Design for what institutions cannot see.
BLIND SPOT
What the system cannot see.
MANDATES
INCENTIVES
INFORMATION
NORMS
CAPACITY
RULES • CULTURE • RESOURCES • INFRASTRUCTURE
Clarity
Foresight
Humility
Action
Not a new discipline. A new posture inside every discipline.
HISTORY
POLITICAL THEORY
ECONOMICS
ENGINEERING
PHILOSOPHY
"The task is not to predict the future, but to be prepared to shape it."
— PETER DRUCKER

CHAPTER ELEVEN

The Four Tools

I want to start the chapter with two specific moments from the past week that show how the framework has been moving through the practitioner audience the chapter is for. The first happened when I was on LinkedIn reading a piece by the World Economic Forum that addressed a specific institutional problem. I read the piece and immediately saw what was wrong with the analysis. The piece was treating the problem as a coordination failure that better institutional design could address. The actual problem was the disciplinary apparatus the analysts had used to identify the problem in the first place, with the apparatus bracketing the cross-domain forces that were producing the coordination failure as exogenous to the analysis. I commented on the post that this was exactly the kind of gap The Aden Effect framework was developed to address. The comment generated engagement that the standard professional commentary on such posts does not generate. The framework was reaching the audience the framework is for, with the recognition happening through visible engagement on a professional platform.

The second happened when a senior fintech lecturer posted about two papers that had been published, with the latest one going up that day. The post said that only in retrospect did the papers point to the same conclusion, which the lecturer summarized as goals are not enough, agreements are not enough, institutions are what separate saying from doing. I recognized in the post the same analytical work the framework supports. I responded by pointing the lecturer to my published paper on The Aden Effect. The result was downloads of the paper from the lecturer and from others who had been following the conversation. The framework was again reaching the audience the framework is for, with the operational instruments the framework supports being what those practitioners now need to do the work the framework enables.

This chapter develops those operational instruments. The framework the previous chapters have built has demonstrated what is happening, what is becoming, and what the conditions require of practitioners and scholars whose work depends on understanding the integrated phenomena the book has documented. What the chapter now provides is the operational specification of the practice that the framework supports. The practice consists of four analytical tools that practitioners and scholars can apply inside whatever discipline they already inhabit. Tempo recognition. Convergence registration. Amplification mapping. Reconstitution awareness. The four tools have been named in the Part Four introduction. The chapter develops each one at the depth that allows the practitioner to begin applying it, with the cases drawn from the previous chapters of this book demonstrating each tool at work. The chapter has a scholarly companion paper that develops the tools with greater methodological depth and with comparison to established methodologies, available at https://papers.ssrn.com/sol3/papers.cfm?abstract_id=6698878 for readers who want the fuller engagement. The chapter is sufficient for practitioners who want to begin. The paper is the technical reference that supports the deeper work.

The four tools are not a complete analytical framework. They are an analytical posture that practitioners and scholars can adopt inside whatever discipline they already inhabit. The discipline the practitioner has spent years acquiring remains the discipline the practitioner applies. What changes is the practitioner's relationship to the discipline's bracketing. The bracketing becomes explicit rather than invisible. The cross-boundary integration becomes registered rather than dismissed as backdrop. The work the practitioner produces becomes adequate to the phenomena rather than adequate only to the disciplinary frame. The four tools support this shift in posture. The tools do not replace the disciplinary apparatus. They extend it with the analytical practice that the conditions now require.

Tool	Core Question	What It Makes Visible	Demonstration Case
Tempo Recognition	What slow events are moving beneath the fast event?	Long-term structural shifts hidden beneath immediate news cycles.	UAE withdrawal from OPEC as a fast event sitting on top of deeper Gulf realignment, petrodollar erosion, and commodity architecture change.
Convergence Registration	What does my discipline bracket as exogenous that may now be constitutive?	The outside forces that have become part of the phenomenon itself.	BlackRock/private credit and the forces standard credit analysis missed: deregulation, yield-seeking behavior, technology scaling, and consumer behavior.
Amplification Mapping	What feedback loops are being produced, and at what speed?	First-order and second-order loops that connect politics, markets, threats, and information asymmetry.	Iran political-financial cluster from Chapter Seven.
Reconstitution Awareness	What will the institution I am building be unable to see?	Institutional blind spots before they become permanent design failures.	Greenland and the institutional inability to register climate, rare earths, technology, shipping, and strategic competition together.

Tempo Recognition

Tempo recognition is the analytical practice of pairing every analysis of a fast event with deliberate inquiry into the slow events propagating beneath it. The disciplinary apparatus practitioners use is calibrated toward fast events that fit the rhythms of the analytical environment, with quarterly reporting cycles, eighteen-month strategic planning horizons, and daily news cycles all rewarding analysis that operates at the speed those rhythms support. The slow events that compound across years and decades, that become irreversible before they become visible, register only when they cross thresholds the apparatus is forced to acknowledge. By that point the analysis is no longer diagnostic but descriptive, with the work having been done by events the apparatus could have registered earlier if the practitioner had been performing the discipline tempo recognition supplies.

The practice has three procedural elements. First, the practitioner identifies the fast event under analysis with the precision the disciplinary apparatus already supplies. Second, the practitioner deliberately inquiries into the slow events the fast event is connected to, with the inquiry going in four directions. Backward propagation, what slow events were already in motion that the fast event accelerated, made visible, or crossed a threshold within. Forward propagation, what slow consequences will the fast event produce that will not become visible within the news cycle the fast event occupies. Lateral propagation, what other slow events operating in adjacent domains the disciplinary apparatus treats as exogenous are interacting with the fast event through feedback the analysis has not registered. Vertical propagation, what structural shifts at the architectural level is the fast event a surface manifestation of. Third, the practitioner writes the analysis with both time scales held simultaneously, with the fast-event analysis remaining intact and a parallel section briefly naming the slow events the inquiry has identified, the rates at which they are propagating, and the analytical limit the apparatus imposes on the analysis.

The UAE withdrawal from OPEC on April 28, 2026, demonstrates the practice. The fast event was the announcement, with markets responding within hours and analysts producing competent supply-and-demand analyses within the day. The standard analysis registered the fast event accurately, with bearish near-term recommendations on Brent contracts pricing the Strait of Hormuz reopening and the additional UAE supply. Tempo recognition asks the analyst to register the slow events the announcement was the surface manifestation of. Backward propagation, the UAE-Saudi rift had been deepening since 2018 and the Abraham Accords had been progressively realigning UAE strategic posture toward Washington and Tel Aviv since 2020, with the withdrawal being the threshold-crossing event at the end of a fifteen-year structural realignment. Forward propagation, the Gulf Cooperation Council itself may not survive the realignment intact, with implications for Brent pricing on a twelve-to-thirty-six-month horizon that the standard scenario analysis brackets. Lateral propagation, the petrodollar's reserve status had been eroding for over a decade, with the announcement potentially catalyzing further erosion through the broader reconstitution of global commodity-trade settlement architecture. Vertical propagation, the post-1945 architecture of multilateral commodity coordination through OPEC and OPEC+ has been giving way to bilateral state-corporate arrangements between major Gulf producers and external partners, with the announcement being one specific surface manifestation of an architectural shift operating at decade-scale.

The position recommendation that the analyst delivers does not need to change in form. The bearish near-term recommendation on Brent stands within the supply-and-demand frame. What changes is that the analysis now includes explicit registration of what the recommendation is bracketing. The slow events propagating beneath the announcement are named. The rates at which they are propagating are specified. The analytical limit is acknowledged. When the slow events begin to manifest in ways the supply-and-demand frame cannot accommodate, the trading book will not be surprised, because the analytical posture from which the position was constructed already registered the dimensions in motion.

Convergence Registration

Convergence registration is the analytical practice of naming what the disciplinary apparatus brackets as exogenous and refusing the bracketing when the bracketed forces are constitutive of the dynamics under analysis. The practice is the foundational analytical move that the other three tools operate in and through. Without convergence registration the practitioner cannot perform tempo recognition, because the slow events are typically located in the domains the disciplinary apparatus brackets. Without convergence registration the practitioner cannot perform amplification mapping, because the feedback loops typically cross the disciplinary boundaries. Without convergence registration the practitioner cannot perform reconstitution awareness, because the institutional design choices depend on knowing what the institution will be unable to see. Convergence registration is the entry point. The other tools are extensions of it.

The practice has four procedural steps. First, the practitioner names the disciplinary frame they intend to apply to the phenomenon under analysis. The economist names the supply-shock model. The IR scholar names the horizontal escalation framework. The business analyst names the regression model or the SWOT analysis or the Five Forces apparatus. The naming sounds trivial but is not, because practitioners typically apply their disciplinary frame without naming it, with the frame being constitutive of their analytical identity in ways that make naming it require deliberate meta-cognitive effort. Second, the practitioner catalogues what the frame treats as exogenous. The economist's supply-shock model brackets the institutional architecture, the algorithmic decision-support systems, and the geopolitical strategic logic. The IR scholar's escalation framework brackets the AI integration, the parallel financial settlement, and the institutional reconstitution. The catalogue is the practitioner's honest registration of what the apparatus, by construction, cannot see. Third, the practitioner assesses whether the bracketed forces are constitutive of the phenomenon under analysis. The assessment is a question of degree, with some bracketed forces being partially exogenous and partially constitutive, with the constitutive share growing as the convergence operates. Fourth, the practitioner writes the analysis with the assessment registered, with the disciplinary apparatus applied as the practitioner's training has equipped them to apply it and a parallel section naming what the apparatus brackets, specifying which bracketed forces are constitutive, and registering the analytical limit explicitly.

The BlackRock private credit case from Chapter Ten demonstrates the practice. The disciplinary frame was the standard credit and banking analysis. The frame brackets the regulatory deregulation that allowed semi-liquid private credit products to be offered to retail investors without the oversight that traditional banking products required. The frame brackets the search for yield in low-rate environments that drove capital allocation toward products designed for the low-rate conditions but not stress-tested against higher-rate conditions. The frame brackets the technology platforms that scaled the products to populations that had not historically accessed them. The frame brackets the consumer behavior shifts that made all of this normal rather than novel. Each of these forces operates in a domain the standard credit analysis treats separately. Together they were constitutive of what was being assembled, with the integration being what produced the two trillion-dollar industry over more than a decade.

Convergence registration would have made these forces visible to credit analysts during the industry's growth phase. The practice does not require credit analysts to become regulatory analysts or behavioral economists. It requires them to name what their credit apparatus brackets and to refuse the bracketing when the bracketed forces are constitutive. An analyst applying the practice during the industry's growth would have produced credit analyses with explicit registration that the standard apparatus did not handle the regulatory deregulation, the yield-seeking behavior, the technology scaling, or the consumer behavior shifts that were producing the industry's growth. The credit analysis would have remained competent within its frame. The registration would have made the analytical limit explicit. Decision-makers reading the analysis would have known what the apparatus was bracketing. The structural development that arrived as crisis in March 2026 would have been visible during its formation rather than only at that moment of its surface manifestation.

Amplification Mapping

Amplification mapping is the analytical practice of identifying the feedback loops the specific phenomenon under analysis is producing, in which directions, at what rates, and incorporating them into the analysis as constitutive of the dynamics rather than bracketing them as backdrop. The practice extends convergence registration into the feedback-loop register. Where convergence registration names what the apparatus brackets, amplification mapping specifies how the bracketed forces interact with each other and with the dynamics inside the apparatus's frame to produce outcomes the apparatus cannot model.

The practice has five procedural steps. First, the practitioner identifies candidate forces, working from the convergence-registration cataloguing and selecting which bracketed forces are operating with sufficient strength to be candidates for constitutive feedback dynamics. Second, the practitioner hypothesizes directional flows for each candidate, asking whether force A amplifies force B, whether the relationship is bidirectional, whether the feedback is positive or negative. Third, the practitioner assesses the rate of feedback for each hypothesized loop, with slow loops requiring different analytical treatment than fast loops. Fourth, the practitioner identifies second-order amplifications, the chains in which force A amplifies force B which amplifies force C which amplifies force A, with the second-order chains typically being invisible to the disciplinary apparatus because each link crosses a disciplinary boundary the apparatus treats as exogenous. Fifth, the practitioner writes the analysis with the loops registered as constitutive, naming the first order and second-order loops, specifying the directional flows and rates, and registering the analytical implication.

The Iran political-financial cluster from Chapter Seven demonstrates the practice. The cluster involved Mohammad Bagher Ghalibaf departing the Iranian negotiating team and stock markets weakening on the news, the Islamic Revolutionary Guard Corps issuing physical threats against eighteen American technology and financial firms with corporate operational consequences across multiple domains, and the Financial Times documentation of suspicious bets on falling oil prices placed minutes before specific Trump policy announcements. The first-order loops are visible. Political signal moves the markets. Physical threat moves the corporate operations. Information access moves the trading positions. Each first-order loop is something the standard apparatus can analyze within its respective domain. The second-order chains are what amplification mapping makes visible. The political-signal loop integrates with the physical-threat loop because the same political dynamics produce both, with the markets responding to the integrated signal rather than to either component alone. The information-access loop integrates with both because the actors with privileged information are positioning ahead of the signals that move the markets, which means the trading is itself a constitutive force in how the markets move rather than a passive response to exogenous information.

The standard apparatus produces three separate analyses. A political analysis of the Ghalibaf departure. A corporate operational analysis of the IRGC threats. A market behavior analysis of the suspicious trading. Each analysis is competent within its frame. None of them assembles what was happening, which was the integrated operation of political signaling, physical threat, and information-asymmetric trading producing market dynamics that no single domain could explain. Amplification mapping would have produced an analysis that registered the integrated operation, with the first-order loops named and the second-order chain specified. The analysis would not have predicted the specific events. It would have given decision-makers the analytical posture from which the events become recognizable as the surface manifestations of integrated dynamics rather than as a sequence of separate occurrences that the standard apparatus treats as coincidental.

Reconstitution Awareness

Reconstitution awareness is the analytical practice of pausing before building, registering what the institution being designed will be unable to see, and designing for that blindness rather than around it. The practice is addressed to institution-builders working in the narrow window before institutional stabilization, when the apparatus the institution will reproduce is still being chosen rather than enforced. The practice does not ask the institution-builder to solve the convergence. No single institution can. It asks the institution-builder to register, in the design of the institution, what the institution will be unable to see, and to make the design choices that respond to that blindness deliberate rather than default.

The practice has four procedural steps. First, the institution-builder names the discipline the institution is being built within, with the discipline rarely named explicitly in institutional design documents but always being presupposed by the language, the categories, the qualifications criteria, and the success metrics. Second, the institution-builder catalogues the analytical limits the discipline imposes on the institution, working from the convergence-registration cataloguing of what the disciplinary apparatus brackets. Third, the institution-builder designs for the blindness, asking for each bracketed force whether the institution can be designed to register the dimension explicitly, to interface with another institution that registers it, or to acknowledge in its founding documents that it does not register it. Fourth, the institution-builder writes the design with the registration explicit, with the institutional design finalized with the apparatus named, the analytical limits catalogued, and the design choices for each bracketed force registered.

The Greenland case from Chapter Nine demonstrates the practice in inverse. The international institutions that have been engaging with Greenland over the past decade, the Danish state apparatus, the European Union foreign policy infrastructure, the United States Department of State, the various climate-research institutions, were each designed within disciplinary frameworks that bracketed the integrating forces that have made Greenland strategically central. The Danish institutions analyzing Greenland's status were operating within constitutional and administrative frameworks that bracketed the rare-earth supply chain implications of Greenlandic mineral deposits. The climate-research institutions analyzing the Arctic ice melt were operating within scientific frameworks that bracketed the strategic-competition implications of the routes the melting was opening. The strategic-studies institutions analyzing Arctic security were operating within frameworks that bracketed the technological-dependence implications of the rare-earth supply chains. Each institution was producing competent work within its disciplinary frame. None of the institutions had been designed with reconstitution awareness, which means none of them was registering what the others were bracketing.

The integrated phenomenon that has made Greenland strategically central was invisible to the institutional landscape because no institution had been designed to register it.

Reconstitution awareness would not have predicted the specific Greenland outcome. The practice cannot do that. What the practice would have done is allow the institutional landscape to be designed with explicit recognition that no single institution could analyze the integrated dynamics, with interfaces between the institutions being designed deliberately so that the institutional outputs could be assembled into integrated analytical pictures that no single institution produces alone. The interfaces would not have eliminated the disciplinary fragmentation. The interfaces would have made the fragmentation analytically navigable, with the integrated picture being constructable from the fragmentary outputs through deliberate design rather than through hope that the fragments would somehow assemble themselves. The Greenland case is one specific instance. The pattern operates across the institutional landscape. Reconstitution awareness is the practice that addresses the pattern in the institutions being designed now, with the design choices being made deliberately rather than by default.

The Practice as a Whole

The four tools have now been developed at the depth this chapter can provide. Tempo recognition pairs every analysis of a fast event with deliberate inquiry into the slow events propagating beneath it. Convergence registration names what the disciplinary apparatus brackets and refuses the bracketing when the bracketed forces are constitutive. Amplification mapping identifies the feedback loops the apparatus does not register and incorporates them as constitutive. Reconstitution awareness designs the institutions emerging from the conditions with explicit recognition of what those institutions will be unable to see. The four tools are designed to be deployed in combination rather than individually. Tempo recognition without convergence registration risks identifying slow events without specifying which dimensions the apparatus is bracketing. Convergence registration without amplification mapping risks naming the brackets without registering the feedback dynamics that connect what is bracketed to what is not. Amplification mapping without reconstitution awareness risks registering the loops without designing the institutions for the analytical posture the conditions require. The four tools form a coherent practice because each presupposes and reinforces the others.

The practice does not require practitioners to abandon the discipline they have been trained in. The discipline remains the apparatus the practitioner applies. The practice extends the discipline with the analytical posture the conditions now require. An economist applying the practice produces economic analysis with explicit registration of what the standard economic apparatus brackets. An IR scholar applying the practice produces strategic analysis with explicit registration of what the standard strategic frameworks bracket. A supply chain executive, a trade analyst, a regulatory official, a curriculum designer, an institution-builder, each applying the practice inside their respective disciplines, produces work with explicit registration of what their respective apparatuses bracket. The integration the convergence requires is no longer asked of any single discipline. It emerges from the deliberate juxtaposition of disciplinary analyses each of which has registered its own limits, in conversation with adjacent disciplinary analyses each of which has performed the same registration. The integration becomes possible at the level of decision-making rather than at the level of the disciplinary apparatus, which is the level at which the integration is needed.

The chapter has provided what practitioners and scholars need to begin. The companion paper at https://papers.ssrn.com/sol3/papers.cfm?abstract_id=6698878 develops each tool with greater methodological depth, with comparison to established methodologies including scenario planning, PESTEL, SWOT, Porter's Five Forces, Porter's value chain, balanced scorecard, the Galbraith Star Model, ADDIE, and Wiggins-McTighe backward design, and with detailed sensory-detailed use cases drawn from international trade and business analytics. Practitioners and scholars who want the deeper engagement should consult the paper. The chapter is sufficient for beginning the work. The paper supports the work as it deepens.

The book has now provided the framework, the analytical demonstrations across multiple domains, and the operational practice the conditions require. What remains is the closing return to the specific child whose name the book carries. The framework has been addressed throughout to readers who must understand the conditions in order to participate in shaping them. The closing chapter addresses Aden directly, with his situation being the test case through which the framework and the tools are shown to be load-bearing for the participants the conditions have produced. The next chapter is the personal synthesis. The reader who has absorbed the framework, who has seen the framework demonstrated in cases across multiple domains, and who has now received the operational practice the framework supports, will arrive at the closing prepared for what the synthesis requires.

CHAPTER TWELVE
THE BOY WHOSE NAME THIS BOOK CARRIES
Forming in the new world.
Living the convergence. Becoming the future.
BEYOND THE FRAMEWORK, INTO A LIFE
Aden is not a case study. He is the generation forming inside the conditions this book describes.
Curious. Adaptive. Unbounded by silos we were taught to accept.
Aden's World
AI Tools
Explains. Creates. Amplifies.
Global Learning
Teachers everywhere. Courses anywhere.
Creative Expression
Music. Video. Animation. Ideas become real.
Information Access
Unlimited information. Unlimited curiosity.
Digital Native
No boundaries between online and offline learning.
Family Support
Questions encouraged. Exploration supported.
He does not see silos.
He sees connections.
He lives the convergence we analyze.
WHAT THIS MEANS
The old institutions were built for a world that no longer exists.
The new formation is not a theory. It is the environment he grows in.
His tools will be different. His choices will be wider. His responsibilities will be greater.
Our task is not to control his future, but to understand the world he will inherit.
Aden's generation will not return to the old order. They will build what comes next.
WHAT ADEN IS DOING NOW
Asks questions. Deep ones.
Uses AI as a learning partner.
Creates across media.
Learns across borders.
Navigates complexity naturally.
Bridges what others separate.
WHAT HE IS FORMING
Cross-domain intuition
Comfort with complexity
Adaptability
Digital fluency
Global perspective
Moral curiosity
THE WORLD HE WILL INHERIT
Integrated Systems
Everything connects. Nothing is isolated.
Competing Civilizations
Choices have consequences. Alignment matters.
Rapid Change
Change is constant. Adapt or be left behind.
New Institutions
Old institutions fade. New ones emerge.
Shared Planet
Limits are real. Stewardship is required.
He will not be a passenger. He will be a participant.
WHAT WE MUST DO
See the whole, not just the parts.
Build institutions that can learn.
Design for resilience, not control.
Educate for wisdom, not just skill.
Act with integrity across generations.
Leave him a world worth inheriting.
A NAME. A MEANING. A FUTURE.
Aden means fire and settlement.
The fire of disruption.
The settlement of what comes next.
He is both. He will build. We must help him see.
He asked a question about sickle cell.
We crossed a boundary.
That is the world he lives in.
The future is not something that happens to him.
It is something he will help create.
This book is for him.
And for all the others like him.
The work continues.

CHAPTER TWELVE

The Boy Whose Name This Book Carries

Aden burst into my study one afternoon last week with a question about sickle cell disease. He had encountered it in his biology class. He wanted to understand it, not at the level the eleven-year-old curriculum was offering, but at the level his curiosity had been sparked to want. I am a professor of economics and business. I write about international trade, business analytics, financial frameworks. To Aden I know everything from math to biology, because I am his father and the categories that organize my professional life are not the categories that organize his understanding of what I know. He stood in the doorway of my study with the question. I had no idea what the answer was.

So, I sat there while my eleven-year-old son made me bridge silos. We worked through it together. I learned about hemoglobin and the genetic mutation that produces sickle-shaped red blood cells. I learned about the heterozygous carriers who have partial protection against malaria, which is why the trait persists in populations historically exposed to the parasite. I learned about the painful crises that occur when the misshapen cells block small blood vessels, and about the contemporary treatments including hydroxyurea and the recent gene therapies that approach functional cure. I learned about bad blood and real blood, with bad blood being a metaphor that English uses for something else entirely and real blood being the medical condition that does specific things in the body. The conversation lasted maybe forty minutes. By the end of it I knew more about sickle cell disease than I had known when I started, and Aden had absorbed information at a level his teacher would not have offered him. The work happened in my study because that is where Aden brought the question. The work crossed the disciplinary boundary between my professional expertise and the medical question he was asking. The boundary did not matter to him. He needed to understand. I happened to be the adult available.

This is the closing chapter of the book that carries Aden's name. The previous chapters have built the framework, demonstrated it across multiple domains, and developed the operational practice that the framework supports. What remains is the return to Aden specifically, with his situation being the test case through which the framework and the practice are shown to be load-bearing for the participants the conditions have produced. The afternoon with the sickle cell question is one specific moment in that life. It is also the analytical work the book has been arguing for, performed by an eleven-year-old with no awareness that he was doing it. He bridged the silo because the silo was in the way of what he wanted to understand. The bridging was the operation. The framework names this as the analytical work the conditions require. Aden was doing the work. He was demonstrating it. The book has been arguing throughout that the conditions require the work. Aden's afternoon in my study was a small instance of the work being done by someone whose formation has happened inside conditions where the silos are already dissolving.

What Aden Is Forming Inside

Aden is eleven. He attends an online school that offers him courses across a range of subjects with teachers located in different parts of the world. He is currently in Spanish 1. I do not speak Spanish. When he encounters something in his Spanish coursework that he does not understand and that I cannot help with, he goes to Claude or Gemini and asks the AI to explain. The AI explains. He understands. He returns to his coursework. The whole transaction takes a few minutes and produces understanding I could not have given him through any effort of my own. The transaction is unremarkable to him. It is how his learning operates. He does not have a mental category for school as the place where learning happens and home as the place where it does not. The learning happens wherever he is, with whatever resources are available, including AI tools that did not exist when I was eleven and that I encountered as an adult professional only in the past several years. He is forming inside conditions where the boundary between human and artificial cognitive resource is fluid in ways that previous generations did not navigate.

He uses other tools too. He creates content. He animates old photographs through AI tools that bring movement and expression to images that were static when they were taken. He composes music using software that generates accompaniment around the melodies he hums into the microphone. He produces videos that he edits on his phone, with AI tools handling the work that would have required production studios when his parents were his age. He consumes media through streaming services that present him with content selected by algorithmic systems whose logic he does not need to understand for the systems to shape what he sees. He has not been to a movie theater in years, not because we do not take him but because the streaming experience is more convenient and the theater experience does not offer enough additional value to justify the trip. The cinema as a cultural institution that organized how communities watched films together has been substantially replaced for him, before he had a chance to develop the habits the cinema required.

None of this is unusual. Most eleven-year-olds in households like ours are doing similar things. The pattern is general across his generation in the conditions they are forming inside. What is unusual is that the framework this book has been building gives me, his father, the analytical posture to see what is happening to him as it is happening rather than only in retrospect. I can register that the cognitive substrate he is forming inside is structurally different from the substrate I formed inside, that the institutional environments he is preparing to enter are being reconstituted at rates faster than the standard frameworks can describe, that the analytical work he will need to do as an adult is work that none of his teachers and none of his curricula are explicitly preparing him for. The framework does not give me the ability to plan what he should specialize in for the conditions he will encounter as an adult. The conditions are not specifiable. The framework gives me the ability to recognize what is happening to him with enough clarity to engage with it deliberately rather than only reacting to it after the fact.

Three Generations on the Same Call

My mother Magda is nearing eighty. She lives in South Africa. She holds a nursing degree from the University of Pretoria and served as an officer in the South African Defense Force where she trained operational medics. She has navigated substantial change across her adult life, including the apartheid transition, the restructuring of the South African military, the arrival of digital technology into the healthcare profession she practiced for most of her career. When she calls us from South Africa through the video connection that did not exist when she was raising my generation, three generations of our family are on the call. My mother in her late seventies. Hla and me in our late forties. Aden at eleven. Each of us has been formed inside different conditions. Each of us has different relationships to the technology that organizes our daily life and to the broader transformation the technology represents.

Hla is a researcher who works on family medicine. She uses AI in her professional work where it is useful and remains skeptical about its broader role in domains where its participation is not yet welcome. She manages our household payments through banking applications on her phone, drives ten kilometers in expensive diesel to find imported beef when she needs it for a meal, sits in queues at gas stations when the diesel runs out at the local pumps. She is the third skeptical voice in this book about AI participation in domains where her caution is appropriate. She is also the person who, on a typical day, integrates more cross-domain operations than most of the analysts I write about, with the integration being how a family functions rather than how a research project proceeds.

Magda told us recently, on one of our video calls, that the new things and AI are too much for an old woman's brain to absorb. She was being honest rather than self-deprecating. She has the comparison frame from substantial previous transformations. The frame tells her that what is happening now is different in kind, not just different in degree. Her response is the response of a person who recognizes that her resources for handling change may not be adequate to what is becoming. The fear is rational. The fear is also the felt experience of the formation operating on a person who has the standing to register what it is doing. Aden has different resources for handling the same change. He is forming inside it rather than encountering it as something happening to a life that was already organized before it arrived. The same conditions feel different to him than they feel to Magda because his formation has happened inside them rather than around them.

What I Am Honest About Regarding This Book

My publisher emailed me a banner recently promoting my earlier book on Risk Management. The banner also mentioned that I had been acknowledged as one of the top fifty most influential authors of 2023 for my book Trailblazing Strategies for Career Growth, published through Notion Press. The recognition is real. The book that earned it described career strategies for navigating a labor market that operated within boundaries the standard analytical apparatus could describe. The boundaries were the boundaries that organized professional careers for most of the post-war period. Choose a field. Develop expertise. Build a track record. Navigate the institutional architecture of your industry. The book gave readers strategies for doing these things effectively. It gave them the strategies competently, with the apparatus being adequate to the conditions in which the book was written.

I co-authored another book published through Notion Press around the same period, Wallet Dynamics: The Spirited Journey to Financial Empowerment, with my colleague Ruban Ganeshu. The book covered financial education for students and professionals, working through the historical evolution of money from barter to digital currencies, the principles of budgeting, the analysis of financial statements, the dynamics of global economics. The book operated within stable disciplinary boundaries that were appropriate to the conditions in which it was published. Readers who used the book learned what they needed to learn within those boundaries. The work was useful. The work was honest within its frame.

The book you are now finishing argues against the boundaries that organized both of those earlier works. Not because the earlier works were wrong for the conditions in which they were produced. The earlier works were appropriate to the conditions in which they were produced. The argument is that the conditions have changed in ways that make the boundaries those works operated within inadequate to what their readers now need. The career strategies that Trailblazing described are partly obsolete already, with the labor market they addressed being reshaped faster than the book can be revised. The financial education that Wallet Dynamics provided is partly outdated already, with the monetary architecture it described being reconstituted at the central bank level and at the household level in ways the book did not anticipate. Both books continue to do useful work for readers who use them. Both books also represent a period of authorial work that the conditions are moving past at a rate that makes any adequate analytical work in this environment have a shorter half-life than authors of previous eras could expect.

The book you are finishing now will face the same fate. The cases I have used will be partly outdated within months of the book reaching readers. The framework will need to be updated as the conditions continue to develop. The four tools will be refined as practitioners apply them in domains the companion paper and this book did not anticipate. This is not a failure of the book. It is a feature of the conditions in which the book is being written. The work I am doing is real work, addressed to readers who need the framework now in ways that justify the work even though the work will be partly obsolete by the time the readers absorb it. The recognition for Trailblazing was real. The earlier work was real. This book is real. None of them are timeless. None of them needed to be timeless to be worth doing. The work the conditions require includes acknowledging that the work will be partly obsolete and doing it anyway, because waiting until the conditions stabilize would mean waiting indefinitely while the readers who need the framework now go without it.

Aden

Aden, this book carries your name because you are the structural horizon of the work I have been doing across many years. I have been writing about the conditions you will inherit, with the analytical work being addressed to readers who must understand those conditions in order to participate in shaping them rather than only being subjected to them. The book is for you in a specific sense. You are eleven now. By the time you can read the book seriously and absorb what it is arguing, the conditions it describes will have continued to develop and you will be reading the book partly as historical document about the moment when your father was trying to make sense of what was becoming. That is appropriate. The book was not written to predict your future. The book was written to be honest about what the conditions are doing now, with you being the specific person whose future I cannot specify but who's present I can describe.

What I want you to know is that the formation happening to you is not happening to you alone. It is happening to your generation across the world, with each of you forming inside different specific conditions but all of you forming inside the broader transformation the book has been documenting. You will need to develop the analytical posture the book has been teaching, not because your father wrote a book about it but because the conditions will require the posture from anyone whose work depends on understanding what is happening. You will encounter many adults who will offer you advice based on the conditions of their formation rather than the conditions of yours. Listen to them. Some of their advice will be valuable. Some of their advice will be inadequate to the conditions you will face. You will need to develop the judgment to distinguish, with the framework being one resource among several that may help you make the distinctions.

I do not know what you will study or what you will become professionally. The categories that organize professions now may not be the categories that organize them when you reach professional age. You may do work that has no name now. You may do work that has names now but that operates differently than the names suggest. You may do work I cannot imagine. What I know is that you are forming inside conditions where the silos are dissolving, where the cross-domain integration the book has been documenting is the structural feature of how the world now operates, where the analytical posture the book has been teaching is what the conditions require of participants who want to engage with what is becoming rather than only react to what has already happened. You are positioned for this in ways your father is not. Your formation is happening inside it. My formation happened around it and I have been working to develop the posture the conditions require, which is harder for me than it will be for you because you are not retrofitting the posture onto a previous formation. You are forming with the posture as part of how you think.

Take care of your mother. Take care of your grandmother. Take care of yourself. Read this book when you are ready. Argue with it. Find what is wrong in it and tell me what you find, because by the time you read it carefully, I will need to know what the book got wrong so I can do better work in whatever years remain to me. Build something with your formation. The conditions are not fully terrible. The conditions are also not fully promising. The conditions are what they are, and you will live inside them, and what you do with them is the work that the framework cannot specify in advance because the framework can only describe the conditions and not predict what participants like you will make of them. The book closes here, at the door of my study, with you having brought me a question I could not answer and with the two of us having worked through it together. That is what the work looks like when it is being done. The work that remains is yours.

www.ingramcontent.com/pod-product-compliance
Lightning Source LLC
LaVergne TN
LVHW070935210926
848482LV00003B/244